Memories of Growing Up In BORGER TEXAS
By Frieda Lanham Pickett
With contributions by Borgans

Memories of Growing Up In Borger, Texas

Forward

In 2006 in preparation for my high school graduating class's 45th reunion I completed a booklet to be sold at the reunion of the history of the town as written by the wife of one of my father's brothers, memories provided by a Borger Blog managed by Susan Parker Miller, and short descriptions of class members detailing what they had done with their lives after graduating from Borger High School (BHS). The book included in the "memories" section, stories of people we remembered or events that occurred which we thought were unique, small reports of places we frequented for fun and socialization, including some of our favorite eating locations, movie theaters, and places like Teen Town and the American Legion first floor meeting room where we held dances most week-ends. After several read the book I received letters about what was NOT included and decided to write a more complete second edition, including a section on Sports at Borger High and interview children of business owners regarding why their parents came to Borger and built businesses.

The original concept of the book was to provide an information source for class members and profits from the book were to be applied towards the establishment of our class's Memorial Scholarship, to be awarded to a graduating senior at BHS each year. At the reunion the Memorial Scholarship was established by a majority vote of those attending and a Board of Directors was determined based on volunteers from the class. The Scholarship Fund was supported by contributions from the class members and the Class Bank Account. It has been sufficient to award a scholarship each year since 2006.

Many of us who grew up in Borger during the 40s – 60s remember infrastructure additions to the community and special events planned by city leaders. Most of us were unaware of the time, financial resources needed and efforts required to set these opportunities in place. We never realized how special our little community was, nor how hard our parents worked to make our lives better than theirs had been as young adults. Our parents sought to earn a decent living, to make a better home for their family/children and prepare them to have successful adult lives. They participated to develop a community that provided healthy options as their children, and they themselves, matured. I hear over and over as my now-grown student colleagues recall our lives then, how secure and wonderful we felt growing up in this small town and how wonderful the memories are of our childhood through teenage years. They lament that their children and grandchildren do not have this atmosphere, and feel a sadness that times have changed and social mores have evolved so that it is not as easy for them as it was for us. This book is intended to be a tribute to the community leaders of Borger, TX in this era of the town development. Many are gone now, so the "thanks" is belated, but well meant.

Frieda Lanham Pickett, Class of 1961

Pg 24

Growing Up in Borger

Memories from people who grew up in Borger, TX during the 1950's and 1960's

Table of Contents

Part One

Chapter 1: History of Borger

The History of Development: Hutchinson County- Borger, Texas

"On the high Texas plains in January of 1926, an oil well called Dixon Creek No. 2 came in as a gusher, and touched off a boom. Overnight, the boomtown of Borger sprang up along the banks of the Canadian River, rife with oilmen of every stripe and fashion, and all the camp followers ready to clean the boomers' pockets." Here is the story:
MCILROY, SHERMAN D. (1871-1945): **McIlroy Finds Oil at Dixon Creek**

After working in the oil fields of Alaska McIlroy relocated to Amarillo TX joining his brother who had a meat and grocery business. In December 1918 excitement over the Masterson oil discovery well swept the Panhandle, and early in 1919 the McIlroy brothers formed the Dixon Creek Oil Company as a joint-stock firm and set out to take advantage of the prospects, despite limited experience in the oil business. After securing some prospective leases on the Smith Ranch in southern Hutchinson County, they drilled their first well, Smith-Capers No. 1, which came in during June 1922 at only thirty barrels a day.

Nevertheless, the McIlroys incorporated the company in 1924 to raise funds and continued to drill. Henry A. and Millard C. Nobles were among the principal stockholders. In March 1925 the Dixon Creek, or Smith No. 1, was brought in and produced 400 barrels a day. In December of that year the No. 2 well on the same lease came in at 3,000 barrels a day. Tex McIlroy then decided to try to increase production by deepening Smith No. 1. On January 11, 1926, after being drilled only an additional two feet, the well blew in at 10,000 barrels a day, an unprecedented success that touched off a boom and led to the founding of Borger.

After completing Smith No. 1, the Dixon Creek Oil Company brought in a number of successful producers, most of them on the Smith Ranch leases. This made McIlroy one of the dominant independent operators during the boom's early days. To use the large volume of casinghead gas produced from company wells, he built one of the Panhandle's first natural gas plants. Later, McIlroy expanded his operations to the West Pampa Field in western Gray County, where he drilled the second producer. There the company eventually brought in eighty-seven producing wells on leases totaling 1,800 acres; at one time the wells were producing more than 20,000 barrels of oil a day.

In all, the McIlroy brothers organized three successful independent regional oil companies between 1919 and 1932. During that time, Tex McIlroy handled most of the oil properties. In an era of shady stock deals and questionable business practices, he became known for his honesty, his determination to keep his word, and his charities.
From: Amarillo Globe, August 27, 1945. Amarillo Sunday News-Globe, August 14, 1938. Canyon News, Special Supplement, February 20, 1986. C. L. Hightower, ed., Hood County in Picture and Story (Fort Worth: Historical Publishers, 1970; rpt. 1978)

"The town blazed wide open until the governor of Texas, Dan Moody, called in the Texas Rangers to clean up the streets; in one day, over ten thousand gamblers, bootleggers, whores and camp followers were run out of town." [from Boomer's Gold by Jack Walker, Thorp Springs Press 1978] The history of the founding of Borger, Texas is one story, but it started much earlier with the establishment of Hutchinson County, of which Borger is a part.

On March 7, 2007 Borger celebrated it's 81st birthday and a special supplement edition of Borger News-Herald was published highlighting accomplishments of the city. The following characterizes the reporting of newspaper journalists and, also, comments from people who grew up here add to the information.

The Early Years

The earliest inhabitants of the area now known as Hutchinson County (HC) were Native American Indians called the "Antelope Creek" culture, a southwest extension of the Plains Indians. These Indians lived in pueblo-like villages with foundations and walls made of stone. This culture were hunter-gatherers with horticulture and bison hunting from around 1200 to 1500 A.D. Francisco Vasquez de Coronado was the first of several Spanish expeditions to pass through Hutchinson County from the 15th through the 18th centuries. Juan de Ornate passed through in 1601 followed by Pedro Vial in 1792. Vidal's expedition appears to have penetrated the eastern boundary of HC and camped on the present site of Borger before returning to Santa Fe. By the early 1800s settlers itching to see the "old West" came by wagon, horseback and railroad, and the Texas Panhandle was becoming "Americanized". Back in the early days of HC, the grassland was an excellent grazing ground for buffalo, antelope and other large animals, and many thousands of them could be seen on land now devoted to wheat growing and oil derricks. I remember as a child while we drove from Borger to Amarillo, looking out on the ranchlands and seeing large herds of antelope moving over the land. Many old-timers in Borger talk of using buffalo chips for making a hot fire, and cowpunchers, while on their lonely vigils, likely kept warm on many a night by a fire of "chips". Thousands of heads of cattle were driven through our area to market in Dodge City, KS—"North of 36—30". Hutchinson County was a vibrant part of the "old West". The first establishment on the Panhandle prairie was built by William Bent and his partner, Ceran St. Vrain as part of their enterprise *Bent, St. Vrain & Company*. As the company's Mexican and Indian trade grew trading posts were established, ranging from Santa Fe to Independence MO. According to Wes Phillips the men established a temporary Fort Adobe in the northeastern part of the present day HC, north of the Canadian River, sometime around 1840-44 (exact date undetermined) as a trading post for trade with the Kiowa and Comanche Indians. The spot had formerly been used by the Hudson Bay traders. William Bent was married to an Indian woman and had a relationship with the Plains Indian tribes. Initially trading was conducted in a tepee. Later better constructed structures were completed. The Fort consisted of three buildings made of double rows of posts set upright in the ground and filled in with packed dirt, across from the White Deer Creek. Around 1848 Bent sent Kit Carson and a group of soldiers, well armed, to bring supplies and try to open the Fort for business. They were attacked by Apaches and had to return to Colorado where Bent's Old Fort was located. Bent later attempted another last effort to reopen the Fort, but the Comanche and Kiowa Indians who resented the "white men" disturbing their hunting grounds, attacked. The buildings at Fort Adobe were eventually destroyed by Bent after trouble with Indians made the trading post an unprofitable venture. Oddly enough twenty years later, on November 25, 1864, in retaliation for Indian attacks on wagon trains and white settlers Kit Carson, Commander of the First Calvary of the New Mexico Volunteers, returned to the Panhandle area and his men attacked Indians camped in the vicinity of the ruins of the Fort, called the first battle, but less well known, at Adobe Walls. Carson and his troops withdrew from the battle, being outnumbered by thousands of Indians, however he is credited with a victory for the battle (http://www.tshaonline.org/handbook/online/articles/AA/qea1.html). It was at a location a few miles from the original Adobe Walls, that the more famous Second Battle of Adobe Walls occurred.

Battle at Adobe Walls

Hutchinson County is best known to history for the famous Battle of Adobe Walls, which took place over in the northeast section of the County back in 1874. The Battle of Adobe Walls resulted from years of disputes between the Indians and white hunters and traders. A treaty between the U.S. government and Indian chiefs prohibited white hunters from hunting south of the Arkansas River which runs its course to the east across the southern part of Kansas. The treaty was disregarded and broken routinely by the white hunters, sometimes paying for it with their lives. Indian war parties raided settlements in retaliation. It was during this period that the Federal Peace Commission was created to convert the Plains Indians from their nomadic way of life and settle them on reservations. The Indian chiefs tried to negotiate with Lt. Col. Armstrong Custer and Major General Philip Sheridan for peace when Custer attacked a Cheyenne encampment killing between 30 to 100 Indians, including women and children, and slaughtering their mule and pony herd. This was to cripple the Indians' ability to live "off the reservations". Conflict continued between the Indians and the settlers and hunters over the next decade but the Battle of Adobe Walls changed this situation. There was a wealth of buffalo in the Texas Panhandle that were strongly desired by hide vendors in Dodge City KS. Hide shipper Charlie Myers put together an expedition of 30 wagons and 50 or more men in March 1874 and tested the resolve of the Indians protecting the area from outside hunting. Among those in the party with Myers were men to do the skinning of buffalo under the direction of James Hanrahan, along with 23-year old Billy Dixon and R.B. "Bat" Masterson. The group reached Bent's abandoned Fort Adobe trading post in May. The post was little more than a set of rock walls. Permanent structures were began as Myers set up a store. His competitor, Charles Rath, opened a store, Jim Hanrahan opened a saloon, while another in the group, Thomas O'Keefe opened a blacksmith shop. Throughout May and June the buffalo herds were spotted and the hunters and skinners, now numbering around 300 people, were kept busy, using the Fort for R&R. Indians killed some of them for hunting in Indian Territory. A half-breed Indian scout from Fort Supply (also called Camp Supply) with the name of Chapman, traveled to the Adobe Fort post to warn the men of an impending attack planned for the end of June. Hanrahan kept the information quiet as he was afraid the hunters might leave the fort unprotected. The evening of the planned attack (June 27, 1874) he set out free drinks at the saloon to keep the hunters at the Fort. The Indians made an alliance between the Comanche, the Kiowa and the Cheyenne for the attack bringing close to 700 Indians to the battle. The Comanche were led by Quanah Parker, half-breed son of a Comanche and a white girl taken by the Indians as a child, Cynthia Parker. The Kiowa were led by Lone Wolf and the Cheyenne by Stone Calf. The medicine man for the alliance was a young Indian called Isa-Tai or Little Wolf. Little Wolf, also known as "Wolf's hind end or Wolf's droppings", had developed what he called "bullet-proof paint" and assured the Indian fighters they would be safe from the white men guns. The Indians watched in wait for an easy victim and saw Ike and Shorty Sadler and their dog asleep in their wagon outside the Fort walls. The Indians killed and scalped these men, also scalping the dog. The Indians then drove off the stock with the Sadler wagon. Most of the hunters at the camp were awake repairing a broken ridgepole when the Indians charged at dawn. The defenders, 28 men and one woman, gathered in Harahan's Saloon. Two white men were shot during the battle: Billy Tyler, shot while returning from the stockade, and William Olds who shot himself with his own gun while coming down a ladder. The initial charge was repelled with the loss of only these two men. One more man was lost in later charges, which continued until about noon, and a fourth man was accidentally killed by the discharge of his own gun. The battle lasted just this half day but the Indians laid siege to the spot. The siege lasted for about four or five days but no more attacks were made on the fort. Before long the Indians found out that Little Wolf's bullet proof paint did not work and at least 150 were killed by the buffalo guns. The Indians retreated to a safe distance to rethink their strategy. On the second day a group of 15 or 20 of the Cheyenne appeared on a high mesa overlooking the post. Their appearance led to the famous gunshot of Billy Dixon. Billy Dixon, a crack shot, was on guard in the saloon, watching for the next attack. He saw the scouts and Chief watching the Fort and took aim with a "Big Fifty Sharps" rifle, firing, then watched as the Indian Chief fell from his horse and dropped to the ground. This event convinced the Indians to give up the plan and leave the hunters in peace. Army surveyors later measured the distance of the bullet and determined it went 1,538 yards, or 9/10ths of a mile. This event marked the last time Panhandle Indians assembled for any large military purpose. This cleared the way for farmers and ranchers to move to the Texas Panhandle and settle the area. The site of Adobe Walls is on the Turkey Track Ranch, privately owned by the Honorable Will T. Coble of Amarillo TX. It can be reached from Borger in a little over an hour's drive. A monument was erected in 1924 on the site by the Panhandle Plains Historical Society.

John White recounts in his book that the Panhandle area was visited by Jesse James and his gang, holding up at the place where the Rock Island Railroad bridge crossed the Canadian River, an area now known as Sanford. "Uncle Tom" Cooley, an old time plainsman states that he knew James and his gang, as they visited his trading post near what is now Dalhart in Dallam County. Kit Carson, noted scout, also visited HC, as well as Col. William F. Cody "Buffalo Bill", Pawnee Bill and Billy the Kid.

The first ranch in HC was established by T.S. Bugbee along the banks of the Canadian River. It was small, however, in comparison with later large cattle companies, like the Capitol Freehold Land and Cattle Company, who, in exchange for three million acres of Panhandle land, built the state capital of Austin. This company brought in thousands of head of cattle, establishing the cattle industry on ranch land. As cattle increased, the need for crops was recognized. The farmers who came to the area set down roots North of the Canadian River, mainly, and before long a county was formed. In the spring of 1901 a petition was granted for organization of the county and the county was named for pioneer jurist captured in the wars with Mexico and Santa Anna and imprisoned in the Perote Prison in Mexico, Anderson Hutchinson. The first elections in HC were held April 25, 1901 and four voting precincts were formed. Billy Dixon who established a ranch on the Turkey Track Ranch area was the first sheriff. He resigned after the first year, disgusted with politics in the county organization. He and his wife, Olive, had several children and eventually moved to Plemons to enroll them in school. He moved to Oklahoma a few years later where he died. A question arose as to where the county seat should be located and it was decided by election that it should be located at Plemons. This site was opposed by the interests of the A.A. Bugbee ranch, which was located three miles north of Plemons on Bugbee Creek. The county was evenly divided between the "Tracks" and the "Nesters". The land question was the issue. The Turkey Tracks ranch owners resented the idea of settling the country and sought to preserve the open range as long as possible. J.M. Coburn was the general manager of the Turkey Track Ranch with offices in Kansas City MO. The Hansford Land and Cattle Company sold their interest in the property about the year 1904 to Patton, Price and Hyde. The ranch then was sold to W.T. Coble who continues to use the old brands.

The only residence in Plemons at that time was that of J.A. Whittenburg, who had filed claim on four sections of land along the Canadian River in the southeastern part of the country, not far from the historical Adobe Walls location.

The first road in the county was laid in 1901, going from the county seat at Plemons to the new county line at Moore County. There were old roads in the county before settlement began, with the oldest known as the Old Santa Fe Trail. This trail passed through the county from northeast to southwest. Signal Hill, just north of the Canadian River, is located on this trail. The Turkey Track chuck wagons followed this trail to their spring and fall roundups. Most of the people of the country attended the roundups and gatherings around the chuck wagon at dinner time where the best of food was served...frijoles and coffee were always on the menu.

The first county courthouse was built according to the style of architecture at that time, being a dugout covered with poles and earth. The dimensions of this building were 14 X20 feet and the cost was $90.00. In the summer of 1901 a permanent courthouse was built for around $2700.00 and the old courthouse was used for a school. The school opened in the spring of 1900 with 20 pupils. Miss Fannie Archer, who later came to be Mrs. George Whittenburg, was the teacher. Later that year a three months term was taught on the Bugbee Ranch, four miles from the first school. The county was eventually divided into nine school districts with short terms and low salaries for teachers. By 1927 the school had 16 school districts, running 8 month terms, and a County Superintendent of schools, a reflection of the rapid increase in population.

The first official act of the first Commissioners' Court was to pass an order designating the entire county as one school district. Soon after at an election called for setting the tax (of 10 cents on the one hundred dollar valuation of taxable property) to pay for the school operation, the bill failed to carry, not receiving the required 2/3 majority of the votes cast. Eighteen voted for and eleven against the measure. HC enjoyed slow, tranquil growth over the next 25 years. Then in 1918 the first gas well was drilled in Potter County, close to Amarillo, bringing speculators to HC; eventually bringing A.P. (Asa) Borger to HC.

Prior to January 1926 there were approximately 300 people living in Hutchinson County (HC), most involved in farming and ranching. In the town of Plemons, the initial county seat of HC, merchants met the needs of these residents, coming from communities such as the Holt community in the northern portion of the high plains or in the small community of Plemons located on the banks of the Canadian river. About 15 families made Plemons their home. Along with a mercantile store, there was a barber shop, medical office, drug store and a two story frame courthouse. Plemons was a river-crossing town for area ranches. These communities began in 1898 when James A. Whittenburg, an area rancher, built his dugout in a hill overlooking a bend in the Canadian River. He named the site *Plemons* for Judge W.B. Plemons, a gifted criminal lawyer in Amarillo, as well as a judge and state legislator. His son, Barney Plemons, had filed on land just below Plemons at the mouth of Moore's Creek in 1898. He lived on one of the principal river crossings and always kept a good river horse to assist people in crossing the river when it was high. In fact, it was a community service as most of the men who lived in the area would meet freight wagons at the river to see them safely across. They would often use about three saddle horses with lariats tied to the end of the wagon tongues. Sometimes the wagon would capsize and it would be necessary to round up the freight and carry it over on foot. Usually the freighters carried a sufficient amount of "cough medicine" and all partook of it freely.
More people drifted into the area and Hutchinson County was organized in the Spring of 1901 with J.A. Whittenburg elected County Attorney, serving until 1926; and with early settlers establishing a school and a post office. Other county officials included a judge, Sheriff (Billy Dixon was elected), Commissioners from 4 precincts, and clerk. The Hutchinson County Herald published a story of a county track meet in Plemons that involved representatives from HC schools (Holt community, Plemons community) on April 9, 1926. Events included tennis, 50 yard dash, 100 yard dash, 440 relay, high jump, chinning bar, running high jump, running broad jump, even javelin throwing. Student competitors names were listed and it seemed several students planned to compete in several events. At the end of the story the winners of the literary events were published. One, Violet Balthrope of the Holt school, had more points to her credit than any other contestant in the meet. Unfortunately rain forced the postponement of all events except the literary events (spelling match, arithmetic match, declamation, and extemporaneous speaking). However all was not lost, as the good people at Plemons served a delicious free lunch at noon, with W.S. Christian preparing barbecued beef and Mrs. Burt Bryan's special recipe for the sauce. Attendees brought home made pickles, salads and cakes. It sounded like "a good time was had by all!" A road was built from Plemons toward Dumas TX to facilitate moving people, supplies and transacting business.

Life was simple, everyone knew everyone, and crime was almost nonexistent, except for a few cattle rustlings. The first 25 years of the County's history shows one capital offense charged. Temple Houston, a son of General Sam Houston, was attorney for the defense in the case and succeeded in clearing the defendant on a plea of insanity. After the county seat was moved to Stinnett a newer courthouse was constructed and remained the hallmark of the county as a beautiful building. Then oil was discovered in HC ... and life soon changed for these early residents!

A Township is Established and Early Woes

The town of Borger was described as a city of lawlessness in the late 1920s following establishment by A.P. (Ace) Borger in March 1926. Ace Borger was a well known and shrewd town promoter in the Oklahoma/Texas area, and in 1927, along with Pete, his brother, and A.S. Stinnett, played a major role in establishing the town of Stinnett, north of Borger, and getting the county seat of Hutchinson County moved to Stinnett. In 1929 Borger built a spacious two-story family home, the first brick residence in Borger.

In Oklahoma he helped to build towns, such as Picher, Slick and Cromwell. The event that initiated the rush of people to the area was that a gusher came in around January 11, 1926 drilled by the Dixon Creek Oil and Refinery Company. This oil well produced 5,000 barrels of oil a day, setting off the search for "black gold". Every place the drillers punched a hole the "black gold" came in abundance. Along came the drillers and the contractors. Rig after rig was erected. In their wake came the merchant, the medical caregivers and the caterer. Dr. W.W. Brooks, a Borger pioneer set up a medical practice in 1927, and served as medical director of the Phillips Clinic until 1949 when he and another physician, Dr. Smith, opened the Brooks-Smith Clinic at 500 West Third St., which served as a medical office and out-patient surgery center. Sadly Dr. Brooks died suddenly in 1955 at 58 years of age.

Other community improvements included churches and the theater, the beauty parlor and the haberdasher; followed by Castleberry Shoes and the Hutchinson County Herald. Within a matter of months, oilmen, prospectors, roughnecks, panhandlers, fortune seekers, card sharks, bootleggers, prostitutes and dope peddlers descended on Borger, along with a cadre of honest workingmen and their families. While some workers brought their families in hopes of establishing a new home with well paying jobs, others had different ideas. "Booger town", as it was nicknamed, became a refuge for criminals and fugitives from the law. It was Borger by day and "Booger" by night. An article in the Kansas City Star in September 22, 1929 started with the words "Boys, she's a ring-tailed tooter, this town of Borger, two miles long and everybody in town pistol-minded. Only 3 years old...but the folks have a record for killings, stabbings, fights and old fashioned knockdowns and drag-outs that Chicago could envy. Thirty murders in three years and only one prosecution."

Borger Township: From ranchland to prosperity

Following the discovery of oil in the area A.P. Borger and his attorney-partner, John R. Miller, purchased a 240-acre section of ranchland just west of the gusher from John and Maggie Weatherly of Panhandle TX for a consideration of $50.00 an acre or $12,000.00. He next obtained a grant from Texas secretary of state Emma

Grigsby Meharg to organize the Borger Townsite Company, with capital stock of $10,000 divided into 100 shares of $100 each. They formed the Borger Townsite Corporation for the purpose of developing a town. The land was in the southern part of Hutchinson County, near the Canadian River. They drafted the land space into lots, after reserving building sites for churches, schools and city buildings. Records reveal that within 90 days of legal application papers for township development the partners had placed advertisements in sources so well selected that the lure of "black gold" brought over 45,000 men and women to the new "boomtown". March 8, 1926 was the first day of lot sales bringing in $100,000.00. Early townsite lots with 25 foot fronts and 120 foot depths sold from $1500 to $2500.00. Prime lots on Main street and Dixon Street sold from $1500 to $5000.00. Within a few moths lots trebled in value. Six months later there were no lots left to sell and Borger/Miller group had grossed over $1,000,000.00. Borger officials established a charter incorporating the city by October of that year, voter registration was begun and John R. Miller was elected mayor. A post office had opened to facilitate communication and a school district was established to educate the children of workers. Borger was a shrewd businessman and it was clear that lumber would be a profitable business. He established a lumberyard in the town named for him and opened its first bank. Often he took out full-page ads in area papers promoting settlement in Borger and other oil-rich sites throughout West Texas and eastern New Mexico in which he had an interest. He also owned a string of Panhandle wheat elevators and 19,000 acres of farmland in Hansford County. Residents who lived in the county before the oil boom avoided the new town and lawlessness that followed so that among the minority of honest, hard-working individuals, the area became a refuge for criminals and fugitives from the law. Ranchers John R. Weatherly and James A. Whittenburg had other land in the area and hoped to reap the benefits of the financial boom in the area. They established two rival townsites next to Borger, calling them Isom (Weatherly group) and Dixon Creek (Whittenburg). Lots in Isom were 50 feet by 140 feet. The Black Hotel was built near to the railroad spur from Panhandle. Oil companies sprang up over the area and established camptowns to house the workers, such as the oil camp of Signal Hill to the northeast of Borger, the Dial Gulf Camp and TexRoy at Spring Creek. In November of 1927 sparks from the drilling equipment initiated a fire at the Dixon Creek Oil Company refinery and destroyed much of the equipment and buildings. These areas were ultimately incorporated into the Borger city limits. Shacks of every type and tent cities dotted the countryside on both sides of the three mile long Main Street. Business establishments were hastily thrown together and business was good from the moment they opened their doors. The Santa Fe Railroad had a track and station in Panhandle about 32 miles south of Borger and building materials were off-loaded there and hauled to Borger overland. When the spur from Panhandle to Borger was completed by the Santa Fe RR, construction was much easier. The prairie between Panhandle and Borger revealed scores of trails and vehicle ruts, which were, at times, almost impassable. Traffic was constant however, day and night. On rainy days the tires on vehicles often got bogged down in the mud and cars were deserted while occupants set out on foot to get to Borger. It was a common site to see cars and trucks mired down in the center of Main Street. People had to have boots for walking down the street, even more so to cross the street. The price of whisky or beer was 50 cents a drink or bottle. Bath houses had showers for 50 cents.

The Post Office
The Post Office (PO) on Main Street was the main meeting place in early days of Borger. It was where husbands met their families coming to join them. Others would meet up with friends or people coming to Borger at the Post Office. There were estimated to be thousands of letters coming into Borger each day in 1926 and the PO space was inadequate to handle the mail. Sometimes the two general delivery windows had long lines extending out the door of the building. Postal clerks worked from early morning to late at night, it is not like today where the post office hours are often "meager". Mail delivery was often days behind as there was no time to sort incoming packages and letters during the day. There was no delivery service. All mail had to be picked up at the PO.

Martial Law and the Texas Rangers
Before long, according to the 2007 Special Supplement to the Borger News-Herald, Borger was firmly in the hands of an organized crime syndicate led by Mayor Miller's shady associate "Two-Gun Dick" Herwig. In the township map the center of vice and the "red light district" was Dixon Street (now Tenth Street) notorious for brothels, dance halls, gambling dens, slot machines, and speakeasies. Murder and robbery became commonplace. Illegal moonshine stills and home brewing were commonplace. Herwig's henchmen included W.J. (Shine) Popejoy, the king of Texas bootleggers. Police were called "the Law" and most were criminals from other areas. They often drove new cars, stolen from someone. Many owned their own bars, operated by their mistresses and would confiscate liquor from other bars after making trumped up charges, then sell the liquor in their places. Prisoners were chained to a post before a jail was built and it was not uncommon for prisoners to be beaten, some dying while in custody. It has been written that the early "laws" had mistresses - unmarried women or wives of other men—and these women operated "joints", the proceeds of which went to the officer in question. Needless to say these joints were never raided by the law. John White describes a typical day in court of the Justice of the Peace in his book (Borger, Texas): "The early court was that of Justice of the Peace who had an office and room next door to the 'jail-house'. His name was George Webb. His word was law—the famous Borger Law—no appeal was possible if the victim desired to remain in HC. A man was guilty in his court as long as he had a dollar. If not, he was told to get out and leave town. Oil Field characters who knew the judge well could get him to allow them to pay their fines later on. It was interesting to visit the 'cote' in those days. A docket having from 30 to 100 names was usual. As the clerk called the names, the prisoner in question rose, the judge, if he had time, would ask what the guy was charged with. If the reply was, 'I don't know' the judge would say 'contempt of court' or 'drunk and disorderly--$18.00 fine. Next case.' On many occasions the clerk would just finish calling the name when the judge would say 'Guilty -- $18.00 fine'. In the Borger court all brought to the JP had fineable offenses, so long as the prisoner had the money to 'pay off'. If the prisoner was a friend of a prominent bootlegger, the case would be dismissed for lack of evidence." Fixers were people who arranged for

someone's release. Lawyers had "poor pickings" in those days as those in authority didn't want "representation" they wanted "fixers".
It was not long before the activities of this group brought governmental investigators to the area and in the spring of 1927 Texas Governor Daniel J. Moody sent a detachment of Texas Rangers under captains Francis Augustus Hamer and Thomas R. Hickman to quiet things down. I saw on the History Channel a program detailing this event. It was a show on notorious places in the history of America and I was surprised to see the story of the early days of the Texas Rangers and their trip to Borger TX! They had footage taken on film of the situation in Borger, the lawmen going into the town, images of some of the "no-gooders" and some of the people in the police department who were in "cahoots" with the organized crime group. It was a real learning experience for me, as I didn't know the details of Borger's early days, just the reputation. They showed the Rangers running people out of town who were engaged in illegal activities and shutting down the houses of "painted women". One scene showed women running out into the outskirts of town on their feet, didn't have cars. They were actually filming people being "run out of town". It was rather humorous. Hamer would go onto later fame as the lawman who killed Bonnie and Clyde.
The Texas Rangers were sent to Borger on more than one occasion. There were 30-39 murders between the years of 1926 and 1929 (depending on which account one reads). Borger's wave of crime and violence was intermittent into the 1930s and climaxed with the murder of District Attorney John A. Holmes at his home at 406 Hedgecoke by an unknown assassin on September 13, 1929. Holmes, just 33 years old, was murdered around 10:30 PM as he was closing the garage door at his home. Holmes, his wife and his mother-in-law, Donna Greene, had just returned home after closing Mrs. Greene's shop in Borger's business district. The women had gone into the kitchen to turn on lights, leaving Mr. Holmes to close the garage door. He received 5 gunshot wounds into his side and the back, three of them deadly. The perpetrator fled the scene on foot, jumping a back fence in the back yard, escaping to a nearby white sedan, never to be seen again. Law enforcement and physicians, Dr. H.D. Irvan and Dr. A.F. Hansen rushed to the scene but Holmes had died instantly. A .32 caliber bullet was found in a neighbor's yard. Holmes had been appointed to the district attorney position one year to the day prior to his death, filling the unexpired term of Curtis Douglas who resigned. It was this episode that prompted the Texas Governor to impose martial law and, *again* call in the Texas Rangers and Captain Hamer who said of Borger "...the worst bit of organized crime I have seen in my career." He explained that many of the Borger police officers are either ex-convicts or under indictment for criminal offenses in other jurisdictions. Captain Hamer was assisted by Brigadier General Jacob F. Wolters in the Texas National Guard, and a Houston attorney. Within 48 hours five Texas Rangers arrived in Borger on orders from Governor Dan Moody (Captain Frank Hamer, Captain Tom Hickman, Sgt. J.B. Wheatley, C.O. Moore and B.M. Gault), checking into The Black Hotel in the Isom area of Borger. Martial Law was declared on Borger at 3 PM on September 29, 1929. Eighty-four National Guardsmen and 14 other officers entered the county, on an order by Governor Moody, as a result of the crime in Borger and HC. All local officers were suspended, with the exception of Judge H.M. Hood, County attorney Henry Meyers and Ranger J.W. Aldrich. Although Holmes's murderer was never apprehended motives behind his death were

discovered during the investigation. Holmes has been gathering evidence for a number of prohibition cases that were to be brought before the federal grand jury in October of 1929. Two Borger police officers, Jim Hodges and Sam Jones, were indicted by the 84th district court in November of '29 for the murder of Holmes. Despite the 80 witnesses that testified, neither Jones nor Hodges went to jail for the murder. John H. White in his book (Borger, Texas) describes preliminary court proceedings on the case. The Governor appointed District Attorney Clem Calhoun to replace Holmes's seat and conduct legal proceedings on the trial. Rep. White describes Calhoun as one of the most vicious prosecutors in Texas and gives this account of the morning:
"On the morning of November 23rd the habeas corpus hearing for Sam Jones, indicted for the murder of former District attorney Holmes came up for hearing. W.C. Witcher, a Borger attorney was representing Jones, and... asked the state to put on evidence in order to determine intelligently what bond the man should be held under. At this juncture, the District attorney stated, 'I know what he wants—he wants us to tip our hand, so he can come to Borger, call his herd, bring over his perjured testimony.' Attorney Witcher replied, 'Your Honor, I resent the last statement of the District Attorney and take it as a direct insult, and brand it as an infamous lie!' The District attorney, Calhoun, then jumped up and reached into his pocket for his pistol with which to shoot Witcher. Deputy Sheriff W.L. Kelley reached for his pistol and told the District attorney to 'Sit down or I'll knock your head off.' Another deputy sheriff at the District attorney's word took attorney Witcher into a side room, where he was presumable searched for deadly weapons, finding only a pen knife, which he removed."
On October 26, 1954 the state of Texas dismissed the murder charges against both Jones and Hodges. Mayor Glen Pace and Sheriff Joe Ownbey were also indicted because they had not aided Holmes in his campaign against crime. John White in his book recounting events at the time portrays Sheriff Ownbey as an old-time Panhandle Plains citizen, ex-cowpuncher and ranch foreman and past sheriff of HC, who only resigned his position in Borger law enforcement to save the city from having the National Guard stay indefinitely. He is described by White as "an honest man." White predicted that when the present Governor of Texas was replaced the next year that Ownbey and many other law officers who resigned would be re-elected to their positions. According to Hutchinson County records, C.O. Moore completed former sheriff Ownby's (sic) term and in 1931 Jim Crane was elected Sheriff for one year, followed by Dan H. Hardee who was sheriff for the next five years. At the time when Ownby (spelling in Hutchinson County Officials Register) was sheriff, the office was combined with Tax Collector (Sheriff/Tax Collector). The records show that after 1931 when Moore completed Ownby's term the positions were separated, and the infamous Arthur Huey became Tax Collector from 1931-1935; his term ended when he went to prison for embezzlement. Martial law was established after numerous requests from Borger citizens to provide relief for law-abiding citizens there. This goal was eventually achieved, but not before Ace Borger himself was gunned down August 31, 1934 by a vengeful county tax collector, Arthur Huey, who had placed the county's money into Ace Borger's bank. The bank failed, leaving the county with no income to pay expenses. The story is recounted by Slim Harrell, barber, who worked in a shop across the street from the PO.

Bad Day to Go to the Post Office
Ace Borger was born on April 12, 1888 in Jasper County, Missouri, the son of a farmer. He married Elizabeth Willoughby of Carthage, MO, his school mate, and the young couple began farming. He then tried work in the lumber industry and this led to "town building". When he came to Borger, he was in a position to have the city as his namesake and he took a personal interest in the town and in the quality of life for the town citizens. Unfortunately, his earlier alliance with John R. Miller led to the corruption and criminal influx of the town. In the first days of the township's development people lived in tents and slept in cars. Within the first year there were numerous buildings constructed, including 48 dance halls. It was estimated that 2,000 dance hall girls were in Borger. As in any town, one sells what people want to buy, and records show the town was flush with gambling halls and liquor lines, some of these being illegal stills (not paying government taxes) under the leadership of Miller's shady associate "Two gun" Dick Herwig. But, back to the Borger story, Ace Borger put his money in 1930 into establishing the Borger State Bank and attracted local depositors, with himself as president and his son Phillip as vice president. The City Treasury deposits were placed in the Borger bank. The town treasurer, Arthur Huey, developed a resentment of Mr. Borger, and that dislike became stronger after Borger's bank failed in 1933. This caused a minor panic among local businessmen and investors and Borger was convicted of receiving deposits in the bank even though he knew it was insolvent, a conviction he appealed. Huey was also jailed for embezzlement of city funds and asked Borger to help him out with his trial. Borger refused and Huey made threats on Borger's life. On August 31, 1934 Ace Borger went to the post office, located on Main Street at that time, not across from the Snack Shack, as in the 50s. Huey walked in behind him, shouted obscenities and drew his Colt .45, shooting Borger five times. He then went over to Borger's fallen body and took Borger's own gun (.44 caliber) and shot him four more times. Lloyd Duncan, farm boss for the Magnolia Petroleum Company, was severely wounded by the gunfire exchange and died five days later. At the trial, held in Canadian TX, Huey claimed that Borger was gunning for him and pleaded self-defense. The jury believed him and acquitted him of the murder charge, however Huey was later convicted of false robbery of county funds (embezzlement) and sent to prison. The city's money could have been deposited in safer banks in Panhandle or Amarillo and tax-paying citizens had to rebuild the city treasury. Ace Borger's body was taken back to Missouri for burial in his family plot. Borger's sons, Phillip and Jack, left the area soon after their father's death. However, their sister, Helen, remained and occupied the brick house with her husband, Fritz Thompson. Ace Borger's dream house, now a Texas historical landmark, has remained a family treasure. The Hutchinson County Historical Museum has many photos of the early days of Borger and readers should visit the museum to see them. The Museum has a written narrative of an interview of Slim Harrell, one of the early Borger pioneers, who put in a barber shop across from the post office where Ace Borger was murdered.

Building the Infrastructure
One important aspect of the development of the township was getting communication resources, electricity, roads and other means of transportation to the area. Before the end of 1926 a telephone system and service, as well as steam-

generated electrical service, was available. The Panhandle and Santa Fe Railway began a spur line to Borger from Panhandle, TX. Roads were mere sod covered passageways through grasslands and travel was difficult. The ability to travel by railway and to bring supplies to the area by rail was a major boost to getting an infrastructure established so business could be conducted. Of course, another major need was to provide buildings for habitation and for feeding the populace. J.D. Williams (known as Big Heart, another story to be told later), set up the first hamburger stand in Borger on the Main street, three miles long at that time. It accompanied other important buildings being constructed, including a hotel and a jail. Drinking water in 1926 was provided by hauling water to the townsite in tank wagons pulled by horses and efforts to drill for water wells began. It has been said town pioneer Big Heart Williams got his name because he sold water for 10 cents a cup. To a thirsty man with little money he was thought to have a "big heart" when it came to preventing one of dying from thirst.
The first newspaper in HC was called *The Hutchinson County Herald* with the first issue April 5, 1926. It was a weekly publication and considered to be the county seat newspaper. The name was changed to "The Borger Daily Herald" with the first issue November 23, 1926. It was established November 23, 1926, as was hailed as "the greatest testimonial ...to a genuine belief in the permanency of the city". The owners were J.L. and J.E. Nunn and D.W. Warren of Amarillo and represented the most modern newspaper enterprise available. No stock was sold to finance the paper as the proprietors took all the risk themselves. The publishing team described in the first edition "The combination of circumstances culminating in the publication of a modern daily newspaper on land so barren mesquite is scarce, on plans rarely viewed by human eyes prior to eight months ago, adds an exciting chapter to the story of Texas achievement. (This event) mimics the struggling printer dragging over the rockey (sic) way his hand press and a few cases of his long primer and brevier. It is almost impossible to believe that right here, on ground seldom if ever seen except by a lonesome cowpuncher until a few months ago, in its own 200 foot building, a fast press is grinding out a modern daily newspaper by the thousands." The newspaper investment was $35,000.00 and brought 22 good jobs to Borger. The newspaper owners leased a private wire from the Associated Press and hired a telegraph operator to receive all the news of the world, presented along with advertisements from businesses in Borger. This newspaper was later owned by the Whittenburg family enterprises and renamed in September 1946 to the *Borger News-Herald*. My mother worked at the newspaper during the early to mid-1940s. The Advertising Manager of the paper at that time was my stepfather, Wayne Lanham. He was devoted to keeping our family money in Borger and we could never go to Amarillo to buy clothes or...anything.

"Boomtown" painting by Thomas Hart Benton

In 1928 the noted artist Thomas Hart Benton visited Borger and painted a famous painting of the Main Street. He titled it "Boomtown". Benton formerly painted in Europe, returning to the United States in 1908, and after the death of his father became interested in painting "the American scene" and murals depicting a "people's history of the U.S., from the earliest settlers to the present". His quest to accomplish this brought him to the oilfields and ranches of Texas. The painting "Boomtown" plays a prominent role in this saga, since it was the most important painting to result from this sketching trip through America. It was regarded as a masterpiece, distilling a distinctive, humorous, raucous vision of American life. The canvas records the boomtown of Borger TX, a town that sprouted from empty ranchland with astonishing speed, in that a gusher came in around January 11, 1926 drilled by the Dixon Creek Oil and Refinery Company. In Benton's autobiography *An Artist in America* he noted

"I was in the Texas panhandle when Borger was on the boom. It was a town then of rough shacks, oil rigs, pungent stinks from gas pockets, and broad faced, big-boned Texas oil speculators, cowmen, wheatmen, etc. The single street of the town was about a mile long, its buildings thrown together in a haphazard sort of way. Every imaginable human trickery for skinning money out of people was there. Devious-looking real-estate brokers were set up on the corners next to peep shows. Slot machines banged in drugstores which were hung with all the gaudy signs of medicinal chicanery and cosmetic tom-foolery. Shoddy preachers yowled and passed the hat in the street. Buxom, wide-faced brightly painted Texas whores brought you plates of tough steak in the restaurants...The hotels that had bathtubs advertised the fact...Out on the open plain beyond the town a great thick column of black smoke rose as in a volcanic eruption from the earth to the middle of the sky. There was a carbon mill out there that burnt thousands of cubic feet of gas every minute, a great, wasteful extravagant burning of resources for monetary profit...Borger on the boom was a big party—an exploitative whoopee party where capital, it's guards down in exultant discovery, joined hands with everybody in a great democratic dance ."

Benton's painting records the view from the second floor window of Don Dilley's apartment (above Dilley's American Beauty Bakery where my grandmother worked) of Borger's Main Street. Years later in 1976 Mrs. Dilley told a journalist "He was an interesting person but I didn't know he would become so famous. He and his cousins were our guests for lunch and Benton did his sketching while we talked about Kansas." Some have described the Boomtown scene as depicting a frenzied energy, can-do-spirit, wastefulness of natural resources, corruption, and sheer manic exuberance of the town.

Development of Civic Services

By March 1930 Borger had a Chamber of Commerce with a president, Guy T. Coffee. In four years since city incorporation the city had grown to a status as "the second city in Texas, just behind Houston". Some businesses failed while others stayed the course and ultimately succeeded, so that in March 1930, during the depression, merchants in Borger were in much better shape than the average business in any part of the country, according to a report in the publication *Nation's Business*. Real estate was selling at high prices and business and residential construction had taken off. Civic pride led to the establishment of many civic and fraternal organizations with men and women working together to build a better Borger. Merchants realized that boom days were

over and boom prices must be eliminated, making for more affordable living in the area. Top quality merchandise, together with staples in all product lines, at a range lower than could be obtained in adjacent cities, was available. Road infrastructure was being planned out to accommodate not only business, but also tourist travel. It was noted in the 1930 article "that while the rest of the country, generally speaking, is suffering from a general business depression, Borger's business will exceed that of 1929 and at the end of this year we predict that the entire community well be prosperous, contented and happy." With the aid of the Work Projects Administration (WPA) streets were improved and the boom shacks were gradually replaced with permanent buildings. Main Street included numerous business enterprises and most essential products could be found in Borger.

At this time part of the investment in Borger was made by The Griffith Amusement Company which invested $100,000 in theater equipment with the Rex and the Rig movie theaters, including "talkie equipment". In 1929 the Rig Theater was equipped with the latest Vitaphone improvements and the theater was considered the best in the entire Panhandle. The Rex was also equipped with talkie equipment in January of 1930, opening to the public February 1, 1930. Both theaters had air cooling devices to provide comfort to attendees, as well as theater managers and uniformed ushers, in the same style as metropolitan theaters. The American Theater (later renamed the Crown) was the third theater and it only showed silent movies. The Rig and Rex Theaters burned down but were rebuilt by the company. (photos courtesy of Joey Wood)

In 1946 the Griffith Amusement Co. built the Morley Theatre, a top notch theater with surround-sound and a screen which accommodated "cinemascope". It had a "cry room" for families with babies to have a place to watch the movie and a balcony for those wanting to be seated there. First run movies were shown there, attracting large crowds, and the balcony was often needed to accommodate all the movie viewers.

In the early 1950s it cost 9 cents for children to see a movie. There were candy options 2 for a penny, so a child could see a movie and have a treat for a dime. The theater has undergone several ownership changes, and underwent extensive renovation in 2000.
Civic improvements included the establishment of the American Legion to honor veterans of foreign wars. It had a dance floor and was the place where the first "Teen Town" was held. The new Teen Town was built after the passage of a bond fund to raise the money for the facility. A modern, large swimming pool was built along with the Teen Town facility and used for many fun events. Before this facility was built Borger provided a large city park, Huber Park, which had a swimming pool, a baseball field, and picnic tables with playground equipment. The Park was for community use, close to the small Huber Camp, a community housed with workers at the Huber Industry, maker of printing ink from carbon black. Huber built the Borger carbon black plant in 1909.

The lawyer, John H. White

John H. White, an attorney who came to Borger 1929, wrote a book about Borger (*Borger, Texas: A history of the real facts about the most talked of town in Texas and the Southwest* was the title) and described his efforts to promote the development of the town. The book was priced $1.00 when it came out around 1930. The book was reprinted, with copyright protection by his children Rosa White Pace and John T. White in 1973 and I paid almost $40.00 for the reprint. The following information and quotes are from this book. He was born in Shippensburg, PA on April 6, 1902, so he was just 27 years old when he relocated to Borger. He enlisted in the U.S. Army in 1917 (only 15 years old), did his reserve training at Travis Air Base in Texas, and served in WWI until 1919. At age 17 he was one of the youngest veterans of the war. After his discharge he returned to complete high school and entered Shippensburg State College, graduating in 1923. By 1920 he began a teaching position in a one room school at Stony Point, PA, and continued with college studies. He also wrote articles for several newspapers while attending college crusading for environmental preservation and that of historic monuments. Following college he took a teaching position at Leesburg and Renova, PA (1923-25) and concurrently began studying law and preparing for bar exams. His goal was to return to Texas as he had developed a love for the state during his military training. In 1925 he moved to Florida with his brother and dabbled in selling real estate. Prohibition was a big issue in Florida during their boom days, and life was fast and hectic, a fitting tutorial for his eventual move to Borger. John moved to Austin TX and was admitted to the State Bar of Texas in 1926. From there he headed to the newest boomtown in Texas, a place in the middle of the Panhandle area where oil was discovered and almost overnight 25,000 people had invaded the area. He arrived in Borger with little more than a license to practice law and a previous experience coping with boomtown events. Within a month he had earned enough to put up his shingle and pay for a typewriter, thus becoming one of the first practicing attorneys in Borger and the first State Representative from the area. He led the effort to establish the American Legion Hutchinson County Post in Borger and became the first commander. In July 1927 the American Legion Monthly magazine reported "When it seems that even the (Texas) Rangers might need help (in Borger), Governor Moody was handed a telegram. It came from John H. White,

Commander of Hutchinson County Post of Borger. If the Rangers needed help to preserve law and order, the Legionnaires of Borger would give that help in accordance with the pledge contained in the preamble to the Legion's constitution...(the Post had) a membership of more than two hundred (and expected) five hundred members before autumn." So, Attorney Representative White could muster the veterans to fight against the criminal element in Borger. Although White was concerned about the criminal element in 1927 that overview had changed by 1929 when he felt Governor Moody's actions on martial law were unjustified. During this time he married Anna Mae Harris and dealt with the issues of a new wife and his commitment in Austin at the Legislature. The session lasted four months and Legislators were paid $5.00/day which had to cover expenses. His young wife was with him and she noted that had they not been invited out to eat on multiple occasions, that small salary would not cover the expenses of living in Austin. He was on the tax committee of the House and kept records to show that no new tax load was passed to burden the citizens during that time. During this four months Rep. White would drive 1000 miles each weekend to take care of obligations in his law practice.

When Governor Moody was considering declaring martial law following the assassination of DA, John A. Holmes; Rep. White was strongly opposed to this action. He introduced legislation to limit the power of the Governor to send the Texas Rangers to cities. Many businessmen felt martial law would be bad for business and for the reputation of the town. This strong opposition to the second influx of the Texas Rangers and declaration of martial law led White to resign his governmental position, returning to private life. His book was written within months of the second withdrawal of the Texas Rangers in late 1929. The book about this "sin city" was published and sold over the U.S., advertised nationally from a Mississippi radio station. Later White served as U.S. Government Appeal Agent in Borger from 1952 until he died in 1965. He received four certificates of Appreciation for his work from Presidents Truman, Eisenhower, Kennedy and Johnson.

Through the years John White and Anna acquired and managed apartments and other housing during the 30s and 40s and invested in uranium mines in Utah. Anna taught in the Borger schools during this period, having received a degree from West Texas State College (WTSC). John continued his education to receive a B.S. and two masters degrees from WTSC. The newly acquired education allowed him to specialize in tax law and patent regulation in 1932. He helped patent many oilfield devices during this time. Through his knowledge and interest in genealogy he helped many establish their claims. During these years he and his wife had three children. Daughter, Rosa Jane White Pace joined him in the practice of law in 1956 and his son John T. joined the practice in 1962 under the name of White, White and White. Daughter Anne (Luginbyhl) married and moved to Virginia. He established the first law office in Fritch TX and practiced law there from 1962 until his death in 1965. He served many clients until his death.

H.H. Crosby, DDS

The first dentist in Borger was Dr. H.H. Crosby and his office was established in 1926. He shared an office on South Main Street, across from United Carbon Co., and later moved to the second floor of the Dilly building on Main Street, sharing space there with Dr. L.E. Petty. One had to walk up a flight of dark stairs to get to his office. The dental cabinet and chair from his office are dated 1904 and were purchased when he lived in Lawton OK. From the vantage point on the second floor of the Dilly building he observed the shooting of Ace Borger in the post office at that time on Main Street. He was the person who informed the daughter, Helen, of her father's tragic end. Dr. Crosby was a veteran of WWI and a member of the Texas National Guard. In Borger he served on the Selective Service Board (bet that didn't get him many new friends) and was a commander at the American Legion Post. Dr. Crosby was a generous caring man who, as the county dentist, treated indigents getting them out of pain due to oral problems. He retired in the 1970s and died in 1981. His dental office equipment and dental chair is in the Borger Museum.

The Alamo Refinery

According to information provided by Elnora Engle Walker, who grew up at Dixon Creek and other locations around Borger, The Alamo Refinery was built in 1926 and consisted of two fractionators. No. 1 Still was put into operation on December 2, 1926 and was essentially the entire refinery since there was no other processing other than caustic washing. The capacity of the No. 1 Still was around 2,500 barrels/day. On October 25, 1927 Phillips Petroleum Company signed an agreement to purchase the Alamo Refinery for a price of $17,818.89 and the sale finalized on November 1. Twelve men were employed to run the unit. Shortly after the purchase the Alamo Refinery was renamed to the Phillips Refinery since it was located in the community of Phillips, TX. By 1929 the refinery capacity increased to 15,000 barrels/day. In 1962 the name was changed to the Borger Refinery, with the new name considered more appropriate because the nearby city of Borger was the center of Phillips's huge concentration of facilities in the Texas Panhandle. During the 1940s it was used as a utility still doing odd jobs of separation to produce special products and it's last year of use was in 1953. In 1958 the original unit was moved to Johnson Park in Borger as a museum piece.

Phillips Petroleum Comes to Town

Phillips Petroleum Company moved into the Borger area in the 1927, bringing jobs and the early day residents who were mostly hard-working people. This influx of law abiding, decent people worked to establish churches, schools and civic organizations.

Labor Unions were formed to represent workers at Phillips and in 1941 IUOE Local 351 was organized and the first contract with Phillips was negotiated in 1942. In 1951 Local 351 negotiated with Phillips Petroleum to secure land, platted and improved by the company and lots were sold to employees through payroll deductions at actual cost, enabling hundreds of employees to build their own homes. This new addition to the city of Borger was named Keeler Heights, in honor of W.W.Keeler, vice-president of Phillips who facilitated the negotiations. The main street in Keeler Heights was Union Street and all the streets were named for officers of the local union. By 1953 the local had 4000 employees in the area. Local 351 presently represents over 3000 members in cities in Texas, New Mexico and Oklahoma (personal information, Joey Wood, Borger TX, Mar 2010). Keeler Addition was constructed on land outside of the Borger city limits, on the prairie where many reptiles habituated. Read this account of living in that location:

Diana Wunsch Denton '64
"We lived in Keeler Heights on Davenport Street , the first street on the North side running East and West on the edge on the canyon. Out of our back windows looking North we were facing the canyon then Phillips, Tex. All kinds of critters crawled out of that canyon into our house. Many snakes. Often the black cloud of carbon floated over our house depositing the black mana over all, including the clothes hanging on lines in the back yard. Once a chemical cloud floated overhead and all the paint fell off our houses on that north side of Keeler.
I spent many hours with Patsy Eason at her house perched on one of the many hills of Keeler Heights. It was very "hilly". Walking and bicycling wasn't easy."

Frieda Lanham Pickett '61
The 1940s arrived and the beginning of WWII came in 1941. My father, W.A. (Doc) Gunnels moved to Borger with his parents and eleven brothers and sisters. His father lost an arm in an oil-field accident and supported the family by delivering ice to homes from a wagon pulled by a horse. He would engage the block of ice with a device that had picks in a semi-circle and carry it on his back into the house, placing it into the "ice box" (precursor of a refrigerator). His mother, my paternal grandmother whom I never met (she died before I was born), ran a boarding house on Coolidge Street. My father's brothers mostly worked in the oil fields. Several members of the family came to Borger during the 1930s as my grandmother's sister and her children grew up there, too. There was not much decent work for women, but my father's sisters could earn a little money by going to the dance halls and dancing with men for 10 cents. My Aunt Lucille was reported to be "the best jitterbugger" in Borger during those days, guess she was one of the 2000! After the war began many of the young men moved from Borger as there was work in California in the munitions plants. My father and mother married in 1939, my older sister was born in 1940. In 1941 they moved to California with my father's brother and his family. My father and his brother said they were "roustabouts" in the oil field, which was dirty and hard work. California seemed to have greater promise for them. Others from Borger went into the military, fought in the Japanese war or in WWII and those who made it back returned to continue raising their families in Borger. Following the end of WWII Borger and the surrounding area prospered as many "set down roots", built homes, established businesses, and looked forward to the future. Patsy Eason (BHS '64) mentioned "My father walked from Keeler Heights to work at Phillips every day (several miles). That generation that grew up in the depression knew the value of a job! They had a great work ethic. Today very few - if any - would walk that far on a nice sunny day!" Patsy is right, our parents and those of our friends all seemed to have the same rules for us, based on honesty, moral behavior and pushing yourself to do your best.

Schools in Borger **[also discussed in next chapter, from THE BIG BOOM: THE TRUE BORGER STORY written by Mae W. Owens]**

Phillips School System
The Phillips community had their own schools, which was the practice in "company towns". Bunavista had an elementary school and the Spring Creek School serviced the outlying oilfield camp housing. In December of 1940, just before Christmas, the 13-room elementary school, located northwest of the Pantex Hospital, was reduced

to ashes by a fire of undetermined origin. Insurance estimates were an $80,000.00 loss, half covered by insurance. The fire swept through the one story building just a few hours before books, records, desks and equipment were scheduled to be moved to the new school building east of the high school. The only articles saved were about 100 folding chairs which had been loaned to a church the day before. A new school had been built and students were set to start school in the new building in January, 1941.

Private Schools in Borger

There were various kindergarten schools in Borger, established by women seeking to earn a living. These may have been no more than day care establishments, but some learning was attempted, I'm sure. I attended Mrs. Stakeley's kindergarten on the corner of East Adams street and a large street. She had a nice home with a large fenced back yard. We played in the back yard, sharing the space with a few goats which were pinned along the side of the yard with a wire fence. If one leaned up against the fence all of a sudden the goat would butt you across the yard, getting your attention, but not causing harm. It happened to me twice before I learned not to rest up against the fence. I guess Mrs. Stakeley milked the goats for the milk. I'm sure I learned something about the ABCs but mainly I remember carrying my lunch and putting it in the back area where we put our coats. Once, I opened my metal container that held my lunch and someone had taken some of my food. I was shocked that someone had stolen from me and reported the incident to Mrs. Stakeley. We never found the culprit but the coat area was monitored after that. My sister, Linda, went to elementary school at West Ward, I think, and I went to Mrs. Stakeley's kindergarten. Our mother worked at the newspaper office.

Winnie Sparrow – Girl Scout and Brownie Leader

As a young child I remember being a part of a community group led by a tall woman, single, and I believe she had a child, a young girl. We called her "Sparrow" and I'm not sure if she volunteered to plan and implement activities for us children or if she was hired by the Girl Scout Organization or some other community organization. She took us on hikes out into the country, got permission from ranchers so we could hike on their properties, camp and hike back. These hikes were several miles and we always had a large group of kids, various ages, on the hikes. We built latrines, put up tents, slept on the ground, made a campfire and cooked our food in foil packets or cans (probably got some lead in our systems as cans were lead lined in that era, I believe) and drank water from the steams. I never got sick and had a great time. Once we found a huge snapping turtle in the creek. It was about 18 inches to two feet across, the largest turtle I've ever seen. Sparrow got a long limb and pushed it's head and made it snap at the pole to show us why we should NOT try to pick up the turtles. That was a good lesson! She took us many places and I wish my memory was sharp to remember all I learned from her generous teachings. She was kind but made us follow her rules, and we were obedient kids.

A New Era: Business Comes to Borger

Following the end of WWII many native sons returned home to work for Phillips Petroleum Company, building their own businesses and beginning families. Still others moved into the area as they embarked upon a new time in their lives. Schools were of prime concern to young families with children. Main Street was a thriving place in the 50s in Borger. Grocery stores providing food for the new residents and clothing stores were in abundance. The Hutchinson County airport was constructed north of town in 1949. During the 50s the town was becoming "cultured" as the Tri-City Concert Association began bringing in many high caliber performers in the Fine Arts. The Hutchinson County Aluminum Dome was constructed in the late 1950s providing a large space for community events. Alfred Skoog was the choir director at Borger High School (BHS) and organized chorales with excellent performance skills. The choir consisted of over 50 vocalists and recorded several records from their concerts. Another special place constructed in the 1950s was the luxurious Borger Hotel, housing small businesses on the first floor and large meeting rooms on the top floor, also enough space for dances. The Rotary Club had a special Christmas Event each year, with the Father-Daughter Banquet where the father with the most daughters was always recognized. One of the members had 5 daughters (Bob Johnson) and my step-father was recognized as having four daughters (the also-rans).The population was listed at 14,000 in 1943 and by 1950 population was almost 18,000; by 1960, almost 21,000 were recorded and Borger was recognized as one of the largest centers for oil, carbon black and petroleum chemical production and supplies in the state. The newspaper headline was "The Carbon Black Center of the World". A long-standing dream of one citizen was the damming of the Canadian River to make a lake for recreational sports. During the 60s the long awaited Lake Meredith became a reality for the local residents. The lake water is not only used for water sports and tourism, it also is a water source for the community. Tourists also are interested in a special type of flint found in this area, called Alibates Flint. It was a hard flint and the local Native American population traded the flint for goods not available here, as it has been found in areas of New Mexico and Colorado. In the 1960s Phillips moved their corporate offices to Bartlesville OK and by 1970 the population dropped to 14,195, although that year Borger was designated an All-American City. Over 3 decades three men represented Borger in Austin conducting state business, Fritz Thompson, Guy Hazlett and Charles Ballman. Borger community leaders worked hard to promote their town and one continuously returning compliment was the people were always so friendly in Borger. By 1980 the population increased somewhat and was almost 16,000 people. These are some of the stores in 1949.

Trip down Main Street in Borger in 1949. Research was done by Zoe McGough class '50 at the library. [Thanks Zoe.]

Business and their locations in 1949 as we remember Main Street
BUS ROUTE -- Starting at South Y - Huber Park Veterans's Memorial
Old Huber Swimming Pool and Tennis Court
Veteran's Memorial (dedicated July 4, 2005)
1335 South Main Street Dr. --Dill Veterinary Clinic, old ZESTO ice cream next door
114 South Main Street (Jolly Pig Drive In - longest in continuous operation, food and beer served).
929 South Main Street Goldsmith Dairy

920 South Main Street Floyd's Grocery Store "Piggly Wiggly" (Winston Floyd's brother Carl owned it)
900 South Main Street Foxworth Galbreath Lumber Company (now Moore's Storage)
801 South Main Street Wicks's Sporting Goods
618 South Main Street McCord Grocery (Tommy and Jack McCord's family's)
521 South Main Street Cecil Darden Service Station
619 South Main Street – Joy-Youts Motor Company
417 South Main Street Black Hotel (originally3 floors with dancing on the roof). Later housed offices of Phillips Petroleum Company.
418 South Main Street Barney's Pharmacy with Isom Hotel upstairs. (This was original area where the township of Isom was established in early Borger)
411 South Main Street Minton's Funeral Home and Flower Shop
410 South Main Street Blackie's Café
401 South Main Street Pennsylvania Hotel
400 South Main Street (corner at Coolidge) Dr. Stephen's Dental Office, glass block windows
331 South Main Street Jerry Keith Electric Company
307 South Main Street Poston /Simpson Funeral Home
207 South Main Street Nu-Way Café
120 South Main Street Smock's Service Station
101 South Main Street VFW Hall and Elk's Lodge
NORTH MAIN STREET
100 North Main Street - Louie Zavernick Tire Shop
101 North Main Street Holcomb Grocery
104 North Main Street Blackburn/ Shaw/ Brown Funeral Home and Flower Shop
2nd and Main – Cities Service Gasoline station (Adolph Schmitz). It was built in 1936, it was the most modern station in Borger at that time, first to have NEON lights, a popular station.
205 North Main Street Borger News Herald
215 North Main Street Yow's Brothers, Grocery (could get cold watermelon from the icehouse there. They would cut you a "plug" so you could taste the melon)
227 North Main Street Darby's Rio Grand Fruit Stand (Donald Darby's family)
231 North Main Street- the site of first building on Main Street? – Haywood Moore Family
305 North Main Street Borger Laundry
331 North Main Street Johnson Bakery (Melnora's family)
324 North Main Street Popular Supply.
400 North Main Street Hunt Motor Company
404 North Main Street "66" Bar
401 North Main Street Furr Food Grocery
407 North Main Street J. C. Penney Company (now the home of "BoomTown" Dinner Theatre).
415 North Main Street Megert Music Company (relocated to Borger Hotel in 1950s)
421 North Main Street Cretney Drug
431 North Main Street Southwestern Public Service Company (Home of Maxine Richards)

500 North Main Street Miller Building (Then Cartwright's Ladies Clothing, now Century 21) –first large building built in Borger (Slim Harrell interview), 3 levels. Elk's Lodge top floor, later moved to South Main.
502 North Main Street Copeland Jewelry
501 North Main Street Charlie Smith Variety Store, upstairs was the Betty Jane Hotel
507 North Main Street Zale's Jewelry
509 North Main Street M. E. Moses 5 & 10-cent store
512 North Main Street Whitlock Drug
519 North Main Street Crown Movie Theatre
521 North Main Street The Diamond Shop (Jewelry store)
523 North Main Street Rex Movie Theatre
527 North Main Street City Drug
524 North Main Street Dilley Bakery -the famous Thomas Hart Benton painting was done from the upstairs of this building. This painting appears in the Texas History books now).
531 North Main Street Panhandle State Bank
530 North Main Street Cullen Drug
600 North Main Street "Pete's Place"
602 North Main Street Oil City Drug and Newsstand "From the Boom Days"
612 North Main Street Rig Movie Theatre (now Crawford Park)
603 North Main Street White's Auto Store (now Johnny's Furniture)
611 North Main Street J & J Show Shop (belonged to Joe Kouri)
613 North Main Street Employment Office (Some of us girls called this "Spit and Whittle" and would always cross to the other side of the street when going to the Morley).
617 North Main Street Big Hart Café (here is where "Big Heart" Williams got his nickname of Big Heart, charging 10 cents a glass for water, very expensive).
618 North Main Street Grand Hardware Store owners Gus Yiantsou (Now the Hutchinson county Historical Museum)
619 North Main Street Dolly's Curio and Pawn Shop
620-½ North Main Street American Hotel (upstairs over the hardware store)
621 North Main Street – Grodzin's Working Man's store (we got western clothes for rodeo dances there!)
626 North Main Street City Cab and City Bus Office
700 North Main Street Morley Movie Theatre built in 1947
710 North Main Street McCartt Super Market (now Dake's Catering Service)
806 North Main Street Holt Food Store (now Frank's Floor Coverings).
821 North Main Street Jim's Grocery belonged to Jim Nix and was open 24 hours a day. (now Popular Supply). Many poor people were given free food from Jim, a real humanitarian.
901 North Main Street Coronado Drug
905 North Main Street Borger Home Furnishings
906 North Main Street Ideal Grocery
910 North Main Street Lindsey Furniture
Historic Addresses of Interest to the 49ers
10th Street (was the infamous DIXON Street known for it's brothels, gambling and criminal element in the earliest boom days).

7th and Deahl Street (The first Skating Rink with a wooden floor, side walls and a tent top).
6th Street between Main and Deahl (American Legion Hall the home of the First Teen Town. During the World War II it had a Memorial Plaque that had all Service Men from the County's name enscribed. The Borger Hotel was built here in 1947. The American Legion Hall was relocated to the opposite side of the Hotel parking lot. High School club dances were here in 50s)
Corner of 6th and Hedgecoke- Big Heart School Store and Hamburger Shop. J. D. Williams known as Big Heart bought the building from Mattie Castleberry in 1930 when she was forced to leave town by the Texas Rangers. The building was her Famous Dance Hall where the dime a dance started.
6th Street between Hedgecoke and Coble- Borger High School, then reclassified as a primary school and called West Ward (Now known as the former Phillips Building).
531 North Deahl (the Borger Bowling Alley (now the First National Bank) the present building was built for the Panhandle State Bank.
111 West 5th Street Snack Shack Dutch Jones Owner and known for his famous cream pies.
120 West 5th Street, Borger Post Office. This was not Borger's first Post Office, as I know of three others before it. The one that Ace Borger was shot in was located in the 400 block probably about 422 North Main Street.

Many businesses that we remember came after 1949, as Borger became a thriving business center, helped by large companies locating home offices in Borger. Here are some memories:

In the 50s **Les Hargis**, Class of '59 reminds us that the funeral homes used to operate the emergency ambulance services in Borger, rather than ambulances from the hospital. Their ads included their phone number. Minton's was "Early or Late, Call 718". Brown's was " Dead or Alive, Call 555". I don't remember Simpson's Funeral Home having an emergency service.
I think Borger's first pizza restaurant was called Tonys and it was catty-cornered from the Morley. That was my first experience with "pizza pie". Also we used to get the glass pack mufflers installed on our cars at Jacksons across the street and South from the Morley. There used to be a Gulf station and garage where the Morley is located. I remember when the station burned down and then they built the Morley. I guess I'm the only one old enough to remember this. The Rig was next door to the current Borger Museum where the park (vacant lot) is now located. The original Whites Auto Store was on the east side of main where Woolworth was located (which is now City Hall). I worked there and Mary Pat Ormon's ('59) daddy was the manager at one time. Charles (Charlie) Hargis was my uncle and he ran ICR (the paint company) along with my cousin Doug who had kids named Wesley and Tracey. Wesley and Tracey both went to BHS but probably graduated in the 80's. My dad's name was Bill Hargis and he was in the Oil Field Business and also the gasoline and propane business. If you really want to know some old timey stuff, you have to ask an old timer!
Jerry Shelton '63
I had forgotten about Bergen Radio. My Mom and Dad bought our first TV there - a 21" black and white Magnavox. Even though we could only get two TV channels

(Channel 4-KGNC and Channel 10-KFDA) at the time and would occasionally joke that it "must be snowing in Amarillo" when the reception was fuzzy, I recall being absolutely mesmerized by shows such as "Range Rider", "Boston Blackie", "The Plainsman", "I Love Lucy", "Amos and Andy", "Ramah of the Jungle", "I Led Three Lives", etc. On the radio everyone remembers the by-line "No one knows but the *Shadow*!"

Ed Stevens '64

Castleberry's Shoe Store was on the same block as the Morley in the early years, shortly before we graduated he moved into the same block on Main Street as the Hub Men's Clothiers, M.E Moses five and dime shop, etc. can't remember what was in the building before he moved there may have been a jewelry store. Castleberry's had an x-ray machine you put your foot into and it measured your foot for the correct shoe size. Buckley's shoe store was popular, too.

Lyncia Landgen '70

Jim' Grocery on Main Street.....Jim Nix also owned (and property is still in the family) Jim's Lake where many people from Borger went fishing......I can see that grocery store just like yesterday......my momma lived there with her parents, Jim and Bessie Nix.

Bob Jackson-'66

I remember one time meeting a man and when I told him where I was from he said, "Borger.....I've heard that they have the longest Main Street in Texas." To which I said, "I don't know if it's THE longest, but I do know for sure that it is long." When you stop to think about it, it does run the whole length of the entire city.

The Big Boom: The True Borger Story

Mae Woodard Owens, written in October 1976, who married the brother of my father [William Aston "Doc" Gunnels]. Aunt Mae was married to Uncle

"The history of the Panhandle is richly endowed with such events as the passing through of the Spanish conquistadors, boundary agreements between Spain and the U.S., the coming and going of the buffalo hunters, and the colorful Kit Carson and the Battle of Adobe Walls. All of these belong to the Panhandle, not to any one locality, such as Borger.

The real history of Borger can be thought to have a prelude, like the organization of a symphony. Let us assume that the beginning was sometime after the Battle of Adobe Walls in 1874. From 1874 until 1901, there were few settlers in this part of the Panhandle, but there were fifteen families that constituted the first semblance of civilization in the area. The range was open, with cattle running freely, and a Scottish syndicate known as the Hansford Land and Cattle Company, was running a sizable herd. These ranchers were popularly known as the "Turkey Ranchers". Most of this land was owned by the state of Texas under their school fund. By an Act of the legislature in 1897, the land was offered for sale, and filing on as much as four sections was permissible. The land was offered at one dollar an acre, one fortieth to be paid and balance payable in forty years at three per cent interest. We now begin to see the nucleus of the organization of Hutchinson County. By 1901 many settlers had come to Hutchinson County. These settlers petitioned the legislature that Hutchinson County be detached from Roberts County and be given a separate organization. The petition was granted, and the first election of county officers was held April 25, 1901. The following officers were elected: W. A. Ingerton, County Judge; S. B. Tarkington, County and District Clerk; William Dixon, Sheriff and Tax Collector; B. C. Miller, Treasurer, T. L. Coffee, Tax Assessor; James Archer, County Surveyor; T. N. Russel, F. J. Brown, J. H. Canfield and A. Megan, Commissioners. The first act of these commissioners was to post an order selecting and designating the entire county as one school district which was later divided into four districts. In 1901, the first road was laid out in the county, running from Plemons to the Moore County line in the direction of the place where Dumas now lies. There were old roads in the county before settlement began, the oldest being known as the Santa Fe Trail, but in 1926, the one road mentioned above was the only one laid out formally. Several of these ranchers, the Thompsons, Claytons, and Cobles who helped organize Hutchinson County, still have holdings there.

In March 1926, the Holmes-Huey well came in, within the heart of what is now known as the Texas Panhandle oil fields of Hutchinson County. With it came people who were to this settled group of ranchers what the fortune-seeking gold-miners were to the peaceful farmers in the California valleys. The founding of Borger was entirely a commercial enterprise. The man who bought the land intended to [and did] make money out of it. The founding of the town was as much a calculated move as the purchasing of leases and property rights, the building of rigs, and operation of drilling machinery. The purchase of the land which was later to become the Townsite of Borger was made by A. P. Borger, a promoter from Carthage, Missouri. He bought the surface rights on two-hundred and forty acres of land from J. F. Weatherly on March 19, 1926, for "six thousand dollars". Fantastic, isn't it? *Six thousand dollars* for what was later worth millions. Mr. Borger secured a grant from the Secretary of State, Erma Grigsby Meharg, to form a private corporation of the directors, A. P. Borger, C. C. Horton, and John R. Miller. The name was the Borger Townsite Company. The capital stock was ten thousand dollars, divided into 100 shares of 100 dollars each. Mr. A. P. Borger then granted to this corporation the two hundred and forty acres he had just purchased, in a deed that read as follows: "All of the west one-fourth of the southwest one-fourth of Section 19, Block Y, Morris and Cummings Survey, consisting of 240 acres located in Hutchinson County, State agreed on behalf of previous grantors, J. G. Weatherly and wife, Maggie Weatherly, all the oil and gas and other minerals be reserved."

A. P. Borger, or as he was popularly known, "Ace" Borger, opened a townsite office on Monday, March 8, 1926. The advertisement ran in the Amarillo Globe newspaper, heralding the advantages of a new town. It read: *"Your opportunity lies in Borger! The new town of the Plains, located in the heart of the Panhandle Oil Fields, 27 miles north of Panhandle, Texas, in Section 19, Block Y of Hutchinson County. Terms of Sale: 30% down: balance in 10 equal payments."* By March 7 of that year the townsite had been surveyed, the streets were being marked off and everything was in readiness for formal opening of the town. The first contract for a building in Borger was the bank building which was to be constructed of bricks. The rush for home sites was on. By March 8, 1927, the lure of oil had spread like wildfire over the Panhandle and thousands flocked into the Borger area. On the first day of the sale, Borger and Miller netted $100,000.00. Workers of the Holmes-Huey well and others sought homesites near the scene of operations. The Ace Borger family produced descendants who stayed in Borger. A daughter, Helen, married Fritz Thompson and had a son named David. David Thompson, grandson of Ace Borger, was an outstanding man with a personality very much like his grandfather. He had a big part in the beautification of Borger's Main Street in the early days. He lived in the old Borger home on McGee St., which was a showplace in Borger. David's father Fritz, was an outstanding man who carried out the work that Ace Borger started when Borger was developed. He had the assistance of many good people in early Borger.

The nearest town was Panhandle, which was 27 miles south of Borger. The people of this ranch settlement did not want this caravan of fortune-seekers, and hence this small town has not grown appreciably, and is still just a cattle settlement and farming community. The gypsy city of Borger was not a phantom of wealth "here today and gone tomorrow", as most people predicted. On the contrary, the depression which followed in the thirties, stranded many and they were forced into the responsibility of building a vastly expanding city...a happy turn on the wheel of fortune. Within six months Mr. Borger had sold out completely, his gross sales averaging over one million dollars where surface rights of the land in 1925 could have been purchased for $3,000.00.

Rough wooden shacks and even canvas covered structures sprang up in Borger, the name being adopted generally from the Borger Townsite's sign that the Missourian had placed on his tent office. Brick buildings soon began to replace the temporary wooden structures. In eight months time the town had a population of 15,000 people.

There were other districts outside of the Borger Townsite. To the south of Borger, W. A. Henderson and J. Smith sold lots. This part of the town was named Isom. To the north of Borger, the Johnson Brothers sold lots, and the town of Dixon Creek started up from these sales. To the east, townships such as Whittenburg sprang up. It is interesting to note that the expansion of Borger eventually absorbed all of these districts by a process of incorporation. The only remnant of Isom, in name, may be seen on a local bar with the name "Isom" and the fact that the Masonic Lodge has the title of the Isom Lodge.

After townsite sales were initiated, Joe Owenby, the sheriff of Hutchinson County, took charge of the city. Eventually, however, the Borger Townsite, Dixon Creek, Isom and Whittenburg citizens realized that they were here to stay, and a petition to have Borger incorporated was signed by the qualified voters. The petition described the land, population, survey, and the situation in the Hutchinson County. The petition also proposed that the town be known as the "Town of Borger", and that the territory described as the "Town of Borger" be incorporated under a commission form of government in accordance with the laws of Texas governing such incorporation. The election for incorporation was called on October 28, 1928, by Judge I. W. R. Goodwin, who at the time called for an election of the officials of the proposed town. After the election for incorporation was carried, Judge Goodwin issued the following statement: *"I do hereby declare such territory and the inhabitants thereof, duly incorporated as a town for municipal purposes of the State of Texas, governing the incorporation of towns under the commission form of government, and the name of such town shall be and is the town of Borger, and same is situated within the County of Hutchinson, State of Texas."* John R. Miller was elected mayor, W. T. Malone and a man with the last name, Fleig, were elected commissioners. The city ordinances were immediately drawn by John R. Miller, and the two commissioners. On the first Tuesday of April, 1927, Miller, Malone, and Fleig were re-elected. Then, on the first Tuesday of April, 1929, Glen Pace was elected mayor, J. E. Elgins and W. Corn were elected commissioners. On November 8, 1927, a charter was submitted to be voted on by the qualified voters of the city of Borger, Hutchinson County, for their adoption or rejection. The charter was adopted by the voters. The charter provided for a commission form of government, composed of three commissioners who were to be elected at large from the city of Borger, one of whom was to be designated as Mayor. All powers vested in the city were executed by the commission.

Now we have a town! We are familiar with the gay 90s, the roaring 20s and now the boom era, with the quest for oil a dream in men's hearts, and a by-word on fortune hunters' lips. We have been introduced to the beginning of Borger, but that beginning was what the name implied, only the first of this fiery saga of a boom town. The town of Borger was a beacon to many colorful individuals, and the scene of many historic, tragic and exciting events. All had heard of the bad in the town [it was called Borger by day, and "bugger" by night!], but little if any audience was given to the social, civic, and cultural developments. The life in Borger during these hectic years will be discussed in the second of this series on the history of Borger, and may serve to display the forces and personalities which mold a boom town, and then turn it into a very respectable lady.

Borger "the boom town", was a town of adventurers. The "mushroom town" whose god was the god of chance persisted. At first, Borger was like a cancer upon the picturesque hills of the Panhandle. The crude shacks and tent town, hastily put up, sheltered the complex crime ring that would shame the old time Al Capone groups with its efficiency. Most old timers take it for granted that everyone knows Borger was "cleaned up" by the Texas Rangers twice during the period between 1926 to 1929. Little has been written about it and most of the information is to be found in old newspaper clippings, Chamber of Commerce records, and County and District Court records.

Early pictures of Borger show a jumble of rude houses and stores lining either side of a three-mile long main street, so muddy that trucks and cars were often stuck and had to be pulled out. Most of the houses of that period were of the "boxcar" type. These were called "shotgun" houses or simply "railroad" houses. These houses consisted of two or three rooms, built one behind the other, without porches, awnings, or architectural ornamentation of any kind. By February 27, 1927, work on the Black Hotel had been completed. This was Borger's most pretentious architectural achievement in that it was "four stories and of fire-proof construction throughout, modern in every detail." Regardless of how much this raised the prestige of Borger in the eyes of traveling salesmen, it did little to assuage crowded conditions of Borger's native population. Rooms were at a premium in those days and many men drove back to Amarillo or Panhandle after a day's work in order to find a place to rest or sleep.

Fires and explosions were everyday occurrences in that early period of Borger history. For example, on February 21, 1927 shortly after 2 o'clock PM, eighteen hundred quarts of nitroglycerin exploded. It was stored in a magazine about one and a half miles southeast of Borger. The town was rocked from one end to the other by the blast. But fires and explosions were merely frequent incidents in the lives of the people of early Borger. If the memories of inhabitants and press reports are to be given credence, there was constant excitement and insecurity from other sources. An old resident gives the following mental and sound images of Borger in the night: noises of all sorts were to be heard. The pop of opening beer bottles, the roar of escaping gas from wells a few hundred feet away, the sound of a siren on an ambulance tearing by as fast as traffic would permit, the backfire of trucks and cars and occasional pistol shots, the continuous grinding away of an automatic piano, the blare of a half-drunk jazz orchestra in one of the numerous dance halls, the voice of the "law"... the whack of a pistol on some poor creature's head, the whine of some beggar wanting the price of a bed [but more often the price of a drink], all of these were to be heard by the visitor spending the night in Borger.

In spite of prohibition laws, the illegal liquor traffic was stupendous. Liquor joints were in every block. They might be found in a restaurant, gambling hall, or behind a camouflaged drugstore set-up. Two kinds of beer [coc and brew] were sold, but the demand for it was so great that it was usually served green. The liquor was of two kinds also – a vile-tasting iodine liquid produced from the local stills, which were known as "lines", and the imported liquor, which was a reddish liquid. As one enlightened Borgan remarked, it was probable that it was imported from as far as the other side of the river. There were "lines" on other commodities, too. There were "line" girls and dope "lines". It has been said that the beer and whiskey "lines" were directed by a notorious criminal, Dick Herwig, later convicted of murder in Oklahoma. It has been also reported that the "line" employed official tasters to visit the various joints selling, and *woe unto them* if the liquor did not have the "line" flavor. Tales of other forms of vice are even more sordid than these. The Borger "Belles" were no less notorious. Reliable accounts estimate that there were over 2,000 of these women in Borger in the early days, some of them serving as hostesses in dance halls – Mattie's White Way, and Pa Murphy being the most notorious. While others were stationed in houses on the ill-paved Dixon Street, and still others were to be found in "night clubs" such as Pantex Sis, Cottonwood Inn, Bevo Mills, the Canadian Club, and the Bucket 'o Blood. The dance hall hostesses charged twenty-five cents a dance out of which they received fifteen cents, and the earnings of the other women must have been enormous judging from the reports of the amount of money they spent with local merchants. One of the "best" jitterbuggers around was Lucille Gunnels, sister to Frieda Lanham's [class of '61] father, Doc Gunnels. People did what they could to make some money to support the family.

Bev's mother

Killings were probably fewer than was to be expected. During the three years from 1926 to 1929, the estimate is thirty. This number included four deputies and one district attorney. Money talked to the courts, and all offenses were assessed fines regardless, except, in the case of the "line", where cases were generally dismissed for *lack of evidence*. It is interesting to note that Dick Herwig, the alleged founder of the "lines" was the first deputy in Borger, and, of course, named other deputies who would generally be congenial. These people were beyond subtle activities and flaunted their business under the noses of the respectable citizens.

The transition period of Borger, like the word itself, is hard to point to with any specific time, but it is generally believed that the initial turning point came with the murder of John A. Holmes, District Attorney. At 10:15 PM, on September 13, 1929, John A. Holmes was shot to death while closing the doors of his garage in the rear of his home. The killers hid in the shadow of a vacant house next door. Holmes had been elected to the post on September 13, 1928. It had been whispered about from the very first that Johnny Holmes would never serve out his term of office. This was, of course, attributed to the edict of the Borger crime ring. Suggested motives were various, but one thing was certain, and that was that Holmes was obstructing the pleasant pursuit of vice. Mrs. Holmes charged that her husband was the victim of an underworld plot. When the sheriff came to see her, she sent him away and later charged that the sheriff and the mayor and all the city and county officials had never given her husband any aid in his campaign against vice and crime. While Borger officials were making a great show of searching for the murderer of Holmes, other parts of the state were becoming interested in this little oil boomtown "up North". With a second murder, this time of a private citizen, 48 hours after the Holmes shooting, Governor Moody certainly felt that an investigation was in order. The first few days after the murders, an official investigation began with the communication which said that Borger could be faced with the possibility of martial law, but that if corrections of the existing conditions could be effected without this drastic measure, such an act would not be necessary. Captain Hamer of the Texas Rangers accordingly made an investigation and reported that it was the worst condition that he had ever encountered in his long career of law enforcement. Hammer also reported that some of the law enforcement officers had either served terms in the penitentiary or were now under indictment. The community leaders of Borger challenged the statement of Captain Hamer and the Borger Daily Herald had the following reply: *"Borger people are anxious for proof or disproof of the statements made by Captain Ranger Hamer to the effect that there exists here the 'worst bit of organized crime' that he has ever encountered. If such a crime ring does exist here, Borger people demand the arrest of it's leaders; if it does not exist, they demand a retraction of the information going out of the city to that effect."* Hamer did not reply. Instead, Brigadier General Jacob F. Wolters was dispatched to Borger to make further investigations and recommendations. He conferred with the mayor, Ranger Captain Tom Hickman, with District Attorney Clem Calhoun, who had taken the office after Holmes' murder, and some Borger businessmen. On the basis of the second investigation, 84 National Guardsmen and 14 officers arrived in Borger and proclaimed the town under martial law. Although this was the first actual proclamation of martial law, the town had been threatened with it before. At the request of citizens, Governor Moody had stationed ten Texas Rangers there since April 4, 1927. Most of the arrests made were for narcotic and prohibition violations, but most of the business people felt that Borger should be allowed to rid itself of crime. The Rangers were never withdrawn, however, and there were reinforcements for them when the town was declared under martial law. The clean-up started efficiently and quickly. All officers, with the exception of Judge J. M. Hood and County Attorney Henry Meyers were relieved. Ranger J. W. Aldrich was appointed acting chief of police while Ranger Sergeant C. B. Wheatley was named sheriff pro tem at Stinnett. Arrests were made on a wholesale basis for liquor, narcotic, and firearm violations. Many of the deposed city officials were arrested, and immediately after, an order was issued for the arrest of the mayor, on the grounds that he forced a witness to leave town during a murder trial. The "heat was on", but by the second day of martial law things were unusually quiet. Very soon after, the newspapers which had been labeling Borger as the Babylon of Blood, were quick to report it's reformation. Seven days after martial law was declared, the Kansas City Journal Post had this to say: *"Borger is a business-like town today and not a place for foolishness or law violations such as preceded the advent of the military. The town is bone dry, orderly as a church on Sunday morning, and women of the former "bright light" districts have found darkness is a blessing. There isn't a saloon, gambling joint, or immoral place open in the town, and in all likelihood, there will not be any open for many more moons. Night life is out of the picture."*

The summary of the achievements of martial law in Borger during this one month is appreciable. Forty arrests were made of persons who had been under suspicion since April 4, 1927. An entire new official city and county force was installed including a new mayor, three new commissioners, and a complete police force. Furthermore, the Texas Rangers obtained affidavits substantiating alleged public official conspiracy in underworld activities in Borger and Hutchinson County. As for the murder of John A. Holmes, he was not apprehended while the city was under marital law, but it was believed that the motive had been discovered. He had gathered a great deal of evidence, it was thought, to be used in a number of prohibition cases which were to be brought before the Grand Jury convening on October 15 of the year he was shot. His assassins were later apprehended in November of that same year. Whether or not martial law did rid Borger of it's crime ring, as was claimed, certainly there has been no necessity in the years that followed for the governor to call out the militia again. Most Borger citizens go about their daily business undisturbed by Borger's past reputation.

The city's first hospital was Malone Hospital at Fourth and Weatherly streets, then a larger one was built at Sixth Street East, just off Weatherly Street. The site of the old hospital was made into the City Hall parking lot. By 1929 Main Street had been paved and sewage and lighting systems installed. Before 1929 gas lights were used and water was hauled in by trucks from the springs north of Borger and emptied into barrels selling for one dollar a barrel. The ice house also sold ice. In 1929 City Hall was built on East Sixth Street and was used for many years. Shortly after this time, Gulf Oil Company, Prairie Oil & Gas Company, Marland, United Continental, and Huber Oil Company set up business in Borger. Each one of these companies built homes for their employees. These homes are still in use today, but most of the companies moved from Borger to other boom areas. Phillips relocated offices to Bartlesville. Huber Oil and Carbon Black ceased operations in the 1980s. Most of the oil companies became discouraged in the '30s in the depression. There was plenty of oil, but sales were slow and money was almost a thing of the past. Stinnett to the north of Borger is a very busy small city, and the county seat of Hutchinson County. Borger is located in Hutchinson County.

SECTION 2: Church building in the city of Borger

It is a cause of some concern to people who realize that only the bad and florid accounts of Borger have reached various parts of the country. Very little is ever said about the cultural developments. Everyone who reads the newspapers knows about Borger's alleged crime ring, but how many know that by 1929, three years after Borger's birth, there were 13 churches in Borger and nine church buildings? Everyone has heard of Borger under martial law, but who has heard of the excellent school systems? If Borger is judged alone from the florid accounts of the past, then, indeed, the town deserves it's name of the "Sodom of the Plains". This side of the life of Borger made such excellent material for headlines, and so fed the inherent love of human nature for the scandalous and sensational, that very little has been said of the more constructive forces in Borger, which from the very beginning, were trying to make an impression upon the seething violence and lawlessness. The religious, civic and cultural influence in Borger, therefore, more properly claim emphasis at this point since they have received less public attention. The rearing of children of these early Borgans deserves a chapter of it's own." For example, Faye Litterell Blanks is the first female County Judge in Hutchinson County. There are many others who have excelled and made a significant contribution to society (Part 3). Looks like the "shady lady of the Panhandle" has certainly gone respectable. Faye contributed her story of how she became the 1st County Judge in Hutchinson County:

Litterell, Faye Blanks, BHS '61

I started working part time in the County Judge's office in 1986, immediately loved the work and all pertaining to that office. However, while I was working part time the Justice of the Peace became very ill and the County Judge appointed me to fill in for her (full-time). That is when I really became interested in law. The commissioners then took it upon themselves to send me to all the training available for JP's and court clerks. That training has proven to be the stepping stone for higher aspirations. I ran for the office of JP at election time and won my election and took office in 1991. I have served in that capacity for almost 16 years. About 8-9 years ago I determined that I wanted to be the County Judge. I visited with the commissioners and one of them stated that our county was not ready for a woman leader! I believe that was the spark that set me to make sure that I became the first female County Judge! So, when the time came that our current County Judge determined to retire, my husband and I had a long talk because he is retired and I did not know if he would want me to continue working. But the great love of my life came through again and said "You will not be happy until you do this so I am behind you all the way". His standing joke is he would rather have a "working wife" than a pumping oil well and he has had both.

So the campaign began and the rest will soon be history. I won the vote by 73% (72.8) and took office January 1, 2007. This is unique, too, because at this point in Texas (or at least last year when I started my campaign) there are only about 30 women County Judges out of 254 counties in Texas. This too is exciting!

Moral to this story is to *never give up on your dreams*, they may come true and I have been truly blessed all my life. I believe that growing up in Borger and Hutchinson County has given me the confidence and desire to serve others. My faith in our God has granted me supportive and loving daughters, husband, grandchildren, siblings and parents.

[back to Mae's book] "It is the purpose of this book to survey the constructive forces leaving their mark upon the history of Borger at the same time that publicity was giving our city it's shady reputation. The road of the church-minded citizens in early Borger was anything but a primrose path. The first church services in Borger were held on the first Sunday in June, 1926, in the store of the Herring and Young Grocery Company. The next Sunday they were held in the Dobbins Undertaking establishment. About 25 persons were present at these first two meetings. By the first Sunday in July, through the energy and determination of Rev. Orion W. Carter, a tabernacle was partly completed and, in it, the Methodist Church was organized. There were 54 charter members. Not without difficulties was the building erected, for, writes one of the early members: "*We finally bought a little lumber and had to sleep with it in order that no one should take it during the night. This being the case, the pastor, who became night watchman, had to leave his bed at the location during the day and, unfortunately, on the second or third day, the bed caught fire and the pastor met with new difficulties."* In spite of these minor tragedies, however, the church became self-supporting by the first Sunday in August. The Baptist Church was the next one to be established and was organized in October of the same year by Rev. Rolfe Barnard. The Christian Church was then organized, followed by the Church of Christ, Presbyterian and Catholic Churches in quick succession. These five churches were established by December 24, 1926, ten months after Borger's founding. They represent the first churches established. Within the next two years congregations were organized in several other churches, both in Borger and the Phillips community.

SECTION 3 – Borger School System

Although no longer the center of a community's life, as was the case in old New England days, a school is an essential part of every American community. Consequently, the citizens of Borger petitioned for the incorporation of an independent school district on July 7, 1926, for the purpose of determining whether Borger should form a corporation for free school purposes to be named Borger Independent School District. The new school board thus elected was faced with the necessity of voting taxes, voting a bond issue, letting contracts for new school buildings and ordering equipment for teaching facilities for the new buildings. The election for the bond issue was held on August 27, 1926, and was passed. The foundation for the present Borger school system was thus laid. By September 1926, there were over 1900 children needing schools in Borger. The first schools were set up in frame buildings, with apple-crate desks. Among the first 19 teachers were Miss Mildred McGee and her sister, Louise, the late Mrs. Henderson O'Neal. They came from Missouri after hearing of the urgent need for teachers. Borger High School, the brick building on West 6th Street between Hedgecoke and Coble Drives, was completed March 6, 1927. This building still stands, but is not used for schools. By 1929 three other schools had been built: East Ward, at Ninth and Weatherly (turned into the School Administration Building in the 1950s), Weatherly school at the west end of Grand Avenue, and West Ward adjacent to the old High School.

The administrative problems of the Borger school system in the early days were many and varied. The conditions which were met prior to the completion of the permanent-type school buildings were sufficient to have discouraged almost any teacher. Flimsy, temporary structures were hurriedly built and were unprotected from the broiling sun until money was finally obtained to build a wooden awning. Enrollment was far in excess of the capacity of the accessible facilities. Since water was obtainable only in barrels, and sometimes this supply ran short, the children were forced to bring water from home in bottles or else do without. But in spite of all these discomforts, school work progressed. Throughout the years, the Borger School System has constantly grown and within recent years the fine Senior High School, the modern Frank Phillips Junior College and several new elementary schools were completed.
In 1942 the high school girls basketball team "The Red Birds" were state champions, coached by Faye Langford.

Faye Langford, Girls Basketball Coach

BHS 1942 Champs, the Borger Red Birds

Few records of that League survive but the summary below was researched and prepared by Dr. Billy Wilbanks for his website: www.TexasBasketballChamps.com --a non-profit venture.

In 1942-43 the Red Birds were 33-1 on the year with only a loss to the Friona "Squaws" (whom they defeated in a rematch) marring their perfect record for 1941-42. Borger won eight tournaments on the year and averaged 38 ppg to their opponents' 19 ppg. The Red Birds won the District 20 championship to qualify for the state tournament with wins over Stratford, 35-11; Dimmitt, 47-16; and Dumas, 32-16. Borger made their only state appearance in their championship year of 1942 at the 16-team state tournament (HSGBLT) from 1939-1954. The 1942 state girls' championship remains in 2007 the only state (boys or girls) title won by Borger H.S. in basketball, though the boys teams was the state runner-up in 1952, 1977 & 1983.

Faye Langford was the 1942 Borger championship coach and became the only woman to ever coach a state championship team in the High School Girls Basketball League of Texas (1939-1954). Langford played at Breckenridge H.S. in 1928 and graduated from the Sam Houston State Teachers College at Huntsville. After H.S. Langford played semi-pro basketball in 1929 & 1930 for the Dallas Golden Cyclones who were national A.A.U. champions in 1931 and runner-up in 1929, 1932 & 1933 games. She coached at Borger from 1938-1942 and had an overall record of 96-23. Her first team won the District and lost in the quarterfinals of the state AAU tournament. She won 27 consecutive games in the championship year of 1941-42.

The 1942 Borger players were: **Dolores Vann, Sr; Helen Miller, Sr; Pauline Taylor, Sr; Pauline Boylan, Sr; Vernell Roberts, Sr; Joyce Taylor, Jr; Julia Ensor, Jr; Margret Newman, Jr; Laurella Ford, Soph; Erlene Atchley, Soph; and Lavonne Bell, Fr.** Vann was the Red Birds' leading scorer on the year at 14.3 ppg followed by Pauline Taylor at 12.6. Vann led Borger in the final with 18 points and scored 68 points in the 4 state tournament games for an average of 17.0 ppg. Taylor scored 51 points in the 4 final games for 12.8 ppg. The Borger newspaper noted that the Red Birds were led by a "trio of dead-eye goal shooters who can hit the baskets with alarming regularity" and scored at state at a rate of 41 ppg and by a "threesome of guards" who held 4 state opponents to an average of only 28 ppg.

The 1942 All State Tournament Team included forwards Delores Vann of Borger, Dorothy Godwin of Emory and Estelle Vrana of Aquilla and guards Helen Miller of Borger, Camille Lester of Gatesville and Mary Asbill of Emory. Pauline Taylor of Borger was voted "Queen of the Tournament" after the awards for "prettiest redhead," etc. Each Borger player received a gold engraved basketball. At the earlier District 20 tournament the Red Birds placed four girls (forwards Vann, Boylan and Taylor and guard Miller) on the 12-girl all-tournament team.

In 1942 Faye Langford left BHS and joined her friend and former teammate, Babe Didrikson, as the only women to play in a professional men's Class D league in Dallas where Langford was a pitcher. She and Babe later toured California playing professional baseball with the Wichita Thurstons. She turned down an offer to play professional golf from her friend, Babe Didrikson Zaharias. Like Zaharias, Langford was also a track star and held the national A.A.U. record in the softball throw in 1929 at 247 ft. (only "five feet off the world record"). She "practically single-handed" won 4th place for her team, the Dallas Cyclones, at the A.A.U.'s 1929 track meet in Chicago in 1929 finishing 2nd in the baseball throw at 234' 8" (to 1st place and world record 258 ft. by Gloria Russell of CA) and the javelin at 98 ft. Faye was a member (with Babe Zaharias) of the 1932 U.S. Olympic Team in the javelin. After serving in the Women's Army Corps in England, France & Germany in World War II, Langford later became a lab technician for Phillips Petroleum, close to Borger. Lillian Faye Langford was born on 5/8/1908 and died in Dallas on 3/28/1996 at the age of 87. She is buried at Restland Memorial Park in Dallas. She deserves to be "in the discussion" of the greatest all-around athletes in the history of Texas and the U.S.

Faye Langford was one in a family of six all-star basketball players. She, her sisters and cousins started in Dublin High School in 1928. The Dallas newspaper also noted that six Langford girls were "star players" on their respective teams. There was some talk of a challenge match of an "All Langford" team playing the winners of the tournament. Faye "Lefty" Langford, later coached **Borger** to a state championship in 1942 in the High School Girls Basketball League of Texas; played semi-pro basketball for the Dallas Cyclones--the 1930 national A.A.U. champions; set a national A.A.U. record in the softball throw; made the 1932 Olympic Team in the javelin; and became a "world class" golfer. Joey Linscott Wood (BHS '61) was her caddy when she worked at Phillips.

SECTION 4 – Culture in Borger

From it's very beginning the people of Borger have displayed considerable interest in organizing various social and civic clubs. In fact, citizens have commented at various times that Borger was "over-clubbed". Nevertheless, the effort shows the desire of the people to provide for city development. The Borger Chamber of Commerce quite naturally was one of the first to be organized and began immediately to initiate efforts toward civic development. The objectives of the organization were: (1) to advance the commercial, industrial and civic interests of the city of Borger and it's trade territory, (2) to promote the development of agriculture, manufacturing and mining industries, and (3) the up-building of all educational institutions; and the conservation of all natural resources, with special attention to petroleum and natural gas. This group claimed to be non-political, but because of some fine differences in regard to this factor, a counter organization calling itself "The Borger Board of Trade", was organized. Finding, however, that two organizations with similar objectives were an administrative and economic waste, the two groups were united into one in September 1927, under the name of the Borger Chamber of Commerce. At present, in addition to the organization just mentioned, there are about 25 active social, civic and cultural groups in Borger including the Rotary, the Lions, the Elks, the American Legion, Toastmasters, a Music Club that met in the library, Adelante Women's Club and many others.

SECTION 5 – Industrial growth in Borger and the surrounding area
Little has been written from early pioneers of the most sensational aspect of Borger – it's industrial growth and diversification. A stranger entering the city in the late 1940s and 1950s from the direction of Panhandle could see for miles around the great plumes of smoke from carbon black plants on the horizon and might have wondered if he was not on the verge of an inferno. If he approached at night and the jets of smoke were hidden by clouds he might have experienced an uneasy premonition for the electric lighting of the city and it's industrial plants, together with gas flares, dotted the horizon for many miles. If he passed safely through Borger proper and ventured out toward the Phillips refinery and Rice plant, he might feel the ground quaking to the powerful "chug chug" of compressors and engines. Exhaust steam poured shrilly into the air and myriads of electric lights outlined towers, tanks, still stacks, and buildings in the distance. Recalling the sight, it was almost like walking into a giant carnival. This is the Borger of industry, the Borger of perpetual activity, the Borger that carries the responsibility of supplying the country with a large portion of it's gas, oil, carbon black and petrochemicals. However interesting Borger's scandals may have been, the town in itself does not live on it's reputation. Borger is certainly no longer a boomtown in the original sense of the word. It has a firm foothold in natural resources and has become, so say impartial critics, one of the industrial centers of this country. It has the distinction of being "the carbon black center of the world". Millions of dollars have been spent on refineries, gasoline, petrochemical and carbon black plants. During the depression of the 30s, the Panhandle was one of the few spots on financial maps not marked in red. Wildcatting has been replaced by permanent industries and it is to these that attention is now turned.

Several prominent oil and gas companies operate in the Borger area, but the most important processing groups have been the Huber Corporation, Phillips Petroleum Company and Phillips Chemical Company. Huber Corporation produced carbon black and printers ink and did basic research on carbon blacks, inks and kaolin-clays. The first carbon black companies, principally United Carbon and Columbia Carbon, built extensive plants near Borger and Sanford. These plants were of the channel-black type and several such installations are still here. United and Columbia, however, do not have many holdings here now as they formerly did. The channel black plants, using natural gas as feedstock, have gradually gone out and were replaced by the furnace-type blacks and their type of furnaces which use liquid hydrocarbon as feedstock. Phillips Chemical Company developed the furnace-type black process and used several types of black, produced by this method, in the manufacture of synthetic rubber. Huber produced furnace-type blacks, and the companies were located adjacent to each other. Both Huber and Phillips provided housing to their employees in the area of their plants.

The smoke abatement program completed in the Fall of 1954 gives the appearance of less activity, but in reality is only a mark of further progress. Borger is still the carbon black center of the world despite a decline in the number of operating plants. Phillips Petroleum Company operates one of the country's larger oil refineries near Borger. It was formerly known, and is still referred to by many, as the Alamo refinery. In the 1970s this unit was the largest of the seven refineries owned by Phillips Petroleum. The company entered the Borger oilfield on December 2, 1932, by purchase of an oil and gas lease owned by W. B. Johnson and Sons. Since then, the company has acquired extensive holding of oil and gas producing leases in Hutchinson county. In the late 1970s the Alamo Refinery had a daily capacity of some 70,000 barrels of crude. Since the installation of a new multimillion dollar fluid-catalytic cracking unit in 1950 the gasoline recovery from crude oil has increased considerably. Adjacent to the Alamo refinery is the Borger Fractionator and Rice Plant. Tremendous quantities of liquid hydrocarbons were separated, purified, and chemically transformed into more useful products at these plants. One of the by-products of the Phillips installations was cyclohexane, a hydrocarbon which was used in the manufacture of the synthetic miracle: nylon. A large percentage of all cyclohexane produced in the U.S. came from Borger.

Shortly after our entry into World War II, the synthetic rubber program came into full swing. Gr-S rubber, the copolymer of butadiene and styrene was produced in the Bunavista area. The plant there consisted of butadiene and copolymer manufacturing facilities. The unit in Borger was one of the most versatile plants in the whole government rubber program, and was capable of producing a varied line of synthetic polymers. *Industry and Borger* – two words which are associated with each other. Borger is an industrial city and is proud of the fact, and the continued expansion of it's industrial facilities promises the continued growth of the city.

SECTION 6: Highways and roadways in Borger

We now turn our attention to just a few of the many developments which have been partially responsible for the transformation of Borger from a raw boomtown into the modern industrial city it is today. The highway system in and around Borger has been vastly improved as Borger's population and traffic increased. A four-lane highway was built between Borger and Stinnett with a traffic circle to help handle the traffic near the north end of Main and Cedar streets. The old Pony Tuss Canadian River bridge, where two cars could barely clear at the same time, was replaced by a spacious, concrete bridge. A four-lane highway now connects both Phillips and Bunavista with the Borger metropolitan area including a modern cloverleaf at the junction of Bunavista road and Cedar Street. The highway to Pampa was improved. The city is also circled with bypass highways to prevent the congestion of downtown streets. The Main Street in Borger was redesigned to promote interest and increase downtown shopping in Borger.

SECTION 7: Community infrastructure, hotel and motels

Building of all sorts has enjoyed an exceptional period of growth in Borger. A good example was the Borger Hotel which was owned and financed by Borger businessmen. In the early days of Borger parks were a dream, now there are several community supported parks that have sprung up in several areas of our community. So the forces that shaped Borger's history: greed, brutality, lawlessness have been replaced by civic pride, religion, culture and the drive of the community leaders inspiring men to pioneering enterprise in the development of Borger. It is these former leaders who built the Borger empire, who came after the adventurers, who saw in an oil well, not just a dirty stream of thick, viscous liquid to be turned into immediate gold, but a force which can be tamed, controlled and sent to faraway places to run every man's automobile, to supply the world with ink and oils and comforts; in a word, to contribute to the underlying movement of civilization that we are pleased to call *progress*. These are the men who shaped the future of Borger and reared their children to seek excellence in whatever they attempted in life.

At the present time prices are high in Borger and many people drive to Amarillo, about 45 miles away, to buy what they need in the way of clothes and other major items. It would help business owners in Borger if people wouldn't do this. Most people in Borger have worked hard to make this town what it is today, an All-American city. We have most everything that big cities have. We do need more places for the young people to have fun, as the city is very slow to provide this type of facility. It wasn't always this way. All of us remember the big park on Cedar street with a community swimming pool replaced by Teen Town and the adjacent community swimming pool, the VFW hall where we had dances sponsored by the High School Clubs and who could forget Post's drive in, the Jet drive in, Cone & Burger, driving down Main Street and cruising around the drive ins. Lake Meredith has done a lot to make this area a better place in which to live. The town of Fritch, to the west of Borger, is a very nice, small, but busy place. Many Borger people have found it to be a nice place to make a permanent home. Mr. Roy Brinson fought very long and hard to make Fritch an outstanding small town, with the Brinson Development Business enterprise. Mr. Tom Deahl, Mr. Max Page, Mr. J. D. Walton, also have had a very large part in developing the city of Fritch, the Gateway to Lake Meredith. Frank Phillips Jr. College has added much to the city of Borger and it's citizens. The college was named after the late Frank Phillips, founder and owner of Phillips Petroleum Company. Panhandle, to the south 27 miles from Borger, used to be the Gateway to the city of Borger, but Fritch to the southwest is now more of a Gateway to the City. Sanford to the northwest of Borger should not be forgotten, as Sanford is a lot older town than Borger. Sanford was in existence when the Indians roamed the Plains. There is a rock house in Sanford still standing where the family by the name of Tate lived and had to fight the Indians to stay alive. Sanford has an outstanding sight that everyone should see, that of the marina on Lake Meredith, which is among the nation's largest marinas."

Dale Lane, early lawman/sheriff who took no bull...

By Frieda Lanham Pickett [`61]
A relative suggested I should look up a policeman named Dale Lane. This is what I found:

Dale Lane came to Borger in Nov 1926, employed by Panhandle Power & Light Co. He became a policeman in 1931 serving under Chief Charlie Price. Chief Price died that year in an explosion of a truck loaded with nitroglycerin, which he was using as a well shooter. In 1939 Lane became chief deputy under Vern Underhill; then chief of police. Lane assumed the sheriff position in 1941-47. He is remembered as a tough law enforcement officer in Borger's early violent days. After leaving Borger in 1947 he served with the Oklahoma Dept. Public Safety and worked in the sheriff's department in Big Spring, TX. In 1954 he became a restaurant owner of the "Pheasant Grill" in Lamesa, Big Spring and Andrews. He spent his last years living in Slaton. He saw Borger grow from tents and mud streets to a beautiful paved main street and downtown area. His pleasure never faltered in looking over the town he once protected.

Borger News Herald - Nov 3, 1944: Sheriff Dale Lane was involved in a wreck on official chase. He received an emergency call about a stolen car, started chase with full siren on Main Street. At section of 4th and Main, a 17 year old Borgan tried to turn corner and hit the sheriff's car. Boy had no driver's license and was taken to jail. Sheriff got gash on eye, but caught up with the car stealing suspect anyway. Man claimed he borrowed the car from his boss. The police car was not insured.

From Borger News Herald 7/30/69 – Former Hutchinson county sheriff, Dale Lane, died of a heart attack at age 62 in Slaton where he operated a private business after retiring from law enforcement. Brother Keith Lane received a call from his brother's wife. Survived by wife, one son Jimmy Dale. Body rests in Lubbock.

Interview with **Sam Thompson**: "I remember Dale Lane, I sure do. If you ever had any dealings with the man...you would remember it. When I was a teenager in Borger we had a curfew, supposed to be off the streets by around 10 PM. Well, some of my friends and I decided to try to go to town after curfew. Sheriff Lane saw us walking on a side street and picked us up, took us to jail, and called our parents. We were pretty scared thinking we were going to have to spend a night in jail. Thank goodness our parents were allowed to come get us and we avoided a night....IN THE BIG HOUSE!

Chapter 2: Education in Borger

East Ward School

Mike Crouch – 58
In the 1940s there were three elementary schools – Weatherly, East Ward and West Ward. I seem to be a bit older than most respondents, so many things I remember include many older siblings.....I wonder how many went to grade school at East Ward? I realize this may not be of interest to anyone who went to other grade schools but a few memories of those days still linger.

I started there when we moved to Borger in 1948 and went there thru 6th grade. My best friend was John Kyle who later moved to the Houston area....and my girlfriends were Betty Price and Linda Sue Leader who also moved to Houston in 7th grade I think.

John and I and several others would meet up at the edge of Coronado addition and walk down trails through a field of high weeds about 300-400 yards to 10th St and the school. In that field was a small pond where you could catch polliwogs and a former soldier had built a rope slide from high up in a tree to the ground.

I can remember faces of teachers but only a couple of names...Mrs. Vaughn, I think and Ms. Kennedy who was a couple of yrs later in an auto accident in which Coach Marvel was killed.

Ms. K taught Geography (and did not have a sense of humor) and one afternoon after the typical East Ward cafeteria lunch of beans and spinach and some sort of (meat?), Rodney Escoe suffered the gastronomic effects of that concoction and the loudest noise we had ever heard reverberated from the area of Rodney's desk. Of course as 6th graders, we all reacted with great glee; Rodney pretended nothing happened, but his red ears and the reduction in the oxygen content of the air around his desk said otherwise. Ms. Kennedy was not amused, as I recall she accused him of doing it on purpose. On another occasion, she asked one of the girls to spell ASIA. I cannot recall who it was, but the girl stuttered and the answer came out "a s (stutter) s i a". Ms. Kennedy accused her of trying to be funny by spelling "ass" and sent her to the office.

So I will tell a story on me instead of Rodney......when I was in the 6th grade the school nurse came around inspecting all of the kids for smallpox vaccine scars. Mine is in the middle of my back, so I had to take off my shirt, and my girlfriend at the time, Betty Price did not have an inoculation scar. (I was deathly afraid of germs at that time). Later in the week, my friend John Kyle whose girlfriend was Phyllis Payne, and I and Betty along with a few others had a "date" and walked to the Morley after school for a movie. John and Phyllis held hands on the way, but (being afraid of the smallpox germs Betty surely harbored) I refused to hold Betty's hand. During the course of the movie, the romance ended and I walked home holding hands with my new girlfriend Josephine (can't remember her last name) who I remembered **did** have her vaccination.

There used to be a hamburger stand across the northwest corner from East Ward which made the best hamburgers I ever ate (Heap A Burger). They were expensive for the time, as I recall they were 20 or 25 cents. Also a number of us, including Rodney, would go to the Coronado Drug which had a soda fountain. We would eat grilled cheese sandwiches and began making what we called Coronado mushes......that translates into food scraps, left over fountain coke and water all mixed together in a glass. The drug store tired of cleaning up our mushes and called the school and asked them to tell us to eat somewhere else.

On the playground it was boys vs. girls.....anyone remember "CHASE"? Girls in Borger, of course, were just as big, many times faster and meaner than boys. Many times, after CHASE, I went home with my shirt torn. My mom (among others) called the school objecting to CHASE.

In the sixth grade, we had some sort of version of Sadie Hawkins Day... the girls made sack lunches and the boys bid on them. Theoretically the identities of the girls who made the lunches were not disclosed, but everyone had a signal. I know my memory is incomplete on the fringes, so I cannot remember who my girl friend was at the time, but I was always pursued by Linda Sue Leader. For some reason I did not like her as a girlfriend, though she was unfailingly nice to me. The bidding started and I kept looking to my girlfriend for the signal....it went on and on and finally I grew impatient and bid 10 cents on a lunch bag that was then being offered. *It was Linda Sue's...* she screamed and I fainted. I had only 15 cents left to buy my girlfriend's, but somehow got enough money and as I recall ended up buying Nedra Larsen's. The three of us had lunch together. I found out Linda Sue was really nice, so ultimately she became my girl friend.

Earnest Kelly was our principal for a while and later Mr. Icenhower. Gerald Hazard, Loretta Griffin, Randy Hudson, Martha Judd, Gary Horton along with Linda Sue, Rodney and Nedra were among those in my class...I apologize to the rest whose faces I recall but whose names escape me at this moment.

West Ward by Frieda Lanham Pickett '61

I went to West Ward in elementary school, until we moved to the Country Club Addition and Takewell Street. Then I attended a new grade school that only went to the 4th grade (Gateway). West Ward was a big school, had a huge school-yard and a place to park bicycles. One side was for elementary grades and the other side was the Jr. High. The building was an H shape with the cafeteria in the middle. Some kids rode their bikes to school. I had to walk, as I only lived 5 or 6 blocks from school. We had lockers to place books and coats. We had to bring a combination lock for the locker. We had one teacher and stayed with that teacher all morning. We went to school half day until a later grade. My 1st grade teacher was Mrs. Paris. She let us have a music time and we got to select an instrument. I played the "triangle", hit the metal with a metal stick. We had recess and played outside, playing tag and running. Across the street was Big Heart's where I loved to go and buy "frozen cups". We had a great cafeteria and most kids ate there. At some point they renovated the school and turned it into the Jr. High School, built a nice gymnasium and probably added some classrooms.

Central Elementary
Submitted by Frieda Lanham Pickett '61

I attended Central Elementary in the 5th and 6th grades. I had Mrs. Etchison who was a good math teacher, red headed (and had a bit of a temper) and I can't recall my other teacher; maybe Miss Smith, who dressed like a man. It was a new school and had a great playground. We often played softball as there was a softball field in the playground. I don't remember any swings or equipment but I remember running and playing in the fence-enclosed area. Peggy Weldon was a favorite playmate and we chased each other and laughed all the time. Both Bobby Connelly and Dennis Caruth were at Central in my grade. They were the tallest boys in school and I think I was the tallest girl. We had square dancing in the school cafeteria on Friday nights. Don Brown's father (I think) was the caller and he played records and sang to the music. He taught the lessons to both adults and children. It was a great time and I went every Friday night. My mother made me a 3 tiered square-dance dress and I would twirl around and felt very special in my dress. I liked to dance with Johnny Markee; he was a great square-dancer. I learned to call *Alabama Jubilee* and Mr. Brown would sometimes ask me to call the dance. We had class officer elections at Central and voted for the officers. I don't know what they did, though. I think Mr. Haynie might have been the principal. It was a great school, though, and I enjoyed going there.

Weatherly and Hine's Hamburger Joint
Submitted by Barbara Ferrill Sims, Class of '61

Since we didn't have a car I walked everywhere I went and Weatherly was one of the first places I was allowed to go on my own, but probably walked with other kids in the neighborhood. My first grade teacher was Mrs. Summers. I thought she was beautiful (and she was). She was the perfect teacher for one so shy as I! Joey Linscott was kind enough to invite her to one of our earlier reunions. She came...was still beautiful and remembered me, along with the rest of us who were in her classes. Quite a lady!

Being the youngest in my family, I was often compared to my older siblings by the teachers and principal at Weatherly, but since we were all pretty good students, I was actually proud to be a part of my family and strived to measure up to them. Mr. Jackson was the principal. We were told that he had an Electric Paddle and that if we misbehaved we would be sent to his office for a spanking. I behaved!! We had a cafeteria but no gym. We had a nice playground for recess.

Another teacher who was quite memorable was Mrs. Vogel, my English teacher in sixth grade. She was very demanding and strict but I learned so much in her class. I was fortunate enough to have her again in high school.

One of my best friends was Sue Hines. She lived just across the street from the school. Her father had a hot dog stand in the back of their house. I wasn't fond of cafeteria food so would use my lunch money for a hot dog and coke for lunch...then if I had any money left over would have a frozen cup after school (frozen koolade in a paper cup). Sometimes Mr. Hines would treat me and I didn't have to pay!!

Another remembrance about Sue Hines: On Valentine's Day we would pass valentines around to everyone in our class. There was a boy; I think his name was Phillip Miller. Very cute and lots of girls had a crush on him. In third grade he gave me a very "Romantic" valentine. I was so excited, ran over to show Sue....he had given her the same one...neither of us was very happy about that!

Looking back I think that Weatherly was a wonderful elementary school and wish that all children today could have the same experience.

Junior High School
West Ward was changed to Borger Junior High School, then Sam Houston Jr High, and the building used for these grades. Seventh, eighth and ninth grades were here. We kept our books and coats in lockers. We brought our own combination locks. We felt we got a good education and felt teachers had strenuous discipline and required us to learn. Classes were regimented and we changed classes for different subjects, so had several teachers. Lunch was 30 minutes and one had to run to the cafeteria, stand in line, get the food and eat it in 30 minutes! We found ourselves gulping food and running to our next class to be on time. That is probably why I eat fast still today. As we got older we would run to the Snack Shack or over to Big Hearts for lunch.
In 1957 I was in the seventh grade at Sam Houston. Every Friday was "jean day" for the girls. They wore dresses all week except Friday when they wore Levi's and white blouses. I can't recall how long the "jean day" thing went on after the seventh grade. There was a record store in the Borger Hotel (Music Box) where we bought the latest Top Forty hits. We could put a record on "lay away" and pay it out, a quarter a week or something like that.

Borger High School
Borger High School was 10th grade to 12th grade. It was the largest school I had ever attended. We had a big cafeteria (with great food as I recall) downstairs. We had a gym where we played at lunch on rainy days. The girls from Spring Creek almost always played basketball at lunch. I had never seen "girls" play basketball, only boys, and it seemed a little strange. Sometimes we would dance in the gym and we had the Jr/Sr Prom in the gym. Also I took Modern Dancing class (instead of PE or choir) and we

danced there. THAT was an experience. Doreen Kirk was the teacher and she taught us very "strange" movements that were so funny one had to laugh as you tried to mimic them. I never, ever danced like that again in my life! She also taught us steps for Fox Trot, Waltz and Tango! That was a hoot, too, although I have used some of those steps in my adult dancing experience! We had good teachers at BHS. Mr. Smoot (now deceased) was the choir teacher. He was overweight and I always thought he was "egg shaped". One year someone threw eggs at his house and he came to school and threatened all of us. He was a good choir teacher and we made a 33 1/3 record one year of the choir. I remember singing "Hallelujah Chorus" and other songs. I was very proud of how the choir sounded. Mrs. Vogel was a good English teacher, although one never knew which eye to look into when you talked to her. One of her eyes was directed off center. Mrs. Malnor Arthur (still living) was my English teacher. She had a poster outside her classroom that said "There is no frigate like a book...". I remember wondering what that meant. I've thought of it many times since as I read about some interesting places. I can't remember whom I had for Government, maybe Mr. Philip Land, but he assigned me a topic to investigate and give a verbal report on in front of the class. The topic he assigned me was "The Intercourse Act". I was mortified!! Upstairs on the 2nd floor was Coach Halter's algebra class. I did well in algebra as I had Mrs. Gillespie in Jr. High and she prepared me well. He was a good teacher. Years later, when I was teaching college and my daughter was studying to "test out" of algebra 101, I took her practice test and only missed two items. I guess he was a *very* good teacher for me to remember those concepts all those years later. We had Bobby James for Biology. He was home from dental school in Dallas (he needed to make some money, so he could return to dental school). If you talked while he was explaining something, he threw an eraser at you. Vance Reed sat across from me and was forever asking to borrow a pencil. WHAP! The dreaded eraser! Once I was elected to be on Student Council and I was in his home room. An announcement came over the intercom that student council would meet in five minutes. I got up to attend the Student Council meeting and he argued with me that he didn't think I was ON THE STUDENT COUNCIL. I always wondered what THAT meant. Then there was Mr. Black! He taught History and Government in 10th grade and my year was his first year out of college. When he talked he "spit". All his tests contained "dates" of events, rather than the actual invention. I didn't like it. Seemed irrelevant. I remember Gayleen Melton, was his nemesis. She goaded him every day, saying things to cause him to "sputter". One day he gave her a compliment, like, "Well, I want to congratulate you today since for once you haven't talked out all period." Gayleen's reply was "compliments will get *you* everywhere...start talking!" Downstairs, around the corner was Homemaking. I took a 6 week summer school class to learn how to cook. It was great! I never realized one could make bread or jelly AT HOME! Down the hall was Mrs. Smock's class for Art. My friend, Larry Dyke, took her class. She frequently wore the color purple! Remember? I never took art as she scared me, she was always irritated for some reason. The basketball coach was Tricky Ward. One day I was watching the cheerleaders (Nancy Shermer and others) and he burst out of the gym doors and yelled "You girls gee on outta here!" Nancy could mimic him perfectly and often did...! It was funny. We had a big parking lot in front of the school as some kids had their own cars (I didn't). I remember Mimphord Jones's car "Behemouth" a black car. I thought it was cool! All in all I enjoyed Borger High School and clearly we got a good education to prepare us to be successful in college!

PEP RALLIES: Football and basketball were supported by the whole town. The pep rallies at school were so fun with the band behind the cheerleaders who were on the stage and a crowd of frenzied students yelling in support of the team! Also, all of the businesses on Main Street let kids paint on their store windows. Nothing was better than a pep rally on a flat bed truck (SUPPLIED BY BUZZY BAKER'S DAD) in front of the Rex Theater. These same townspeople regularly crowded onto buses to make the out of town game trips. We had awesome assemblies regularly, sometimes with movies, occasionally students would perform original dances to music popular in the day. Much fun.

CH. 3 TEACHERS IN SCHOOL

Mrs. Vogel – English teacher par excellence!

Sandra Zimmerman '62 (Page, St. Amand)

Mrs. Vogel...... Mmmmmm, have been debating on whether to tell this story. Before teaching at BHS, Randelin Marie Vogel taught at Weatherly Elementary. During my years there baseball was the sport to play at recess. One day when at bat I hit a gorgeous high fly to center field. I excitedly prepared to run the bases for a home run, but the ball hit Mrs. Vogel. It's a freeze frame in my memory. That poor woman...It was a hard hit and the ball struck her in the head. She was unconscious. The hit was the cause of her misaligned eye and other medical problems through the years. I've always felt terribly guilty about that. I also broke David Wise's arm when he tripped over my foot on his way to second base. He lived across the street from me until we graduated and I counted him among my best and most loyal friends and still do.. I did, however, quit playing baseball that year and took up tennis. Too bad they didn't offer Hockey........)

As an observation: Mrs. Vogel was actually the best teacher I ever had. I had her for 6th grade and senior year. She had us diagramming sentences in our sleep and reading college level and she made us think. Am sad she was so volatile emotionally and could be outrageous....she lit into me several times and most everyone else in turn during my senior year. She walked out on our class once, too. But, she got us ready for college in spite of ourselves and I am grateful. I can't remember whether I was in 3, 4 or 5th grade ('53, '54 or '55) when I hit Mrs. Vogel in the head with the baseball. Anyway, it caused her to have permanent eye problems.

Malnor Arthur – English teacher

I asked Malnor Arthur, English teacher at BHS to write down some of her memories of teaching at BHS. **Letter from Malnor Arthur, English Teacher, BHS**

I love all of you, but you know that. I did not grow up in Borger, just almost. I came to Borger with my husband and 7 month old son when I was 25 years old. Now, at over 90, I am still here. Our daughter was born in 1944. I have lived in the same house for 63 years. It had to be moved from Phillips after the big explosion.
When my children were old enough, I started teaching full time. It has been said that English teaching is not a profession, it is a "predicament". Sometimes it felt that way. Most of the time, I loved it. Getting to be with, and to know, teenagers, kept me alert. I never knew what to expect. I was never too surprised at anything.

When the guys stole the Tascosa Victory Bell, guess what they did with it? They did not know where to take it, so they called me! I didn't want to get involved --- I sent them to the band director. Sometimes I was piqued by my reaction to a situation. One day there was a jockey strap in my chair. I saw it from the door, which gave me a chance to decide what to say before I entered the room. I said "One of you fellows seems to have lost a garment. I am going to the office to check my mail. If the garment is not gone I'll have the principal come check to see who needs it. " Needless to say, it was gone when I returned.

I have always been proud to say I taught English at Borger High School. I am very pleased with the success of our students. I feel that I am part of that success. Students have always been welcome in my home. Some of you still frequent my home.

Some sad things happened along the way, as one student accidentally killed another one in a hunting outing. One accidentally killed his mother's boyfriend, for which he was "no-billed". On a bad day a teacher and a student committed suicide – no connection. A student drowned during a Spring weekend. Two more teachers killed themselves. Not I, I liked you.

Most of my experiences were great. In the learning center a young man walked past a group of teachers, and someone remarked "I don't know that kid." I spoke, "I know him, he is in my class." One of the coaches said "Honey, there is no one in your class." Made my day!

Several students lived with us at times, for various reasons. One of them, years later, reciprocated by buying a round trip ticket to Hawaii for us, so I could visit a grandson who was in the Navy. I had not seen him in three years.

That reminds me of this cigar box that was sitting on my desk once, facing the students who were whispering and giggling. When the class was dismissed I checked the contents of the box. A sign said "Send Mrs. Arthur to the moon....one way!" Only in a town like Borger! Those were my good years.

Coach Halter – Algebra teacher

Submitted by Frieda Lanham Pickett '61

One of the football coaches, Jake Halter, taught algebra and advanced math in high school. He was a strict disciplinarian and drilled us in memorization of formulas and logic. He called them "stated problems" and it required a different part of the brain to write a formula based on information given. Students had to study the text several times to understand the concept and it was difficult, very different from previous math courses where we just memorized how to solve math problems from formulas. I believe learning logic in this way helped me with "logic" later in life when I began to write scientific papers. Coach Halter tried several strategies to help the upper classmen learn algebra and be able to pass the exams. The smarter students were placed at the front of rows in the class and it was our responsibility to gather our row into a group and we would show the ones at the backs of the rows how we solved the math. This was unique as no other teacher I had at BHS did this. I used the strategy later when I became a teacher. I'm not sure how many students were helped but it was a different teaching style. He was a nice man, very encouraging to students who tried to learn and evidently was a good teacher.

Ernest Kelly, School Administrator, Principal

Students who were in the Borger school system in the late 1940s through the 60s remember Mr. Kelly. He was much respected. His two children, Patty and Mike, were good students and behaved judiciously. I'm sure he was proud of them. I asked some people to give some memories of Mr. Kelly.

Memories of My Father- Principal Ernest Kelly (Mike Kelly, son)

My dad was discharged from the Air Force in 1947. He was offered a position of coaching and teaching in Perryton, Texas. While traveling there he and my mother stopped to visit friends in Borger.
The Borger school superintendent heard about my dad and offered him a position similar to the one in Perryton. He also offered my mother a teaching position in Borger. Since it seemed to be a perfect situation, they accepted.
Initially, he coached and taught at Borger High School. In 1950 he became a grade school principal, first at East Ward Elementary, then at Buena Vista Elementary. In 1956 he was promoted to principal of Sam Houston Jr. High. In 1957 he became the Borger High School principal, where he remained until moving to Dallas in 1966.
One of my memories that stands out now is that, as the athletic director, he was responsible for arranging all travel and accommodations for the sports teams. As you know, even though Borger schools were integrated many other schools (and society in general) were segregated during that time. Much behind the scenes work must have gone into planning for meals and lodging for the teams. This was accomplished in such a way that everyone, regardless of race, was made welcome and comfortable whenever we traveled.

Mr. Kelly at East Ward by Mike Crouch

Well, this was before Mr. Kelly's tenure at BHS.....he was principal at East Ward the year we moved from Iowa. My family had moved to TX from IA about 18 months before..... upper mid-west winters were WAY TOO COLD....anyhow, I was in the first grade in IA, and we left in Jan 48 (I think) and made our way to 1315 Haggard St, in Borger TX. At that time I enrolled in 1st grade at East Ward to finish out the year.

Much of what we had at EW was a repeat of what I had already learned, so I was disinterested most of the time.....then time came for 2nd grade! After about 3 weeks in 2nd grade my teacher took me to Mr. Kelly and said she could no longer interest me in class... Now, Mr. K, although I came to know him later as a good guy, a fair and compassionate and understanding administrator, had this **stone face** much of the time (at least when he was in his "principal's chair") so I expected at least a stern talking-to and, quite possibly, some hideous form of corporal punishment being visited upon my quivering, skinny little butt for not working hard in 2nd grade class work! Mr. K looked at me and smiled and said "OK, let's try him in 3rd grade" ... to say I was relieved would be an understatement! In fact, as I recall I did have to go get bathroom relief on my way back to class.....and so, my parents agreed and WHAMO I was in 3rd grade. ....All of which is how come I am a graduate of the class of '58 instead of '59 AND all through school was the next-to-youngest kid in my class (I got Randy Hudson beat by a day).

Ernest Kelly was one of the good guys, with wisdom beyond most administrators in recognizing the "reason for the crime".

More Memories of Mr. Kelly, principal by Danny Stephens –

Mr. Kelly was the fairest of all the school administrators I ever had in the Borger ISD. That said, he did have a few "problems" with me along the way. I did give him some grief. Interestingly, when my daughter Sandi went through the Richardson, TX school system, Mr. Kelly was HER principal, too (20 years later +/-). Sandi asked whether he remembered her mother (Linda Alexander) or me, and by her accounts he admitted that while Linda had been a model student, I had furnished a few "memories".

Velma Gillespie and Zelma Root by Mike Gillespie

Education, the critical need for education, was the central theme of life for identical twins born three generation after the Civil War. They came from a desperately poor family from northern Louisiana. It is hard for us to conceive of the struggle to improve one's life in those hard times. The standard was six or nine years in a one room shack of a school with few books. Early dismissal occurred often so the students could slave on the cotton farms.

Velma and Zelma Freeman struggled financially and, perhaps even more as women, in a family of ten to become the first college graduates in the family. Fortunately, a new college, Louisiana Tech was founded nearby their home. Both began careers as teachers in the miserable school system of Louisiana at that time. Moving to south Arkansas later, at least provided some books, a slightly better building, and a barely livable wage.

Zelma married a former Texas Ranger, Leon Root, who later worked as a special investigator for Phillips Petroleum Company; thus the move to booming Borger, Texas. She and Leon had no children, but they reared Leon's daughter from his first marriage, Bobbi. Velma married a roustabout, Wade Gillespie, and self-educated carpenter from the Arkansas oil field. She, too, was desperate to leave Arkansas and Louisiana for the better life in Texas. She brought her family to Borger with few expectations of what she would find.

Driving into Borger in a 1946 Ford with her two young sons, she spotted a splendid brick building on a hill! When told that this was a new elementary school (Weatherly) she broke down and cried, exclaiming "My boys can get a good education now!"

Both Velma and Zelma were hired into the Borger Independent School System. Zelma taught business courses in the high school and Velma settled into 9th grade algebra. Each taught 35 years at Borger, though Zelma continued teaching for four more years at Frank Phillips Junior College after leaving BHS. Velma served on a volunteer basis in many ways at the First Methodist Church for most of those 35 years. She loved to garden and had many flowers around her home on Austin street, which was a real feat in water-starved Borger in those days. She also loved traveling and music. Her sons, Hamp and Mike, were a joy and comfort to her, as well as her three grandchildren. Mike entered medicine and became a surgeon, retiring in 2006. Hamp is retired from a medical lab in Houston.

These two exceptional teachers prepared Borger schoolchildren for competition in state university systems and with graduates of high schools in large metropolitan areas. The Borger grads consistently made the grade and found they were well prepared for whatever came before them. All of us who grew up in the era of the 1940s and 1950s in Borger can reflect back on the opportunities afforded by so many like-minded educators to whom we owe so much.

Upon the death of Velma (1992) and Zelma (1994), the Gillespie family established a memorial fund to award an annual prize to an outstanding K-12 teacher. Nominations would come from their peers. We invite you to consider a donation to the Velma-Zelma fund or a similar fund honoring the new generation of dedicated teachers.

Memories of the "twins" by Edith Guynes Stanley

I didn't know Zelma very well, but Velma (Mike's mother) was my 9th grade algebra teacher at Borger Junior High. I am algebra challenged and therefore was not a very promising student for her in that class. I took other courses in high school to avoid 'higher' mathematics. I was not a student of Mrs. Root in high school.

My family went to Calvary Baptist Church while I was growing up, but after my youngest sister married a Methodist, they attended First United Methodist Church and a new Sunday School class for young marrieds being taught by Velma (Philadelphia Class). She talked my husband and me into attending that class. Velma had studied the Bible extensively and was eager to pass on the knowledge she had obtained. I was at a time in my life where her teaching found fertile ground and her classes were so amazing that this hungry student found much to enrich her heart and spirit. Truly, Velma's talent and calling from God was teaching, both in public education and in Bible teaching. I was blessed more than I can tell by her response to that call. I look forward each year to knowing the teacher who has been selected for the Velma and Zelma Award.

Mrs. Gillespie – A Great Teacher by Frieda Lanham Pickett, '61 BHS
I have said many times that Mrs. Gillespie was one of my favorite teachers. She was strict and a disciplinarian in the classroom, making it clear that we were there to learn and we needed to put our best efforts forward in that regard. She taught Algebra I in Jr. High, and her clear explanations supported by many examples on the chalkboard were successful in helping the students to understand the concepts we had never known existed before the class. I remember thinking, "Well, this is

new!!" As I watched her explain and demonstrate examples I was able to memorize the formulas and do the problems. Because of her teaching style I was able to excel in coach Halter's Algebra II class at BHS. In fact, he had me tutoring some guys ahead of me in school, trying to help them do better on tests. They weren't interested...they just flirted and teased...and kept making poor grades on the exams.

The Band at Borger High and School Plays by Linda Lanham Andersen '59

BHS had award winning bands in 1950s. We always got "1"s in performance and sight reading, and also marching. Band contests were held at West TX State (Canyon) and in Enid OK. In 1959 the competition was in Borger and we had 79 students in the band. Bands from all over the Panhandle and part of OK came in 1959. BHS band officers that year were Chuck Ramsey (Pres.), Linda Maggart (Sec.), Janet Bryan (Treas.), James McDaniel (Sr. Rep.), John Markee (Jr. Rep.) and Dale Ballard (Soph. Rep.). The twirlers were Merle Walker, Pat Hayden, Sandra Bogan, Carolyn Dickerson, Pat Fisher and Kay Turner. **Steve Hefner** was an All-State student, being chosen from "all region band" students in Texas to be in the All State Band in Galveston. The students selected for All-Region honors in 1959 were **Joe Wilkinson, Jimmy Anderson, Harriett Libby, Carolyn Dillard, Steve Hefner, Stanley Latman, Louis Strovas and Wayne Tucker**. Mr. Rex Shelton followed Mr. F.W. Carpenter as Band Director and he arranged for the contest to be in Borger. **Linda Maggart** was Band Queen. The candidates were **Dorothy Bryan, Janet Bryan, Linda Maggart and Linda Lanham**. The prior year Dorothy, Linda M. and Linda L. were dubbed by Mr. Carpenter as *The unholy three*. "We talked too much and got into trouble in band. The next year Mr. Shelton put us in charge of the Sight Reading part of the contest." It was held at a church at the bottom of the hill, close to the school. The judges watched the sight reading performance there. "Linda M. had a Nash for a car and we "drug Main and Post Drive In" in her car. Her father owned Post's at that time." Drum Major was an important role in band and Borger had good ones. In 1957 the DM was **Jerry Strovas**, in 1958 the DM was **Jack McGlaun** , and in 1959 (my senior year) our DM was **Tony McGowan**. We played at all the home football games and some of the away games. When we had a trip a long way from Borger we left school early. We talked and visited on the bus but were expected to stay in our seats. For band contests we got to take the "flex" bus which was a much better bus with better seats. The sports teams usually took the flex bus. Our uniforms were purchased by the school. We checked them out, kept them clean and turned them back in at the end of the school year. Instruments had to be supplied by the band students but some large instruments were supplied by the school.

Mr. John Banvard was our speech teacher and we had great plays. The Senior Play in 1959 was "Cheaper by the Dozen". I played the character Mrs. Gilbreath. The best play we did was in 1958 when we performed "Our Town" where I played Mrs. Webb. Capy Stamps played "Emily", the lead character. Everyone said it was very professional. Almost 40 years later I played the same character in Houston at my church. Mr. Banvard directed the Junior and Senior plays and had a good debate team, as well. He was a great teacher.

"We spent a lot of time at Marcia Derr's house. They had a large house on the corner of Third and Hedgecoke. We would spend time on the back porch and her mother was always glad for kids to stop by." Marcia had two younger brothers, Eddie and Leslie ('61). Leslie was mischievous and often got into trouble. He was very cute and had a winning smile so he probably got out of being punished. "We met at Marcia's because the house was very convenient, right in the middle of town." Marcia's father came to Borger with his father during the Borger boom days. He was 12 yrs old. His dad started a car repair business, also selling parts, when Borger had a tent city. Marcia's dad did odd jobs to help with family income. Once during martial law times he was hired to go to Amarillo and pick up supplies from a pharmacy in Amarillo. The products were for a pharmacist in Borger to use for medicines. He was transporting malt to be used in these medicines and the TX Rangers stopped him. They thought it strange that a young teenager should have "malt" and thought he was surely *bootleggin'* and hauled him to jail. The pharmacist had to bail him out.

Marcia wonders if anyone knows why the first brick structures in Borger all had the same red brick? She recounts that the three first brick buildings all had the same dark red brick. There were no freight lines supplying Borger in the 30s so it was difficult to get supplies. The U.S. Post Office planned a permanent structure and the postmaster told others they could order their brick with the PO supply to be delivered by the USPO. So everyone who needed a brick building got together and ordered the same bricks planned for use by the PO, delivered through U.S. mail. The result? All these buildings look the same (West Ward, Ace Borger's house and the US Post Office).

Red Velvet Cake Recipe by Marcia Derr '59
Linda Lanham's mother traveled to far away places on occasion and brought the original Red Velvet Cake Recipe to Borger. It went all over Borger as people made the unique cake. Marcia recalls that her mother always made the RVC on Valentine's Day as it was brother, Leslie's, birthday. It was a big hit, having this recipe. Soon the homemaking teacher was helping BHS students learn how to make the cake and...who knows?...it probably went far and wide.

Chapter Four
Commerce in Borger

Civic Leadership in Borger

As with any organization, leadership is required for advancement to occur. The following highlights some of the civic leaders in the 40s and 50s in Borger. The city currently has a website (http://www.ci.borger.tx.us/) and shows the direction of the city in the right path.

The Associate Editor, Donald S. Stroetzel, of a publication called *Pathfinder* (published in Washington D.C.) printed a story November 15, 1950, pp. 34-40 on the development of Borger and titled it "From bankruptcy to model city—the Borger story of five years". He chronicles how Borger got new industries, new schools, pavements, churches and better store features in five years without passing bond issues. Here are some of the facts from this article:

He begins the piece by describing the headlines in Oklahoma City (pop. 242,000) proudly advertising that the city's first escalator would be placed at a bank in the city. In the next line he reports that the C.R. Anthony Co. department store was putting in an escalator in Borger TX (pop. 18,000). He reports that during the same week of the escalator installation, Borger Hotel's new 106-room facility ($900,000) was dedicated, an $80,000 American Legion building became available for use along with a new armory, and a $500,000 airport opened for business. He goes on to report that three new grade schools were almost completed and in the past three years a $1.2 million junior college and high school was built, along with 55 new or remodeled stores coming to Borger. All this in October, 1950, in a town 1/10th the size of OKC! The writer contrasts this small town that is not a wealthy boom town with other areas supported by big money enterprises, noting Borger's economy resting on the income from a few industrial plants and from sales to near-by farmers. Per hour earnings are around $1.50/hr for most workers, he says, and there are no millionaires in Borger, although there is a well-to-do class. He says that the short life of Borger (only 24 years) serves to demonstrate what a small town can accomplish with the right leadership!

Joe Cooley, City Manager

Borger is described by this writer as "Five years ago Borger was a dreary town of dark, mostly unpaved streets. Children went to school only half a day for lack of classroom space. Merchants had no permanent hope for the town, demonstrated by stores of corrugated-iron and shabby brick buildings. The fact that Borger today is a modern well-lighted city of beautiful stores can largely be credited to a quiet, unassuming Oklahoma A&M graduate, young Joe Cooley." Joe Cooley was assistant manager of Amarillo's Chamber of Commerce before moving to Borger, upon invitation by the Borger Merchant Association. The Chamber job paid $500.00/ month and initially Joe turned the offer down. However, after thinking it over and seeing the challenges of bringing the city forward, he relented, and moved to Borger in January, 1944. The first few months were slow and the phone rarely rang in the Manager's office at the Chamber of Commerce. This open time was used to visit merchants, labor leader meetings, industry leaders and talk about the outlook of Borger. He found out who the organizers were and got them into leadership positions of various Chamber Committees. An interview of Cooley revealed that "I tried to give them something to dream about—a picture of Borger as it could be. But always I came up against the same things: nobody really was sure that Borger was going to last very long. They feared that industry would pull out." Records show that many took their profits and moved on, as the city became deep in debt after building paved roads, a small sewer system and a city hall. Tax paying citizens had fallen by 1933 to about 7,000 people. Taxable property had dropped in six years from $7 million to less than $2 million. The city was bankrupt in 1940 and the court awarded bondholders a judgment against Borger of $556,000. Then WWII broke out and Borger was given a badly needed lift. The U.S. Government built a synthetic-rubber plant and an arsenal nearby. Phillips Petroleum expanded its refining and other facilities. War workers streamed in, boosting the population close to 14,000, and increasing payrolls from $7.8 million in 1940 to more than $30 million when the war ended. Retail sales were good but still Borger merchants did not spend money improving their store buildings, fearful of risking capital or effort on a permanent Borger. People didn't know how long the oil and gas would last and no one could predict how long the country would need synthetic rubber. In an effort to calm this uncertainty, Joe Cooley and a delegation of Borger businessmen visited Bartlesville OK in 1947 to speak directly with K.S. Adams, President of Phillips Petroleum Co., the largest employer in Borger. They asked Mr. Adams to speak to the Borger businessmen and residents and tell them directly that "Phillips Petroleum is here to stay!" Mr. Adams was so impressed with the sincerity and aggressiveness of these men that he went to Borger and spoke at a public meeting, saying "It is strictly up to you in Borger whether Phillips stays here or not. Your community has never quite caught up with the pace of the industrial domain that supports it, as there are many hundreds of potential Borger residents who do not live in this locality because certain...community facilities and services are not available." Adams continued to make improvements at the Phillips plant by building two pipelines to connect Borger refineries with the oil fields of West Texas, thereby avoiding production cutbacks. Local farmers were becoming more prosperous and Borger merchants began to see evidence of the farm prosperity in cattle and wheat ranching in the North Plains. There was a common joke told at that time "Up here, the only way you can tell a rich man from a poor man is that the poor man washes his own Cadillac." By the end of 1950 practically everything Adams had asked for had been started, with most completed.

A new spirit began to grip Borger's merchants and things began to change. E.J. (Pop) Lewis put up a large glass and brick hardware store next to the original stucco-plastered shack. Frank Jennings, the slow-talking furniture dealer who came to Borger 21 years before with only $6.50 in his pocket, built a new $80,000 store. Hudson Davis, who had run a $500.00 stake up to a $1.5 million a year Chevrolet dealership, sank $170,000 into a service center. The number of merchants willing to pay up to $25.00 to join the Chamber of Commerce rose from 117 (1944) to over 700 by 1948. Now Cooley saw the time was at hand to develop a better city infrastructure and jumped on the opportunity. Some were obvious needs: better paved roads, all roadways needed street signs, and Borger needed a high class hotel. The hotel facilities were so poor that most industrial groups kept guests at hotels in Amarillo, 45 miles away. Borger had a tiny, hilly airfield but it needed a better airport to accommodate landing for Phillips's DC-3s. The City Manager of Borger, A.A. Meredith, worked hand in hand with Cooley to develop infrastructure in

Borger and Meredith made significant strides in paying off Borger's bankruptcy debt. The city's money was earmarked for debt repayment and salaries, so it was clear that additional monies would have to be raised by the Chamber of Commerce. Cooley organized Committee Heads of special Chamber committees to identify improvements and establish strategies for getting the money for each one. The first step was to look at what other communities had done and copy that strategy. They looked at their own resources and asked those companies for suggestions, then had weekly luncheon meetings to report on findings. These meetings were without entertainment, and deadly serious.

Road paving: D.M. Spector's Street Paving Committee came up with an idea to lick the problem of no city money for paving. Why not have each resident on a street foot the bill voluntarily for paving in front of his house or store? Staff at the Chamber were sent out to talk to housewives about the idea, and pretty, persuasive Lou Cooley, Chamber secretary (no relation) took on this job of "knocking on doors". If a resident balked, Manager Cooley or Chamber President Hudson Davis dropped by for a chat. If they didn't sell the idea to the balker, there was always the indirect approach where neighbors were told that "so and so" is holding up the paving on our street! For those with low incomes the Chamber set up a fund so the home owner could pay the paving bill out each month. Between 1947 and 1950 this technique paved more than 200 blocks in Borger.

Street Lights and Markers: In 1944 Borger only had 27 street lights. Chamber Manager Cooley and the Street Lighting Committee members went to the City Commission and worked out a deal whereby Southwestern Public Service Co., the local utility for Borger and surrounding areas, would buy and install the system for free. The city had only to pay the light bill. By the year's end, Borger had more than 500 street lights. To get the 300 metal street markers needed, Chamber members each put up a little cash and the city workers installed them.

High Class Hotel: Initial efforts were directed at enticing a large hotel chain to come to Borger and build the needed facility with office space, convention space and comfortable rooms. The hotel chains were interested but only if Borger would put up the lion's share of cash for construction, reducing their risk. On September 27, 1947 Borger's Chamber decided to finance the hotel by selling common stock. For weeks 150 businessmen rang doorbells in the search for stockholders. Barber Slim Harrell sold shares while shaving customers. Nearly 500 workers, doctors, large and small businessmen bought enough $100.00 shares to bring in $422,000. Most stock was sold on installment, with 10% down, nine months to pay the rest. In the end only $6300.00 pledged was not paid. The chamber looked at state loan funds for reconstruction and got approval for $900,000 from state representatives with the Reconstruction Finance Corporation (RFC), however just when Cooley thought the deal was done, RFC's board in Washington turned down the request, a crushing blow to the Chamber Committee. Not to be thwarted, however Cooley flew to Washington twice to challenge the bureaucratic red tape with no luck. Finally Cooley led a three-man Chamber delegation to Washington and they insisted on a personal hearing with the Board. They explained the logic of Borger's case. The hotel would repay the loan by assigning income from the stores and offices to be built within the hotel structure. The RFC gave in and...the rest is history!

Modern airport: The airport finance committee at the Chamber came up with a workable idea to arrange joint county-federal financing. The problems did not end with financing, however as airlines needed to fly into Borger and bring passengers in and out of the airport. Two airlines were identified as potential customers and who had feeder-line capability—Pioneer Airlines and Central Airlines. To get them to commit Cooley must have good evidence they would make a profit in Borger. Cooley's investigation started by getting hard data from Braniff Airways that flew into Amarillo. From them he was able to identify the number of people from Borger who flew Braniff, and that was only one airline! He documented an average of 70 Borger residents a month flew on Braniff. By the end of 1950 both commuter airlines were competing for Borger's business.

Cooley kept his finger on the pulse of other city projects and learned from Reverend J.G. Glenn (First Presbyterian Church) they had hired a full time recreation director to organize a softball league and other activities for plant workers and their children. Members of the Ladies Garden Club in cooperation with the Chamber had helped develop parks where shacks once stood. Businessmen had risked rattlesnake bites to carry rocks from the Canadian River canyon to build a Girl Scout Little House. Phillips Petroleum expanded operations in Borger and constructed a catalytic cracking plant, providing many new jobs. Phillips financed a large exhibit showcasing the chamber's activities in 1950 and for the first time, Phillips put a man on the 15 member Board of Directors for the Chamber, demonstrating Phillips's interest in being involved in community activities. In the 1950 interview Cooley identified new goals (1) get the Santa Fe Railway to extend its Borger spur, (2) get the U.S. government to build a dam on the Canadian River at a cost of $85 million, and (3) entice new industries to come to Borger so the economy can be diversified. Science had shown the sand around Borger would be good for glass making and also in the construction of brick. The Chamber hired a firm of Industrial Engineers in the 1950s to investigate the natural resources around Borger in order to identify potential industries that may relocate to Borger. The same strategy of identifying problems, assembling facts, looking what others have done and discussing this with Committee chairpersons one by one was used to develop the Borger infrastructure. Cooley accomplished these feats for Borger in the building years of the 1950s.

A.A. Meredith, City Manager

One of A.A. Meredith's difficult jobs as City Manager was collecting enough tax income to pay off Borger's debt. To do this he brought in out of town experts to make property appraisals equitable, then collected new, higher taxes. He did this despite threats "to take a gun to him", a behavior obviously left over from the "old days". Mr. Meredith was famous when I was growing up in Borger for promoting the idea of building a dam across the Canadian River to form a lake for recreational activities and to bring in tourism to the Borger-Fritch area. When Mr. Meredith died from cancer in 1963 his biography included this information on his accomplishments.

MEREDITH, AUSTIN A. (1891–1963). Austin A. Meredith, conservationist and city manager, was born on January 24, 1891, on a farm in Caldwell Parish, Louisiana. After graduating from high school in Monroe, he attended Meridian Military Academy in Meridian, Mississippi. There he was stricken with malaria, and doctors advised him to move to the drier climate of Texas. Accordingly, in 1909 Meredith enrolled at Texas Christian University in Fort Worth. Two years later, while taking malaria treatments at Mineral Wells, he met Grace Bernice Haynes, whom he married on December 25, 1911. They had seven children. After completing his college education Meredith began working for the Gulf Refining Company at Fort Worth. In 1916 he was transferred to Amarillo, where he became active in the local Rotary Club and was involved with Boy Scout and Girl Scout programs. Meredith moved to Plainview in 1931 and returned to Amarillo a few years later to take charge of the Potter County relief program. In 1935 he was appointed area director for the Works Progress Administration, which helped pave streets and construct sidewalks, tennis courts, and a grandstand in Amarillo. Some $400,000 in federal funds that Meredith obtained went to support building projects at West Texas State College (now West Texas A&M University) and the Panhandle-Plains Historical Museum in Canyon.

In 1941 Meredith moved to Borger and was elected city manager. In that position he engineered tax-reform measures to curb financial instability brought on by the Great Depression. Under his leadership thirty-six miles of Borger's streets were paved, Main Street was widened, and a water system and sewerage plant were installed. Meredith saw the need for a dam and reservoir on the Canadian River to furnish water for the Panhandle and South Plains areas. He promoted the project in numerous speeches and was foremost among the organizers of the Canadian River Water Users Association on June 17, 1949. In August 1952 he resigned as Borger city manager to devote himself full time to the association as its executive secretary. As part of his promotion campaign he published pamphlets, held meetings, and lobbied in both Austin and Washington. In addition he coproduced a color documentary film, entitled *Water: Our Greatest Natural Resource*, showing how a dam would benefit area agriculture, industry, and recreation. His efforts came to fruition with the state legislature's approval in 1953 of the Canadian River Municipal Water Authority. Meredith was a member of the Texas Water Conservation Association and the National Reclamation Association. Governor Marion Price Daniel, Sr., appointed him a delegate to the forty-fourth annual National Rivers and Harbors Congress at Washington in 1957.

For his work in soil and water conservation Meredith was given the sixteenth annual Save the Soil and Save Texas Award. For his work as a civic leader he was named Borger's **Man of the Year in 1950**, **Citizen of the Year by the Borger Kiwanis Club in February 1961**, and the **Borger Altrusa Club's Outstanding Citizen** the following year. At a special ceremony on July 1, 1962, Meredith and United States Secretary of the Interior Stewart Udall officially opened construction of the new Sanford Dam on the Canadian River. The next March, Meredith received the nation's highest conservation award from the United States Department of the Interior, but he did not live to see the reservoir project completed. He died of cancer on April 13, 1963, and was interred in Llano Cemetery, Amarillo. Construction of Sanford Dam began on March 11, 1962, and was completed in 1965. Lake Meredith supplies water to eleven West Texas cities: Amarillo, Borger, Brownfield, Lamesa, Levelland, Lubbock, O'Donnell, Pampa, Plainview, Slaton, and Tahoka. In 1965 by request of the Borger city commission and the Canadian River

Municipal Water Authority board, Congress named the reservoir formed by the dam Lake Meredith National Recreation Area.

Business and Professional Women's Club

Civic leaders in Borger formed the Business and Professional Women's Club, a prestigious group that looked for needs to be managed and found financial resources to implement those needs. One of their projects was the Children's Home, a short term facility to care for children of parents who were taken to jail for various reasons. The establishment of the BPW Children's Interim Home was described by Lou Cooley. "In 1953 or 54, Hal Baumhofer, county officer, came to see me and explained the need for a place to care for children of parents being arrested...saying it was difficult at the time of arrest to find a place for the children. The community was planning to start the United Way and Hal explained how great it would be to have a place to take the children where they could be fed and given a bed until the court decided if the parents could regain custody. Hal and I met with the BPW Women's Club and they agreed to present a budget to the United Way Directors. It was approved and financed for 22 years." The children were cared for at a home rented in the Rock Creek Subdivision, five children at first cared for by a widow who was paid a small sum plus room and board. "Later, the Optimist Club had a building they gave for the home. It was on county land and the members of the Optimist Club, plus many volunteers, remodeled this for us and we could handle 15 to 20 children, although we seldom had this many." After the larger home was secured, Nan Warren, wife of Dave Warren, routinely prepared a hot meal once a week for the children. "For 22 years the BPW women cared for this project, but the Government Agency required later that the Matron could no longer be in charge without having a Master's Degree and the court reverted to using private families, and the home was closed." In the late 1960s a day care center opened to care for children of working mothers who either because of race or financial circumstances could not use existing day care centers. It was called The Buttercup House and the effort toward establishment was led by Marie (Mrs. Harry) Jackson. The Jacksons owned a painting, decorating and refrigeration business in Borger. The day care center is a project jointly supported by the Borger Housing Authority (established to provide low income housing), and the Altrusa Club which will be the continuing responsible body to operate the center and ensure financial liquidity. Other clubs, church organizations and individuals help pay for original costs of furnishing and equipping the center and operating deficits. All families of children registered at the center pay a fee based on income levels and number of children in the family. Prominent Borgans leading the effort to establish Buttercup House are Marie Jackson, Mrs. F.C. Spence, Mrs. I. Jarrett and Mrs. J.B. (Pat) Andress.

BARNEY'S PHARMACY

Cathie Andress Kimbell, Class of 1965 submitted this historical review of her father, Barney Andress and his business known to many people as BARNEY'S PHARMACY. Cathie has provided a photo of the pharmacy.

I can hardly write about Barney's Pharmacy without writing about the integrity of the man who was my father. John Byron (Barney) Andress [June 14, 1907 – October 6, 1971] celebrated that his birthday was on Flag Day and always joked that everyone flew the flag on his birthday! This was appropriate for the proud American man which describes my father. He was born in Dallas and was probably born at home as I researched the courthouse in Dallas and could not find a record of his birth. Barney came to Borger during the Oil Boom days in the 1920's. His brother-in-law, Scott Hatcher, was a pharmacist and the son of a physician in Amarillo. He encouraged Daddy to become a pharmacist. Daddy worked at Dugan's Drug Store (photo) in Isom before he finished school. He bought the store in the 1930s and gave it his name. Daddy was one of a family of eight children who became the family patriarch helping his younger sisters go to business schools or college. He provided a home for and cared for his parents until their deaths.

The Barney's Pharmacy building was on the corner of Main Street and Grand Street. I recall that at one time Daddy held one-third interest and sold one-third interest in Barney's respectively to L.M. Davis and Guy Crawford (Gary Crawford's – class of '65- dad) who were also pharmacists. I believe Daddy completely sold out his third when he bought the Black Hotel and remodeled it into the Phillips Building across the street from Barney's in the 1950s, but the pharmacy kept the Barney's name until Ken White sold it and closed the drug store business forever in 1993. I vaguely recall that the pharmacy had a liquor license at one time and sold liquor as well as pharmaceuticals. He expanded later to include cosmetics, books, magazines, comic books, fashion jewelry and, of course, the soda fountain we remember fondly. Daddy owned a portion of Hawkin's Ice Cream plant with Dick Hawkins. I have distant memories of going to the ice cream plant somewhere south of Barney's in Borger. He sold this delicious hand-packed Hawkin's ice cream at the Drug Store. I was told that Daddy borrowed $5,000.00 from former President Lyndon Baines Johnson to buy or buy into the Hawkin's Ice Cream plant long, long ago.

I believe Daddy was the first of the Andress family to come to Borger and was the reason his two brothers, Joe & George, his parents and one sister, Jimmie, made Borger their permanent home. He married Evelyn Shultz (December 16, 1911 – February 2, 1995) in 1930. At one time there were many Andresses in Borger, but when Elsie, George's wife, died in 1997, the last of the Andress family were gone from Borger. Daddy also served as mayor of Borger and financially supported Mr. A.A. Meredith so he could go to Austin and fight for the birth of Lake Meredith. My dad was very proud of his children and grandchildren: Dr. John Barney Andress (July 14, 1936 – February 8, 1993), his son, was a dentist in Borger from the time he graduated from Baylor College of Dentistry; and Catherine Ann (me), his daughter. He was absolutely crazy about his grandchildren: our twins, John Byron

Andress and Dana Troy Andress, and other grandson, Paul David Andress. He lived to see his only granddaughter who is my daughter, Leasa Lenore Andress Duggar, as he died when she was only three month old. I was very fortunate to have him and my mother for parents.

After Barney's closed for good, my cousin, Linda Andress Earnhart (George and Elsie's daughter), and her husband, Jim, oversaw the painstaking task of removing all the red vinyl covered stools and the entire soda fountain and installing them at the First United Methodist Church's Youth Center. This is available for enjoyment even today. In an antique store in Amarillo, my daughter came across the three foot tall glass medicine bottle with a Barney's Pharmacy sticker on it that stood for many years in front of the prescription window. I was cornered into paying a small fortune to buy this giant green medicine bottle which, of course, I couldn't resist buying.

Barney's Pharmacy remained a favorite meeting spot for many long after high school and college years and the Hitching Post Drive Inn passed into history. It remained a main place to serendipitously run into family and friends from the past: Buddy and R.E. Haynes (Judy's brothers), Ray Sosebee (Dusty's dad), Bill Love (who worked for Daddy and was like family), Dickie Epps (Toni's mom and my 'second mother'), Ruth Bogan (Marlyn's mother) Margaret Lanham Weddington (Frieda, Linda, Waynel and Kim's mom) and many other "old-timers" whom I was always delighted to see again at the beloved soda fountain. I recall that my best childhood friend, Suzie Bagwell (May 22, 1947 – August 11, 1995), and I would buy a whole box of bubble gum...a thousand pieces...and chew them all up on trips to the cabin near Creede, Colorado. No wonder I spent so much time in J.B.'s dental chair! I hold many special memories at Barney's and all involved laughter. Daddy always called me & my friends "you little engineers". A good laugh is priceless...it is very healthy, so they say, and has most certainly been the Rx of my life.

After his death, many people I didn't even know came up to tell me that Daddy had given them free rent and free medicine when they came upon hard times in Borger. This is something my modest and private father never told me and something I never would have known had they not shared this with me. May God bless all who loved Barney and Barney's Pharmacy. I loved them, too. As Daddy often said "Be of good cheer."

Barney's Pharmacy and soda counter
Mary Lynne Bishop Tiner '64

How could anyone forget Barney's Drug Store – they had the best chocolate malts. Does anyone remember "suicides" – a squirt of everything from the soda fountain into a coke or root beer. Can't believe we actually drank those! My personal favorite was Pineapple Dr. Pepper while everyone else was drinking Cherry Cokes. Remember the little cardboard pill boxes with a little square of cotton on top – they didn't use the plastic bottles. I remember going to a play or something at the high school auditorium with my Mother, my sister and Peggy, George Ann and Vera Jo Aull (I think our mothers were trying to expose us to a little culture!)

and then going to Barney's afterward for banana splits. You could always find whatever you wanted at Barney's. When Julie and I went to the Morley or the Rex, on Saturdays, we would walk home. We always stopped at my Dad's office and he gave us money to get a comic book and a Cherry Limeade at Barneys. Barneys used to sell Booze in the back. You would see men and women leaving with brown paper bags.

BARNEY'S CHURCH by **Mike Crouch**

As I recall, Barney's Pharmacy was open on Sunday mornings, ostensibly to provide prescription medications for those who had such need on Sundays....but for many of us it was a safe harbor from Sunday School which had long-since become "uncool". As we acquired driver's licenses, a part of our teenage rebellion was to skip Sunday School and/or other church services and convene at Barney's.....which we irreverently referred to as "Barney's Church".

There were so many, I can't remember all the backsliders who could be counted as regulars at Barney's Church, but quite a gaggle of BHS students from various religious persuasions could be found every Sunday at Barney's Church hanging out and indulging in Barney's various soda fountain concoctions for which there was no equal in Borger.

Sandra Zimmerman '61

Barney's was the center of my universe. It's where I would go to have a cherry lime squeeze after having my braces tightened at Dr. Waldo Beckley's office. It was where I would go to buy 'Seventeen' magazine and where I picked out my first lipstick. Your dad was much beloved, Cathy.

Susan Stephens Bolton '64

I remember sitting on the low shelf in Barneys for hours reading funny books. We would get a nickel for a cherry lime and read all the comics to our hearts content; also going behind the counter with Dad when he went to buy booze.

Susan Fagan Johnston '65

Barney's, you could go to the pharmacy and ask for rose water and glycerin and it would come in a brown medicine bottle. You could also get a small bottle of cinnamon to put toothpicks in. I remember Dottie Butlers Clothing Store. It was my first charge account. I would go faithfully every Saturday to pay $ 25.00 on my bill after I got paid and I would usually charge more than that before I left. We had several 5 & 10 stores that were so much fun on Saturdays. Woolworth's had aquariums and lots of fun eye shadows.

GRODZIN'S "Working Man's Store"

Written by Susan (Susie) Grodzin Heywood

Morris & Sally Grodzin moved to Borger, Texas on April 8th, 1951...my 10th birthday. I'm Susan, better known as Susie in Borger. I wasn't a bit happy about the move, leaving the lovely, quaint, historical, and cultured town of Guthrie, Oklahoma for the ugly 'Boom' town of Borger. Daddy had decided our business would do better in the growing town of Borger and much to my Mother's dismay we left friends and family in Guthrie. Daddy opened 'Grodzin's, The Working Man's Store' on Friday the13th, 1951...and to our disappointment it was located between 2 pool hall /beer joints, with a flop house over head...621 N. Main. The store inventory was basically work boots, Levis, and a brand of khaki work pants named 'Tuf Nuts'. (I got teased a lot about that name.)

My sister, Sandy, and I got to go to the movies every Saturday, sometimes to the old Rig, across the street, or up to the Rex in the 500 block. (We always snuck in our own box of popcorn.) Finally the Morley Theatre was built and we felt the town had arrived. Daddy would go to Heard & Jones Drug store every afternoon and have a 'short Dr. Pepper'. He always took me, when I was around, and would pay me to drink a milkshake because I was so skinny.

My Dad, Morris, was a short Jewish man, maybe 5'4", always with change rattling in his pocket and always good for a .50 cent piece for me. Most of the day, Daddy stood outside the store, sometimes under the awning, sometimes leaning on a parking meter. Our family joke later in life was centered around Daddy standing outside the display windows and when a potential customer started looking at the merchandise in the windows Daddy would walk up to them and ask what size they needed...then automatically say, "Well, we are all out of that size today". You ask why he would do this. Daddy did not like waiting on customers. Of course the fact that Mother or a paid salesperson was waiting inside to help the customer didn't really faze him...he just didn't want to be bothered.

Morris was 52 when I was born, and mom, Sally, was 36, so often my parents were mistaken for my grandparents. Regardless they were wonderful parents, giving Sandy and I a love of travel, a respect for all religions and races, and a secure home life. For me the store was everything. I loved waiting on people, selling merchandise, and Daddy got a kick out of watching me becoming a little 'Morris'. Mother was in the store daily now, and she did all of the altering from Levis to Jackets, while continuing her role as full time Mom, making most everything we girls wore...right down to my twirling costumes.

Since my parents were part of a small Jewish population in Borger I have special memories of Christmas. And I can tell you what most of the other Jewish family's did on Christmas Day; they came to our home where we had the biggest Christmas tree, presents Mother would buy and wrap for every child, and have the most wonderful dinner of the year. Mother would make all the traditional Christmas goodies, plus many Jewish dishes that everyone exclaimed were the "best" Jewish dishes in the Panhandle. That was a huge compliment to Mother since she was a Gentile, raised under a Confederate Mother, Emma Reed and a Cherokee Father, Milton Reed.

Not all my memories of being Jewish in Borger are happy ones; There were the times I would hide under the counter as some drunk ignorant man would come in the store and threaten Daddy for being a 'Goddamn dirty Jew'. While I was accepted in school and enjoyed wonderful girlfriends, when I left Borger to attend college, I was told I could not accept the bids I had received from sororities because "no Negro, Mexican, Indian, or Jew was allowed to belong to a national sorority." When I proclaimed I was a member of the Presbyterian Church in Borger, nothing changed. My girlfriends who were attending other colleges and had been accepted into sororities and their mothers were up in arms...to no avail at that time.

I graduated from Borger High School in 1959, my sister Sandy finished BHS a few years earlier. After a couple of years of college I married high school sweetheart, Don Box on his birthday, August 12, 1961. Don was a track star and we left immediately for California where he could further his running career. My high school years were filled with drama classes where Dick Guthrie introduced me as 'Dogface Grodzin' and the ritual of Saturday night dances at the VFW. I loved to dance and have continued that passion throughout my life. Of course high school was a time where we formed deep and long lasting friendships. I still have my charm bracelet with the disk of each of our circle of 10 girlfriends name on it. We would leave campus for the Snack Shack where our lunch was usually hot pie and or French fries...sometimes we would deviate and go to Heard & Jones drug store for the best grilled cheese sandwiches with lots of mayo.

My father died when I was 24, and living happily in Northern California. At my Mothers request I returned to Borger to help her run the store which was deeply in debt. Once again, I was not happy to move to Borger, this time from sunny progressive California. I had remarried and my husband thought it was a good opportunity for him to get out of the hard labor he was doing. Arriving in Borger in January of 1969, I found much had changed, including me.

I immediately went about changing Grodzin's to a Western Wear store and caught it up to the changing times. Hip huggers were in, girls wearing pants to school was a fight I helped win, and I found myself a pioneer in the women's movement. I bought my first MS. Magazine at the grocery store in Borger. We eventually moved the store to the old By-Rite location in the 500 block on the corner. It was a hit, with rodeo queens there to greet customers and radio ads blasting our new image. I immersed myself into local charities and business organizations, while also free lancing for radio station KBBB.

The best thing to come out of the Panhandle of Texas is my daughter, Nicole...born in Amarillo, March 1, 1971 arriving in Borger 5 days later. My high school buddy, Judy Blackburn Gurley, came over to help me give Nicole her first bath. Our girls had birthday parties together just as Judy and I had when we were in school in Borger. Nicole and I went on the road in January, 1975, looking for bright lights, and a chance for me to fulfill a career. We landed in Phoenix AZ after a trek across California, and here we have grown and loved together. Our fate was sealed by meeting Bill Heywood. Bill and I were married in Phoenix on Valentine's weekend 1977, Nicole was 6. Bill was in radio over 40 years retiring a few years ago. I found my career in Advertising and Marketing owning and operating my own agency for over 30 years. In 1997, I founded a nonprofit organization for homeless dogs & cats. Our creation **Scratch & Sniff** became an umbrella fundraising organization distributing over 4 million dollars in 8 years to 13 shelters and pet therapy organizations. I retired in 2005. It's all been an adventure, and Borger was certainly a part of it. My mother Sally moved to Phoenix to spend her last 7 years close to us. Mother died at 87, and her services were held in Borger at Minton's. Mom was laid to rest next to Daddy in Amarillo. High school buddies Mary Pat Orman Knight and Jimmy Dawson came to see us there. That was the last time I have been in that part of the Panhandle, but that part of the country will always be a part of me.

Cafes in Borger - Recollections of SNACK SHACK.... and more

Submitted by Mary Bess Moore '64

Tooms served plenty of people at the Snack Shack

By Melissa S-Herald Features Editor/News Herald

The little cafe served fare such as hamburgers, french fries, sandwiches, chili and stew to many people who came in with a hungry belly and left with a full one.

The Snack Shack, which was located where the Xcel Energy building is now (at Fifth and Deahl), was a bustling hub of activity, with Borgans from all over, but especially students and workers from the post office and electric company, making frequent stops at the cafe.

For 17 years beginning in 1944, Minnie Tooms served as the cook behind the counter who dished up meals for hungry customers. Tooms, who married in 1935, was raised in Wellington and came to Borger in 1942.

Tooms said the restaurant was usually very busy, especially with school kids coming in for lunch. The place would be so crowded sometimes that there was standing room only. "If there were no seats, the kids would stand up and wait," Tooms said.

When asked if she enjoyed her time at the Snack Shack, Tooms replied, "Yes, very much so." "I had a good boss. His name was Dutch Jones," she said.

In addition to Tooms, there were four girls who worked in the front, a man named Windell who washed dishes, and the woman who baked pies, despite the fact that many over the years have thought it was Tooms who made the pies.

"Edna Sharber was the pie baker," Tooms said. "Everybody to this day thinks I was the pie baker. I have no idea why."
At the Snack Shack, Tooms had to stay on her toes to keep up with the orders that came in - all of which were spoken and not written down.

"I had a shelf where I served from, and the grill was right behind it," she said. "When you wanted a hamburger, we'd say 'make one.' If you wanted french fries, we'd say 'half order' or 'order,' and if you wanted hamburgers and french fries, we'd say 'string one.'"

One would think that it would be difficult to keep up with all the orders without writing anything down, but Tooms said she had a system. "I placed plates in a certain place so I'd know what was turned in," she said. "It was fast-paced ... and I was fast."

When asked if she had a special memory of her time at the Snack Shack, Tooms mentioned a longtime friend she'd met there. "I met Edith Koontz there, and she became a friend of mine," she said. "We were friends for 40 years."

After she left the Snack Shack, Tooms opened her own store called "Minnie's Sweet Shop" that sold cookies, cakes and pies and made orders to go, she said. It was located in the old Cunningham cab stand building across from the bus station, Tooms said. During that time, she had to have gallbladder surgery, and once she recovered from that she went to work for the college as their baker. She served as the baker for seven years at FPC before retiring.

Her time as a cook and baker to hundreds of Borgans over the years was time spent doing something she loved - baking and working. "I like to work," she said. "I miss it very much."

Windell Holder, the dishwasher was my uncle. Everyone remembers the french fries served at the snack shack. Uncle Windell peeled the majority of those potatoes. Yes, they were real potatoes. I remember when Dutch finally bought a potato peeling machine.

Nancy Shermer Grimes '61

SNACK SHACK:_ When the bell rang in Jr. High for lunch, people broke and ran in a dead heat to entire distance to the Snack Shack. In the winter when there was snow on the streets, I remember people holding on to car bumpers and being pulled on their way to the SS. No one's children should ever know this! My knowledge of the English language was broadened when I learned that when Minnie Tooms said "Palm Beach Walking" someone had ordered a pimento cheese sandwich to go. I will forever measure the quality of hamburgers and cherry cream pies by the standards set at the SS.

Les Hargis, Class of '59

Mrs. Sharber baked the pies at the Snack Shack and was also a family friend. When asked for a recipe, she was glad to give it out. Only problem was it was for about ten pies.

Bobbie Green Barton '64

How well I remember Mrs. Sharber. I learned so many things from her. She worked for my dad as a cook, when he owned the Chat & Chew Café. I couldn't have been more than 12 years old when she had me standing next to her, watching & listening. She started me out on Bread Pudding, using up the days leftover doughnuts, sweet rolls, dinner rolls and Texas Toast. Nothing was wasted in her kitchen! The day she made her wonderful 3-layer German Chocolate cake...I was right there. Would I give up my front seat at the hockey game to be able to recreate her mile-high lemon meringue or chocolate pies? You bet I would!! The Snack Shack was across the street from the post office. How did we keep from gaining a lot of weight, eating that food.

Larry White '64

I agree about Snack Shack. (Best coconut cream pie in the world). Hines Cafe, second best hamburgers and fries in Borger (second only to Snack Shack's). The pool hall on Main St. (Mother could always tell I had been there because of the cigarette smoke in my clothes). A&W Rootbeer. (Those frosty mugs were the best).

Talhia Anderson Vanlandingham '64

My mother worked at the SS as a waitress when I was in the sixth and seventh grade after my dad was burned in an oilfield accident. The owner Dutch Jones pretty much kept my family from going hungry during that time.

BIG HEARTS Café and MEMORIES

Ever wonder how Big Heart got his nickname?

The archives of the Borger News Herald relay a story about the early days of Borger in 1927. Many entrepreneurs saw opportunity for business in the new town of Borger, Texas, risen up from a recent oil boom. There were no good roads to Borger and no rail service. Water wells had not been drilled, only oil wells. Merchants had to drive all day to Panhandle to get barrels of water and take another day returning to Borger over mud-rutted roadways across the prairie. J.J. Williams sold water for 10 cents a cup from his hamburger store on the main street of Borger. One customer, surprised that he was asked to pay for "a drink of water" looked at Mr. Williams and said "Well, you really have a big heart!" Well, the nickname stuck and before long Mr. Williams had signs constructed with a big red heart and the name of his business within the sign. Many who attended West Ward, then Sam Houston Jr. High recall the sign. In the late 1940s Big Heart purchased a building on the corner of 6th and Hedgecoke and started Big Heart's School Café. He sold school supplies and food items, such as hot dogs, sandwiches and frozen koolaid cups, known as "frozen cups"! Yumm.... On November 12, 1948 fire gutted the frame stucco structure, destroying the café and 3 apartments which were part of the building. The Borger newspaper reports the story, listing the loss at $30,000.00. According to the newspaper "Flames broke out in the kitchen, and spread to the attic. Firemen answered the call at 9:50 AM, smoke and fire were thick and at 10:05 AM walls bulged out and the roof caved in. The response to the fire was hampered due to low water pressure, however at 10:34 AM water pressure increased and flames were brought under control." The building was rebuilt and many of us who attended school in the 1950s remember the café.

Mike Harrington '65 (cousin to Merle '61)
Just last week, my father, Claude "Dutch" Harrington, was reminiscing about Big Heart's eatery. Dad graduated from BHS in 1935, and he'll be 90 next year. His memories aren't the sharpest nowadays, but he does recall Big Heart's fondly. In Dad's day, BHS was located on the site we knew in the '50s and '60s as Borger /Sam Houston Junior High. Dad says that, as a BHS student, he had lunch most days at Big Heart's with his buddy and classmate Jack Brum, who died within the past couple of years. Big Heart Williams, himself -- was the chief cook as well as the owner. The joint served up blue plate luncheon specials and not just the snack food of later years.

Melinda Eason Stephenson '61 My social life revolved around the youth group at Calvary Baptist Church mostly after church. My parents only gave me thirty five cents for lunch and did not permit me in "Big Hearts" because of stories they had heard about the boom days, it was the place I wanted to eat but Heard and Jones was the best I could manage, and drank water to make the money last. I was the nerd eating in the Cafeteria most of the time. The laundry across from Jr. High had a vending machine with snacks in an emergency.

Tony Poole '64

Yes I remember Big Heart across from old Sam Houston Jr. High. I used to get fries with mustard on them there. That was a place that the youths used to hang out and eat. Do you remember Big Georges across from the Library? Remember Georges 5 cent burgers, they were great. Big George died in his 30's and I never saw another hamburger like Big Georges. How many remember Big George?

Cathy Andress Kimbell '65
I remember the little wax soda bottles with a sweet liquid inside and wax front teeth and the discovery of Big Hunks at Big Hearts...Suzie Bagwell (deceased in 1995) and Darla Cooley were my buddies in elem. school but we knew about Big Hearts then... and we'd share all the goodies at Big Hearts!

More good memories from Joe Kesterson class of 63

I REMEMBER BIG HEARTS FRENCH FRIES WITH MUSTARD SERVED IN A BROWN PAPER BAG AND THE GREASE COMING THROUGH THE BOTTOM OF THE BAG. I ALSO REMEMBER THE BUNAVISTA DRIVE IN WHEN MR. FAGAN WOULD FLASH ON THE SCREEN THAT THE DONUTS WERE READY!! HOW ABOUT THE JET DRIVE IN , CLOVERLEAF, AND WHO CAN FORGET THE POST WHERE WE SPENT SO MANY HOURS SITTING IN OUR CARS AND JUST TALKING TO THOSE AROUND AND WITH US. SO GREAT (GOOD AND BAD) ARE THE MEMORIES.

Reggie Parsons '70
I remember Big George. He used to spit on the grill to see how hot it was. My dad used to laugh when he would do it. It didn't matter...the burgers were great. maybe that's why. Ha! The food safety folks would have a coronary now...

Danny Stephens '62

The "Zesto" which, in my family at least, became synonymous with "ice cream". Then the A&W frosted mug root beers! Ummmm!

Cafes in Borger

Hines's Hot Dog Stand across from Weatherly School

by Jimmy Hines, Class of '57

Somewhere around 1945 our family moved to a house on Grand Street, two houses east of Weatherly Elementary School. My dad remodeled the back porch of the house and built a small store where he sold hot dogs, chips, candy, gum and bottled soft drinks. It was open at noon and after school hours and was so small there was no room for seating. Everyone got their food and stood around outside, visited and ate.

Since Mom ran Blackie's Café, Dad ran the school store and all four of us kids worked at doing something to help out, either in the morning preparing food, at noon or after school, serving food, cleaning up and restocking for the next day.

For a quarter you could get a hot dog (steamed bun with mustard and onions), a bag of chips, a candy bar ***and*** a soft drink. Drink choices consisted of Coke, Pepsi, Dr. Pepper, Royal Crown, Delaware Punch and Nehi drinks (Root Beer, Strawberry, Orange Crush, Crème, Strawberry and Grape). In today's world, this meal would be a nutritionist's nightmare. How did we ever survive? "Frozen Cups" were a very good seller when the weather warmed up toward the last of the school year.

Just out of curiosity we counted 93 different kinds of items on the menu one day, all of which were on display separated by a wall where my brother and I had our bedroom. Needless to say, we were the envy of most of our classmates when they found out about it.

The little store must have had a financial impact on the Weatherly Cafeteria, because it seems we were always at odds with the administration. Over the four or five years we operated the store, several attempts were made to keep the students on campus during the lunch period. But kids will be kids and I don't think it impacted our little family business very much. Due to Dad's illness we had to close the store but I know a lot of folks still have fond memories of it.

Barbara Ferrill Sims - Hine's Hog Dog Stand

I have MANY memories of eating at the hot dog stand. The hot dogs were wonderful....really fresh and yummy. I had forgotten that you got the drink, chip and candy bar also. I'm sure I got a butterfinger!! I also remember playing with Sue in a yard they had behind Blackies (I think). Sue and I spent quite a lot of time together after school as both of our mothers were working. Her dad was, of course, usually around since he opened the hot dog stand for kids to come by for snacks. I was always very intrigued by everything going on there.

On Saturdays I would go to Blackies, then later on to Hines Cafe which was further down from Barney's to get a hamburger and french fries to take home and eat while I was watching baseball games on our new TV!!!! I don't remember seeing her brothers working there...they were probably back in the kitchen, but I know Sue did work there often. Her mother was a wonderful cook and did make the greatest pies....very similar to Snack Shack.

Bobby Dennis '64

Does anyone remember eating at Hines cafe? At noon Jimmy Brown & I never could decide which was best 2 jumbo burgers or chicken fried steak so when we had the money we ate both all in a 20 minute lunch period. Can't believe we ate so much, fond memories of Jimmy and Hinds café.

Patsy Eason Phillips '64

What about **Hine's Hot Dog stand** by Weatherly?? Served wonderful hot dogs. Also were able to buy bubble gum with baseball cards. Whenever I see a baseball card, I can still smell the gum. We used to put the cards on our bike spokes so they made a "racket" as we rode. I wonder what valuable cards were mistreated???

Hine's Businesses in Borger by Jimmy Hines, son

Our parents made a living operating a roadside café on Route 66 in Bristow, OK until the Turner Turnpike put them out of business in 1941. The family packed up everything, and moved in with my grandparents in Borger. My grandparents owned the **Unique Café** in the 900 block of Main Street, north of **Lindsey Furniture** Co. Tenth Street was the north end of Borger at that time, long before Hughes Pitts, Gateway and Coronado Additions existed. My grandmother, Jessie Frump later baked pies and cooked for "Miss Mac" during the beginning of the **NuWay Café**.

A couple of years later we leased **Blackie's Café** on South Main and all six of us moved into a two room house next door. Mom ran the café, Dad worked for C.E. Ruby Wholesale and all four of us kids worked in the café to help ends meet. My older and younger sisters cooked and waited tables, while my older brother and I did the kitchen chores, mostly washing dishes. Our business neighbors included Minton's Funeral Home, The Black Hotel (later became the Phillips Building), Barney's Drug Store, and three different Dr. Stephens's offices (medical and dental).

The next family business venture was managing the **St.James Hotel** (also known as the Isom Hotel) located just south of Blackie's Café. I've written about this in another related article. I t was quite an "adventure".
During this time my Dad operated the **Past Time Pool Hall** in the 600 block of North Main. I was barely tall enough to see over the pool tables. My brother and I were given the unenviable task of cleaning out the many brass "spittoons" each week. As far as I was concerned, we couldn't get rid of that business quick enough!

During my junior high years we leased and operated **The Hiway Café** on South Cedar, across from Huber Park. Business neighbors there included Eason's Service Station, WesTex Lumber Co. and Producers Chemical and Well Service. It was about this time that my brother got smart and found work outside of the family business which left me with the title of "Head Dishwasher and Potato Peeler". Our sisters continued to be a prominent part of the business during this time.

We found our way back on South Main a couple of years later in an establishment called Hines Café (how's that for originality?). It was located a block south of Grand Street and now the surroundings were Joy Motor Co., R and R Sheet Metal and Darden's Gulf Service Station (later Clyde and Scottys).

Looking back on the various businesses a few things come to mind that might bring some memories to some folks reading this. Mom's specialties always included hamburgers, hot dogs, homemade soup and stew, chili and pies. Her pies were always cut into four equal pieces and any pie left at closing time was given to the employees to take home at no charge. It was her cardinal rule that no "day old" pie would ever be served in her café. She always purchased groceries from local merchants, mostly McCord Brothers and Piggly Wiggly (Carl Floyd).

All of us kids worked in each of the businesses at one time or the other. We were all paid wages and were allowed to keep one half and had to put one half in the bank (this fund was used at the beginning of school for clothes and school supplies). Looking back on this arrangement I realize how wise our parents were in teaching us the value of a dollar...and how to manage one!

Although I didn't realize it while growing up in this atmosphere, I was also the recipient of an enormous education on public relations. This proved to be invaluable years later when I owned my own business.
My buddies never ceased to remind me of all the advantages of being allowed to eat my Mom's cooking any time I wanted. I hate to admit it, but it really wasn't a bad deal after all! This writing will give you an idea of early businesses in Borger and how hard people had to work to make it in those days. It will also illustrate a glimpse of "using one's resources" to make it in our little community. All my siblings worked in my parent's businesses without complaint. All would agree, I'm sure, that we were better for it.

St. James Hotel, submitted by Jimmy Hines

My parents, Rube and Georgia Hines packed up their stuff, including four kids, and moved from Oklahoma to Borger in 1941. Three years later they signed a one year lease to manage the St. James Hotel and it became our castle! After living in a two room house this place seemed like a mansion, and at age five, this building became my home for a year! The hotel was located on the corner of Grand and Main directly across the street from the Black Hotel. It was known at different times as the St. James Hotel or the Isom Hotel. It occupied all of the floors above Barney's Pharmacy (South end) and the doctor's offices of Dr. W.G. Stephens and M.M. Stephens (North end of the building). Access to the Hotel was made through the entry at the center of the building between the two businesses.

If you don't remember this edifice, upon entering the front door, a spacious lobby greeted each guest. For me it was a wonderous place with a high ceiling that supported a large black, four-bladed fan that seemed to have only one speed...superslow. Behind the large check-in desk was an endless wall of "pigeon-holes" which held door keys for the lucky guests. A small hand activated bell was located on the desk above the obvious sign "Ring Bell for Service". A couch was located on one wall directly below a huge map of Texas where I spent a lot of time planning endless travels for the future!

The left side of the lobby revealed a magnificent stairway to the second floor. The dark brown, highly polished banister was a never-ending source of entertainment for all of the youngsters in our family. My mission in life was to keep it shining by devising innovative ways to ascend and descend the stairs without using the steps!

The top of the stairs revealed long hallways in both directions flanked by rooms on both sides. A combination "shower/bathroom" was located on the left, the only such facility available to all residents. At the end of the north hallway a door led outside to a wooden stairway which eventually led to ground level on the west side of the building. I soon overcame my fear of this rickety set of steps when I learned it was a convenient way to come and go without Mom's prying eyes!! This area also served as a means to access the roof, a very neat place to watch the goings on in the neighborhood, especially the annual parade which always ended at Grand Avenue, just below our handy "observation deck". You could see a tent city, too.

My folks shared a combination bedroom/office at the head of the stairs. My sisters, Sue and Betty shared a bedroom on the right side of the hall and my brother, Bob, and I shared the most important room in the modern world...No. 15! It is of no small significance that this was also the number of the greatest home-run hitter in Borger Gasser baseball history, Gordon Nell (needless to say, one of my childhood idols!). A small external switch on the wall lit the single exposed bulb in the middle of the ceiling. The view out of the window facing the Black Hotel across Main Street accounted for countless hours of "people watching". We soon learned that the temperature of the room could be controlled, somewhat, by adjusting the transom above each door in all of the rooms.

It is truly amazing how much bigger, taller, wider and brighter things are when viewed through the eyes of a five year old. Maybe I should try it more often....!

Sutphen's Bar B Q and the other BBQs

There is disagreement among Borger grads regarding where Sutphen's first began. Most of us remember the small café on the corner in Phillips, on the site of a former gasoline station. We recall when Myer's Fried Chicken closed in Borger, on Cedar Street, Sutphen's BBQ took that space and this is the present location. In the old days we knew the two boys in the family (Joey, Scott) as they went to the same places as we. Many of us, when we visit Borger, still make special plans to eat at

Sutphen's (even though it no longer is owned by the Sutphen family.) Here are some memories of eating Margie's food and knowing the owners!

Les Hargis '59

Joey Sutphen Jr and I have been friends since 1949. Margie and Big Joe lived in Borger and sons, Joey and Scott, stayed in Phillips with their grandmother, Mrs. Turner. The first 6/49 Sutphen's BarBQ was in Borger on Tenth street, just off Hedgecoke. Big Joe built a pit there and sold ribs and beef to go. You could also get a sandwich and sit on a stool like the Snack Shack had. Joe and Margie bought a going restaurant in Phillips called Pete's Café for $1750.00 that had living quarters in the back. In December 1949 they moved into the back of Pete's Café and started the family style restaurant that you remember in Phillips. Also, for a short time they had curb service. Can you believe family style in your car? Their son, Joey, does do BBQ cookoffs and currently appears on TV a lot. He has been on several channels, but now is only on the Travel channel. You can look him up at texasthunderbbq.com and see what he looks like traveling around. He and I have won a lot of bets on where Sutphen's first got started, mostly from Phillips folks. Phillips people just don't want to admit that Borger had them first.

Bob Stephens '65

Sutphens started in Phillips......1946....Mr. Sutphen worked at Phillips.....and he and Margie and Margies mother...Mrs Turner worked there....I worked there ...Larry Don remembers....when the kids were at teen town on Friday nights and Sat nights I many times was there working....Scott worked there or got to come in when Margie or His grandmother were not watching and take 5 bucks or so....out of the cash register...I would cover for Scott....after work I would high tail out of there ....to teen town or the Post or main street...in my 55 Chev....I was even with Scott when his granddad died and he and I drove his grandad's 58 Ford....a black fast sucker to the funeral at about 13 yrs old....cause we could back then...so believe me Sutphens started in Phillips...ask Mike Webb...I used to walk over there from Phillips elementary school in the 3rd grade and Mrs .Sutphen...on a good day would slip me a piece of pecan pie.....when she wasn't mad at big Joe....Ha!

Many of the messages remember great food from Sutphen's. My memories are a little different. My folks owned **Adele's Cafe** on the Phillips Highway and for many years Margie and my mother acted like enemies. However, they shared a mutual respect for each other and many nights at closing, Margie and Joe would come down and want a steak and my Dad would drive to Phillips and come home with a big sack of ribs. At my mother's funeral 40 long stem red roses arrived from Margie . The card read "40 Wonderful Years of Friendship". When Margie died I sent 40 roses and signed the card. Steak and Ribs are a great combination.

I remember Sutphen's BarBQ in Phillips, later in Borger and the basement at Scott Sutphens house and all the fun we had.....Sutphens and Mrs. Margie Sutphen yelling at "Scottie"....I also worked at the one in Phillips....Big Hearts was off limits to some of us because of the trouble and the smokin and cussin....and the "hoods" that hung out there......*oh it was wonderful....*

Bob Holmes '64

Sutphen's. Oh, my, my all time favorite restaurant. Margie started that when my family lived in Phillips, before we moved to Borger in our 7th grade year. That was the first restaurant I ever paid my own check...sorta. The story: I must have been 10 or 11...got the bright idea of getting a pal and going to eat "all by ourselves" at Sutphens. We asked our parents for the money to cover dinner, got it (you can imagine the laughter...that I never saw), and my pal and I walked the 1/2 mile to the place. You were right, it was in a former gas station, on the road toward Borger, about a block from the first light, on the South side of the street. We went in, got a table, ordered, ate, and when done, kinda wandered out...and started walking home. About half way home, it occurred to us that we hadn't paid. We turned around and went back and told Margie what happened. She took our money, giggling, and told me, "I knew you hadn't paid, but I know your Daddy". What a hoot! I also remember riding my heavy old bicycle over to a friend's house right on the Huber Golf course from Phillips...what 6 or 8 miles? What a trek. How our society has changed! Would you let your kid or grandkid wander that far unattended with the way things are today? Neither would I.

White Way Bar B Q, better known as Etta's Bar B Que

We used to go by Etta White's BBQ which she sold out of her home in the late 40s and early 50s. I was a child but went with my father on occasion to get the food. We would drive to her house, on McGee street, around the corner from the washeteria; park the car, and dad would go into her house and get ribs and beef. This African American family had a clean yard and a house the same quality as we had over in Hughes Pitts Addition. As a child I did not know about prejudice against this race, just recognized the different skin color. My stepfather, Wayne Lanham, was not prejudiced and always led us to be respectful of others and appreciate differences among races. When I was very young my mother worked and we had a woman we called "Black Mary" who took care of us while mother was working and my father, "Doc" Gunnels was away in the war. We loved Mary and she sometimes brought her daughter to play with us. They lived in a different section of Borger close to where the Government housing area was built.

Chris Willerton '65

The **White Way Barbecue, Etta White's place**, was special to my brothers and me because we grew up across the street at 920 N. McGee. Etta and her daughter Lillar, watched us year after year as we walked to Central Elementary. I was the oldest and set out for first grade holding my mother's hand. Two years later, Keith started and walked with me. Four years later, all three of us. They watched every day. Borger's protectors...people did that for each other then.

By the time we'd leave around 8:00 a.m., Etta had been up for three hours cooking barbecue. When we'd cross the street to visit, she and Lillar would offer us a rib. And usually tell me that I was a nice looking boy but needed to lose weight. Every Easter Sunday, they would clip roses so each of us could have a boutonniere. They were the first black people we really knew. On that stretch of McGee St., our side was white and theirs was black, but there was lots of visiting back and forth. Borger still had some segregation when we were little (somebody check me on this). I seem to remember that black people could go to Borger theatres but had to sit in the balcony. Seems like there was one store downtown with white and black drinking foundations, but I'm even hazy on that. Schools were integrated by the time we started. But, being a refinery town, Borger was heavy on Phillips employees, and at the time that was a white workforce. So I'm not sure many kids had the advantage I did, knowing Etta and Lillar before we knew much about the race barrier.

When we grew up and went to college, we'd drop in on them when we were home on break. Once we had a little dinner party there, all three of us with our fiancées and girlfriends. It was the only time we were ever allowed to pay for ribs.

The Hutchinson County Museum, down the street and across from the Morley, is doing a little better with exhibits on Borger's black and Hispanic history, but it doesn't have much yet. The best monument to the White Way Barbecue hangs in the little restaurant that sits where the Post was. It's Etta's "Barbecue Sold Out" sign.

Sharon Kaye Johnson Nichols '61

I remember when the building where Sutphens is located in now, was Meyer's Fried Chicken. Everyone tried to go there after church on Sundays. In the Amarillo MFC they had a train that circled around the top of the ceiling. I remember being fascinated by that train. This was in the 1950s.

DELUXE Café

Mary Lynne Bishop Tiner '64

Another place that hasn't been mentioned is the Deluxe Café that Sharon Kuroki's parents had on Main Street. I remember Sharon and I going into the kitchen and cutting potatoes into French fries - thought that was just too cool (I think we were in the fifth grade). We were talking yesterday about the hurricanes and people helping each other thru the tough times - I remember Mr. Jackson at Weatherly taking kids who couldn't afford them to the store to buy shoes and/or clothes with his own money. Many years after we left Borger, Daddy also told me about Dr. Dyke providing glasses for those who wouldn't otherwise be able to have them. As Cathy said, her dad also helped those who couldn't afford medicine. I'm sure there were a bunch more who did things like this but nobody ever knew about it. There were some mighty nice people with awfully big hearts in Borger that would do anything to help someone in need. Wouldn't it be a better place if there were more Mr. Jackson's, Mr. Andress's and Dr. Dyke's in the world now? I can't think of a better place to grow up than Borger.

Joey Wood '61
The Kurokis ran the Deluxe from 1939 to 1963. It was in 3 different locations in the 400 block of Main. It started in 39' at 410, then moved to 404, & finally to 428 where it was when Mary & Sharon peeled the potatoes for Sada, Sharon's Mom. Claude is one of my best friends these days, he & I have been bowling on the same team at Cedar Lanes now for 25 years.

Blackie's Café
Shirley Castagnetta wife of Joe Castagnetta '64:

I didn't graduate from Borger High, but my husband Joe Castagnetta did. Class of '64. I also enjoy all of your memories. We still live in Borger so I thought I'd let you know that Blackies Cafe is still standing. It has been remodeled and is rented by a man named Kerry Manning. He cuts hair there. He cuts Joe's hair. It's called Kerry's Hair Headquarters. I talked to him and he told me he has several pictures of Miss Blackie and the cafe. Her name was Cleo (Sanders) Winton. He also said the house between the cafe and Dixon's Glass is where she lived. When it burned down she lived in the back of the cafe until it closed.

Mac's Café across from the Morley

Mac's Café was owned and managed by Gwen and Tony Poole's mother, a single parent.

Tony Poole '64

Does anyone remember Mac's Café? That was my mother's cafe back in the 50's and early 60's. Some people called mother Miss Mac back then because of the name of the Cafe. We think she was a real sweetheart of a person. You know to this very day when I smell Clorox my memory brings up those old stainless steel sinks there in the Cafe where I washed dishes when I was a kid. I can still see all those white cups and saucers under the suds. Isn't that wild!

I know Bobby Amador remembers Central Elementary. I had fond memories of Central even though I only spent a very short time there. I was so unruly that the Principal told my mother that I was retarded and should be in a special class. She moved me to East Ward. Turned out later that my I-Q was actually high and I was bored. I don't blame the Principal, because I would have just shot me and put me out of my misery.

Anyone remember Smokey Hall the scout master? Ole Smokey took us on some of the wildest scout trips during that time. It's a miracle that we survived, but we all learned a lot from him about how to survive, literally.

Remember the Plains Drive Inn? And those old sound boxes were something else too! They hung on your car window. I want you all to know that without a doubt that today is the greatest time of our lives! We all had good and bad times as kids and young people, but today is the time that should be our most special time of life.

Susan Fagan Johnston '65

Does anyone remember the coffee house that was in Borger? It would stay open late, had folk singers, It was one of the only places to go after I worked at the theater. Also the **Round the Clock and Triangle Restaurants**.

Patty Kelly Collins – Other cafes in Borger

Does anyone remember the **Charcoal House** on Cedar, 1 block south of the **William's By Pass Grocery**? Also the smell of fresh bread from Tendercrust bakery on North Main street across from **Darby's steak house**. I loved **Adele's Café.** I recall Tendercrust bringing mini loaves of bread to the grade schools around town and passing them out. I went to HUBER grade school, then to Weatherly, then Stephen F Austin the first full school year it was opened. I remember going to lunch at **HINES CAFE** and the **CAMPUS CORNER** for lunch when attending Weatherly grade school. Mrs. Oxley gave me an "F" in World Geography, first grade under a "B" I'd ever made. In later years Mrs. Oxley was a dear friend and neighbor. Does anyone remember the CAMPUS CORNER on the corner between BHS and Weatherly School? Served the best cherry cokes I'd ever had and real french fries. Mr. Raff gave me a scolding in the parking lot of Austin for passing his bus one morning. I slowed down and didn't do it again...ever. I remember the BHS band practicing early in the morning, seems like you could hear them all over Borger and they were the best.

Castleberry Shoes Viewing Machine By Frank and Joe Castleberry

Paul J. Castleberry Sr., was the owner of Castleberry's Shoes in Borger. The store had originally been opened as a Smith's Shoes store in 1948 as an expansion of the Smith's Shoes chain in Pampa, TX. Paul bought the store from Frank Smith in about 1952. The store was a franchise outlet for selling International Shoes in Borger.

Paul carried all the International Shoes brands including the kid's shoe brand, "Poll Parrot". In about 1954 International Shoes sent the Castleberry Shoes store a fluorescent viewing device to aid in the fitment of children's shoes. In fact, it was simply a device to drum up interest in International Shoes.

The viewer that International sent my Dad was a fluoroscope. It was about the size of an under cabinet dish washing machine with a viewing scope on the top that was contoured so that a person could put the face down to it and have the light blocked out from all directions, except from below. When someone stood on the fluoroscope and slipped one's feet into the viewing area and looked through the viewer, the person could see the outline of the shoe and the foot of the user, including flesh and bones. I believe it used electrons from some low power tube to show the structures. When the electrons passed through the user's foot and shoe, they struck the fluorescent screen. The resulting glow could be seen through the viewer. It was a big hit with kids and all customers of the store.

Paul Castleberry retired from the shoe business in 1975 and sold the store to another man. He and his wife then moved to Canyon to be near his son, Frank. They lived in Canyon until his death in 1992. Our mother lived until January of 2007. The younger son, Paul Jr. (known in Borger as "Joe") moved to Canyon to join his brother and mother in 2002.

Davis Chevrolet

Most of you will remember the attractive structure and car dealership on the corner of Tenth Street and what is now Highway 207 through Borger, leading to the circle. A big graphic was right up front inviting the customer to come in and get "Friendly Service". I used to walk by there on my way home from Central Elementary and look at the cars placed where they would spark one's interest. Here is the story of Davis Chevrolet written by one of the daughters of Mr. Hudson Davis, owner and operator.
I asked Mr. Davis's daughter to write the history of this dealership.

Davis Chevrolet by Dolores Dell Griffin

According to the *Borger News-Herald* of November 14, 1947 "The new Davis Chevrolet home – one of the finest in the Southwest – will have its formal opening on Saturday, November 15 and Sunday, November 16 from 2 to 6 p.m. Dedicated to "Friendly Service", the new building hosts complete facilities to do the job. It is on the corner of Highway 117 and 10th street."

Hudson Davis and his family, wife Ruby Dell and their two daughters Dolores Dell "Dolly", and Catherine Burr "Tootie", moved to Borger from Amarillo in April 1941. He had purchased the Chevrolet dealership, which was situated at 820 North Main, from Bob Bradshaw. The dealership flourished in spite of the declaration of World War II in December of that year. By 1947 business had increased to the stage that a new building providing more space was needed. Walden E. Moore of Pampa was the designer and builder of the beautiful structure. Local vendors were used for the building materials and laborers.

Mr. Davis began his career as a school teacher in the town of Des Moines, New Mexico where he met his wife, Ruby. He taught business and typing and Ruby was the debate and drama coach. After a move to Clovis, NM he continued with the teaching profession, but became a part-time salesman for McCrory Chevrolet in Clovis. His talents were quickly evident as the District Manager offered him an opportunity for employment in the Chevrolet Motor Division. Consequently the family moved to Oklahoma City, then to Amarillo, before making Borger their final stop.

In Borger Mr. Davis was active in community and civic affairs. He was a leader in the Chamber of Commerce and the business community recognized him as a man of vision. Hudson headed the building committee for the new Borger Hotel which was opened with much fanfare in the fall of 1950. The hotel had beautiful furnishings, comfortable rooms, space for small businesses and a large ballroom for community dances and events. There was a large area for parking and an easy "in and out" design to the parking area. Mr. Davis was an early supporter of the Lake Meredith project, participating on the board and serving as a primary instigator for the formation of the Canadian River Municipal Water Authority. As president of the Lion's Club in Borger he was the driving force in getting the Girl Scout Little House built so there would be a nice place for the girl scouts to meet and for other youth groups. Many groups rented this facility which was in a prime location close to the high school.

The First Baptist Church was built during the early 1950s with Mr. Davis as chairman of the building committee and Winfred Moore, pastor. He was selected to head the building committee because his past activities had given credence to the reputation that he was a forward thinking man with boundless energy! It was exciting to see a man be able to direct the needs of a community, while at the same time manage a business with new cars coming in and moving out on a weekly basis, plus directing a complete service and repair shop taking care of Borger automobile needs. He was a wise man who hired good talent to work with him in his business. Davis Chevrolet served the people of Borger and the surrounding counties for 50 years.

[Ed. Note] When Borger alumni were asked to submit their fondest and wildest memories of Borger this story was shared. It is too good NOT to include with this story.

Does anyone remember the 1956 Chevy El Morocco that was on the lot at Davis Chevrolet? It was an after market new 1956 Chevy with a Cadillac look. I asked the salesman what it was and he said "Son, it's 1/2 Chevy and 1/2 Cadillac-- wild car for 1956!" Needless to say it didn't go over too good, but today is the rarest of the rare Chevy's...and worth mega bucks.

I remember going to Davis Chevrolet to look at a 1954 white corvette with red interior it was there for a long time, then it was gone and I was very sad. A few years ago I talked to Bill Griffin and he said Mr. Davis couldn't sell it so he gave it to his daughter to drive to college. Bill said that was what she was driving when they met.

Jim's Grocery Store, Jim's Lake and other grocery stores

Roger Dale Smith '61

Jim Nix owned Jim's Grocery on Main Street. Rumor had it that he was very soft hearted and during the hard economic times would help people get food, taking away from his profits. In the first grade to the 9th grade my first girlfriend, was Linda Nix, granddaughter of Jim Nix, who owned **Jim's Grocery** store. Linda is deceased now but I use to go with her to Jim's and she would always get us candy, gum and ice cream. I thought she was stealing it and I didn't want to take it, until one day her grandfather, Jim Nix, told me he let Linda get that stuff for us. Then I would take it.

Melinda Eason Stephenson '61

I remember Jim's grocery. Sue Prescott's parents charged there, I thought that was the "bomb"

Danny Stephens '62

Funny, funny, funny. It all seems so real to me. My mind did a dance a bit on the mention of Sue Prescott, though. Sue was our next-door neighbor when Bob Cobb (Stephens) and I lived at 1121 Valley Drive. Sue and I had a love-hate relationship almost like a brother-sister thing that went on for years and years. She was older than I, though, and SO TALL!. And the Prescott's really did have a charge account at **Jim's** grocery store; I remember going down there several times with R.C. Prescott (Sue's dad). He would go inside and not do any shopping at all – just write out a check for $10, and down in the "memo" corner write the word "beans." Then we'd go down the street a couple of blocks to the bar at 6th and Main or so – R.C. would go inside for about five minutes (long enough to drink a beer?) and then come back out to the car and remind me I wasn't to tell Mrs. Prescott. That has remained a secret until I just told it right now. When I practiced my cornet in the evenings, Mrs. Prescott would holler out the window at me "play 'Pretty Redwing'." For many years afterwards (twenty-plus), I would write the word "beans" on almost every check I wrote, thinking about good ol' R.C. ("are-oh-see" as Bob called him) each time.

Jim's Lake....revisited by James Cornelius

My granddad was Jim Nix, aka Jim's Grocery & Market. He bought the 320 acres where Jim's Lake was developed in 1938. There were 2 ponds and the water table is only 15', so he had to dredge the spring fed lake. He sold material dredged just to get it out. My dad, Grover Cornelius and my uncle F. E. Langdon, established Borger Redi Mix in 1950, (sold it in 1962) and they utilized the sand and gravel operation before they moved it to it's location north of Spring Creek School in 1955 (Borger Sand & Gravel).

Jim Nix's oldest child was my mother, she died September 3, 2006 at 93 yrs old. Jim's wife, Bessie lived here until she died in 1992 (age 100). I married Peggy Huskey on December 25, 1962, and we buried her Dec. 26, 1992. We had one daughter.

Frieda Lanham Pickett, '61:
I remember Jim's Lake. Sue Anderson lived up the street from me in Country Club Addition. Her father took us there to fish. I had a pole but had never used it. I cast off and threw my entire fishing pole into the lake. Needless to say, I didn't catch any fish. The others did catch some, but you had to pay 50 cents for each fish you kept! Ha! It was a pretty place. I'd enjoy going back. Anyone know the directions on how to get there?

Holcomb's Grocery – Sandra Zimmerman '61
One more business that I would like to remember. Do you remember Holcomb's grocery? In the mid forties when I was born it was called Shaw & Holcomb's. During the war there was rationing of canned milk that mom was to use in my formula. It was near to impossible to get, but Mr. Holcomb used to set aside a case for us. He also used to let people "charge" groceries when there was a strike or hard times. Of course in reality he never gave thought to the repayment. His daugher, Michelle, (class of 62) and I became friends through school and are still in touch. She has said that up until his death Mr. Holcomb would still occasionally receive a check and a thank you card in the mail from someone long forgotten to whom he had given groceries. We had some awesome dads in our town, didn't we?

Lindsey's Furniture and Brightly Decorated home at Christmas!

Every year at Christmas people in Borger packed the kids in the car and drove around the town looking at the Christmas lights on Main street and down neighborhoods. One of the most memorable sites was the annual display at the home of the Lindseys. They owned a home on a large corner lot and had much space to decorate. They added new scenes each year until they filled the space. It was a sight I looked forward to each year as a child, always will be in my memory. Other homeowners had beautifully decorated yards in Borger, but on a smaller scale. Merchants in Borger decorated the storefront windows, too, and it gave a very attractive look to the business district. At Halloween they decorated, too, and once had a "Witche's Brew", giving out hot beverages to trick or treaters.

Cathie Andress Kimbell '65
I know everyone remembers the fabulous Christmas decorations on the Bob & Jackie Lindsey home on Cedar Street. I also remember many good times with the Lindsey family at their cabin at Pearl Lakes Trout Club north of Creede, Colorado, where my family also had a cabin and which is where I met my first husband, Greg Duggar, and even though the marriage failed...Pearl Lakes memories are some of the most special in my life.

Jackson Air Conditioning and Refrigeration

by Marie Jackson

The country was beginning to recover from the Great Depression and the dust storms and drought. There was little money and people worked very hard to make a living. When Japan bombed Pearl Harbor, life changed for thousands of people, including Harry and Marie Jackson.

Realizing he needed a "war job" – that a Phillips Petroleum bulk agent was not adequate – Harry got his family in tow and took off job hunting. Several days were spent in Houston. The ship docks were in chaos and no one was hiring at that time. Discouraged and distraught, he headed back to Beaver, OK. On the way he came through carbon-black covered Borger. Phillips was hiring so he signed on. The following Monday, he reported for work. It was May of 1942.

In his spare time he searched for housing for his family, wife Marie and daughter Charlene and son Gary. He found only one empty house but could not find the owner. Not to be deterred, he found an unlocked window, climbed in and his family followed. "We lived there a month in this house on North Hedgecoke wondering who we were supposed to pay for the rent!" In the meantime Harry continued to work and used his "off time" frantically searching for a house before he was evicted from the recent find. Finally, the search was fruitful, and a house turned up on Monroe Street. The family stayed there for several months until housing became available on Lemp Street in the small community of Phillips. Charlene joined the neighborhood children and off to school they went. Daughter, Bette Ruth was born while the family lived in Phillips. At this time, Hughes Pitts addition was being developed. Houses were sold by the bid process. "We bid on a house under construction on Meredith Street. While we waited for the house to be finished we lived in a small, but new home on Valley Drive." Finally the family was settled on Meredith Street.

In the meantime Harry began doing refrigeration and air conditioning work after hours. While still in Beaver, Harry had answered an ad asking for young men to enter the refrigeration and air conditioning field, a new industry geared for the future! This sounded like something Harry would be interested in, so he signed up for the training, first by correspondence, then "hands on" instruction at the factory. For months he got up at four A.M., studied until six, and after breakfast he went to work hauling Phillips gas to customers in Beaver County. When he finished the course he spent a month in Chicago with more "hands on training". He excelled at the work and understood the engineering for the new technology and units, but the depression was upon the country and not many people could afford refrigerated air conditioning. At that time it could not have been predicted that this was the beginning of a career which would last over fifty years. When Goodrich Tire began operations in Borger Harry went to work there and remained until the war was nearly over. As the population of Borger increased and more people came in, Harry decided now was the time to go into the refrigeration and air conditioning business full time. They opened a shop on Main Street, up from the Morley Theater.

In about 1947 or 48 Harry and Marie were approached to sell paint by the Pratt and Lambert Paint Co. Marie's father had been a decorator for many years and she had learned from him how to mix and color paint and how to hang wallpaper. So, Marie was enthusiastic about getting into the paint business. Two sessions at the Pratt and Lambert Paint factory in Chicago gave them confidence and led to their first paint store location was at 813 North Main in Borger. Harry's air conditioning repair shop was in the back of the store. Soon a line of wallpaper was purchased. Marie spent two sessions at the University of Houston taking decorating classes to add this skill to her line of services. Soon a better property became available on Borger's Main Street and the business moved to 719 North Main Street. Marie began to make draperies, curtains and home decorating items. Clara Berrien managed the fabric department in the store. Business continued to come to the Jackson team and it was soon evident that a larger space would be needed if the business was to grow. During this time a lot and building on the corner of Tenth and Cedar, at that time known as the "old by-pass", was purchased from a Mrs. MacMillan, who had the NuWay Café on Main Street. Harry planned to move the store into this building. However, someone else was wanting to use the space so Harry was persuaded by Sophie Page to let her put in a restaurant. She operated her restaurant for a few years then decided to sell out and go to California. Immediately the place was equipped for the paint, wallpaper and fabric store, and called Jackson's Paint store, with Harry's refrigeration and air conditioning shop in the back.

During this time Harry had been busy changing "walk-in" boxes in grocery stores into refrigerated boxes and display counters in grocery stores were becoming refrigerated to preserve the fresh foods. The economy was better in the country and homes were putting in refrigerated air conditioning. In the beginning of the technological evolution of refrigerated air conditioning the units were large and cumbersome and took much attention and service. While yet involved in refrigeration and air conditioning, Harry became interested in ice machines which were becoming popular in motels, refinery offices, restaurants and any industry which hired many workers. Phillips Petroleum Company sought out Harry's services to provide this equipment for their workers. By 1955 Harry needed help to fill the business needs so Marie's brother, Kenneth Niles, came from Oklahoma to help, bringing his family and son, David, to Borger. Kenneth remained with Jackson's Refrigeration until Harry retired and Kenneth took over the business. Other family members were taught the business and daughter Charlene's husband Glen Buckles became an employee.

In 1993 Harry's daughter Charlene and husband Glen Buckles resumed the management of the rental business at the corner of 10th and Cedar. The building had been remodeled into small office spaces. Glen also provided refrigeration services and became owner of the ice machine franchise and equipment which were placed in Kansas, Oklahoma and the Texas Panhandle.

Harry Jackson died at the age of 97 in Borger. Marie still lives in Borger and enjoys pretty good health for a vibrant woman in her 90s. Since his time in Beaver when he hauled Phillips gas to farmers, to his time as an employee at the Refinery, and then his years in the refrigeration and air conditioning business, followed by the commercial ice machine business, Harry received a pay check from Phillips on a monthly basis for over fifty years. His contribution to the growth of Borger was significant.

SANDRA ZIMMERMAN (Page, St. Amand) BHS class of 62

The photo below is an old photo of the Phillips 66 station from my grandmother Dowell's collection. The Phillips 66 gas station stood at West Adams (the street I grew up on) and Main. At that time it was owned by Mr. Smock. Did anyone else have his wife, Naomi Smock, as their art teacher BHS? Do you remember that her favorite color was purple? This gas station was an important source of summer revenue for me as a child. It is where I would redeem my "found" glass cola bottles. Notice the oil well on the left. As children we would use it as a jungle gym. I remember the working oil well by the post office, too. We were indeed a boom town. (I hear they are thinking of drilling in urban areas again).

PHILLIPS 66 SERVICE STATION

Far ahead of its time in architecture and convenience, th Phillips 66 Station at the corner of Main and Adams Street has served Borger customers for many years.

Built in 1928, Phil Phillips was the first operator of this station At the time he was a construction inspector for Phillips Pet roleum Company. He later hired Herman C. Barnes of Denve to replace him, and it was Mr. Barnes who talked T. S. Smoc into moving from Denver to Borger. And so, in April of 1929 Mr Smock took over the lease and operated this station unti recent years. Richard Wilson has the lease at this time.

During those years, Phillips Petroleum Company was buildin many new stations and they were all very fine looking struc tures. Even though this station has been remodeled, it stil retains much of the original lines.

THE WAREHOUSE

by Sue Schmitz Lattig, Borger High School Class of 1955

In the early decades of 1900 you often heard the expression, "Go West, Young Man!" it was hoped young men would expand our country and our economy and build futures on barren lands still undeveloped.

In 1928 Adolph Leo Schmitz heard this call and, being an ambitious twenty-five year old man, heeded the call and went to Borger, Texas when the town was just a baby. Borger was a boomtown at that time and as undeveloped as a small oil field town could be. Wooden shacks here and ragged tents there, up and down it's one main street was the lay of the land. Land was cheap; supplies were non-existent and, although food was plentiful, water had to be trucked in by the barrel from nearby towns. Adolph purchased a lot in the South part of town from Ace Borger, the founder of the town. This lot did not have an address at that time, but later was tagged "1101 South Main Street."

Adolph looked at this piece of dry land; this empty lot and imagined what it could be, the product of his dreams. Determined to make this his home for himself and for his family (and future family) he lived in a small tent while building a warehouse on this location. It must have taken a lot of blood, sweat and tears to build in that day. All materials had to be hauled in from Amarillo 48 miles to the south. In an effort to establish a business in Borger he had obtained the dealership of Cities Service Oil Company for all of Borger, and oh, was he proud!

He worked without complaint and as his warehouse neared completion. Soon he moved out of his tent and into the warehouse for shelter. He lived in the warehouse for nearly three years, sleeping on a cot, cooking food on a hot plate and washing in a galvanized tub. He had a wife and son in Gainesville, Texas, but this was no place for them...yet. He had to build his business, and then a home for them....and this he did.

While building his warehouse, Adolph ran and operated Cities Service Station on Weatherly street, near the water tower. When it was the right time his wife, Tommie and little son Adolph Junior joined him. They all lived for a while in a tarpaper shack behind the station. In 1936 he built a modern and beautiful service station at 100 North Main Street. It opened for business on April 23, l937 and as the Borger News-Herald described it, it was the "New Cities Service Station, Most Modern in This Section of The Country." It was white with green and white neon lights outlining it's art deco architecture and two large front windows. The station had the first neon lights in Borger! It had an office and two large doors, one for the grease rack and the other for a car wash. Three gas pumps stood in the driveway like soldiers guarding the castle and a huge green and white Cities Service sign hung on a pole by the street. Around the pole he built an oval flower bed for Tommie to plant all sorts of flowers, things easy to grow in this dry town. She cultivated morning glories, hollyhocks, marigolds, zinnias and a rose or two. Let it be noted that these were the first flowers growing on Main Street and it made a beautiful sight! This woman was my mother and she refused to live in an ugly town and so she drove up and down the bare dirt alleys every fall throwing out seeds for morning glories, hollyhocks and marigolds. That next Spring our town had the prettiest alleys in Texas!!

Adolph and Tommie built their home behind the service station with a lovely yard and garden between the two and soon, Adolph moved his growing family into another house at 103 West Second Street. He also built a couple of duplex apartments on the other side of the house and he rented these. His first daughter, Marilyn Sue was born in 1936 just before they moved into their new home. In 1943 the second daughter, Mary Ann was born.

The business prospered. The family grew up. Life was good. Work was hard, but it was worth it. Adolph put in an office in front of his warehouse with a showroom for Tommie's "Ceramic House", which later became her reducing salon "Lady Be Lovely". This arrangement provided a situation so that her business was always attached to his office and they could be together. Adolph realized his dream and was a highly esteemed businessman in Borger. His entire family was well thought of and admired. They were in businesses of various sorts for fifty years in Borger. Their last business being "The Wooden Indian" which they were able to operate in the old office building for eleven weeks in 1976 before they both became ill for the last time. They had an elaborate Grand Opening attended by all the other businessmen and women in the community. All this time, the old warehouse stood behind the office, not much in use anymore but more like a reminder, "I am still here and it all started with me."

It is interesting to note that an entire family's future began and grew with a mere empty lot and a small and somewhat primitive warehouse on South Main Street. The warehouse became a landmark and people grew used to seeing it there and considered it just another part of their town. Time went by, weather and circumstances turned the warehouse into an abandoned, old structure. I suppose it became a liability and an eyesore. On November 2, 2003 I learned that the old warehouse had been torn down. Having stood there for 75 years it had become part of everyone's perception of the town. Suddenly it was gone, just gone. To many who were accustomed to seeing it guarding the city over the years, it was a great shock to suddenly see an empty lot there. To others who did not grow up with it, it did not seem such a loss. After all it was just an ugly old building. It had served its purpose; it had founded one family's future in Borger. It had sustained their lives for years. It had made it possible for the family to grow with the town and become separate individuals, as well they should have done. Maybe it was time for it to go.

But I think that Adolph's warehouse is still standing somewhere. I can see it, can't you?

Borger Airport

Frieda Lanham Pickett '61

Borger had an airport, I believe to accommodate the Phillips plant executives airplanes. There were community events there. I bought a ride on one of the airplanes once for $2.00---a chance to see Borger from the air. It was advertised as an opportunity to take a picture of your home's rooftop from the plane. I didn't have a camera, just wanted to see what people's rooftops looked like, and ours of course! When I returned for the 20th reunion of my graduating class in 1981, my aunt, Barbara Kay Ferrill Sims and I flew into Borger and landed at the airport, being taken there by an oil company executive jet. Barbara worked for the head of the company and he and the wife were flying up to Colorado and they said they didn't mind "dropping us off in Borger". I'll never forget my mother driving her Cadillac right onto the runway, stopping by the plane, and picking us up! I was shocked they would let the locals drive their cars onto the runway, but...hey...we were relaxed up there!

Bob Holmes, '64

The Huber airport was located on the South side of town, but the larger one was off the "circle" part of the highway between Phillips and Stinnett. When I was a kid, that was where you "went to the airport", though it wasn't much. The airport on the north side of town, Griff's place, was known to us as "the NEW airport." Brother Bobby and I grew up with a strange, almost parallel view of planes landing at the airport from the old Patburg Camp (Patton/Whittenburg) just above Electric City. I have this vague recollection of having been there when the very first plane came taxiing in ... but that may be my mind playing some sort of sordid trick, because I have no idea why we would have been there, unless everyone in Borger went out that day/night.

My Dad spent the hours of his life doctorin', but his avocation was flying. I certainly remember Mr. Griffin and the Borger airport. One of the series of airplanes Dad owned (seems like he'd either upgrade or wreck 'em, every so often), was an aluminum-skinned one that he determined (???) needed polishing. I have no idea why, but he decided, and everybody got to "help". Do you have any idea how much "skin" is on a medium-to-small 4-seater private airplane. I remember power drills, polisher attachment, chrome polish (cases of that stuff), ladders, and aching arms/shoulders.

Larry White '64

Chris Crouch mentioned the airport in an earlier story. How many remember M.E. (Griff) Griffin, the airport manager for many, many years? Well Griff lives here at Hilltop Lakes and is still active at the young age of 93 in the community. He is a member of the Men's Golf Association although he doesn't play very often and sings every Sunday as a member of the chapel choir. He is a member of the T-38 Club (a club consisting of airplane owners and enthusiasts at Hilltop Lakes). And if you have a few hours of idle time, Griff is never out of stories to tell.

Mike Harrington '65

Glad to hear that Mr. Griffin is still enjoying life at 93. My late father, Claude Harrington, BHS'35, was a good friend of Griff's. After WWII, Dad owned several private planes, including a surplus P-52 Mustang. A friend crashed Dad's last plane in the early 1950s, and Dad was lucky to escape the crash with only a broken ankle. Anyway, that put an end to Dad's flying his own plane, but not his enthusiasm for flight. Well into the Sixties Dad would still occasionally rent a plane from Griff and fly it around Hutchinson County. I want to say that Griff's son graduated near the top of his BHS class in the late 1950s.

Chris Crouch '64

Also a memory concerning the airport was the time when an Air Force jet fighter had to land at Borger due to perhaps a mechanical or fuel problem. They got the problem fixed after a few days and I think a pretty good crowd showed up at the airport when the jet took off.

The Playhouse by Frieda Lanham Pickett '61

Many of us Borgans who grew up in the 50s and 60s will remember a special dancehall on the highway to Panhandle, called the "Playhouse". It was a rambleshack building with bottoms of egg cartons for the ceiling. I suppose that was to provide better acoustics for the music. There was a bar for beer and a great dance floor. The operator was named Jainie Whittenburg. Jainie was a good businesswoman. She ran the establishment with an iron hand and never let the "rowdies" get out of hand, which can occur in a place where alcohol and people meet up. This was a place where many of us went after graduating from Borger High, and staying in Borger for college at Frank Phillips, or not. Often the engineer interns at Phillips would come and dance. We went to dance and see others, as Teen Town and the dance at the American Legion was below us in age group. The older crowd in Borger came here to see others, listen to music and to dance. One band that was popular was from the local area (Borger, Stinnett), The Arcades, and composed of John Henderson, J.P. Jones, Joe Atherton and Kent Tooms. Kent was the lead singer, but John and Joe often sang, as well. Their music was mainly in the rock and roll style as the era was the "Elvis Presley and Roy Orbison" era, the Beatles had not shown up yet. They played every Friday and Saturday nights. If you wanted to dance Monday thru Thursday, there was a coin operated music player, too.

Jainie was a gregarious, single lady, with a winning personality. She watched and listened to her customers so she could supply what they wanted to buy. She was a friendly person with an engaging smile, although not pretty, by most standards. She suffered from a genetic condition called neurofibromatosis where multiple small nodules grew on her face and neck.

People noticed it, but overlooked it, so as not to embarrass her. She had a low, gruff voice and would not hesitate to step in if anyone was getting out of line, saying "Let's take it outside!" on a regular basis. Before Jainie took over the Playhouse it was owned by another woman, Mrs. Tadlock. The place had a seedy reputation since it sold alcohol and was associated with "loose women" and those who enjoyed that. Most of us who went there to dance, didn't know anything about that. It was just a great place to dance and have fun. I never drank alcohol when I went there, only cokes. I don't think I would have been served alcohol as I was not 21 years of age, and Jainie or her staff would let you know up front "no alcohol to minors".

Don Chase '64

Does anyone remember the "Playhouse" bar out on the Panhandle highway? Maybe not because if you were 16 or 17 year old like we were you couldn't get in the place...unless your name was Mike or Steve Butler, Larry Beamguard or, occasionally me, who made up the group that Jainie Whittenburg, owner, needed to bring in cowboys and roughnecks to sell beer to. So, she was not too picky about the age of the members of the band she hired. In her defense she would never sell me beer but pointed out some guy of legal age could buy two beers, one he didn't want.
Old timers may remember Janie Whittenburg, owner of the Playhouse and her early history in Borger. Not a lot of good said about her because of her first "profession" but still interesting.

Phillips Petroleum and all those Carbon Black plants

PeeYuuu, what is that smell? Smells like rotten eggs or an outhouse! "Honey, that's not the smell of a sewer, smells like money to me!"

Sharon Kaye Johnson Nichols '61

One of my memories from Borger is definitely not glamorous or fun, but one, I am sure is, etched in the memory of each and everyone of us....CARBON BLACK!!! I remember having to check to see which way the wind was blowing before the clothes were hung on the line to dry. Before you could hang the clothes out, the lines had to be washed to get the carbon black off them. I even remember when the government made the plants put in filters so that the carbon black wouldn't come over Borger so much, but...**they put the filters in backwards** and it was even worse. I can still remember seeing carbon black granules blowing down the street. Thank goodness, that didn't last too long. I remember how happy my mother was when she got a clothes dryer!

You couldn't hang clothes out on the clothesline in Borger without checking to see if Phillips was spewing carbon black. If you touched the granules and then touched your face it would leave a black line on the skin. There would be black granules on windowsills. You had to wash the carbon black and dust off the lines before hanging sheets and clothes on the line. When we were doing that chore, it allowed us to "get lost" in thoughts, letting the sheets hit us in the face...cool sheets in the hot Borger summer. What a wonderful memory!!

Roger Smith class of 61

Carbon Black & "Can you smell Phillips?" Sometimes, it was dangerous to wear white or have a white car. The smell was often bad, but when I was in France, I smelled something similar so I followed it to some truck. It smelled liked Phillips and made me homesick.
I remember (since a little boy coming to Borger at the age of 5) growing up among the carbon black granules in the air, and the dirt coming in the house on a windy day. The bedspreads were all sandy and had spicules of carbon black all over them.

Nancy Shermer Grimes '61
CARBON BLACK: I learned early on never to lean against a car or put my elbows on a flat surface, lest I ruin whatever I was wearing. I can truthfully say I never owned a piece of white clothing until something was done to remedy the situation.

Ella (Morris) Sewell '63
We still have carbon black settle over the town. It happens most often in the Bunavista & Borger Country Club areas, at night. My daughter lives on Inverness (close to Broadmoor) and she has to wipe the carbon black off the swings and slide before her children play outside. It is not as bad, but it is still there. Go to: www.googleearth.com put in Hutchinson County, Texas and look at the black areas.

PART TWO ---PEOPLE & PLACES

DEAHL STREET 1950s

Chapter 5 – Walking Horse

In the 1950s there was an unusual bearded man who walked down the alleys in south Borger, off Main Street, gathering junk and various things from the trash cans. He pushed a cart on wheels in which to place the materials he gathered and sold. My step-father, Rodney Weddington, told me that many men in Borger recognized the need of the man and would set out valuable "junk" for him to pick up and sell. For us children, the bearded gentleman who was rather tall (to a child), who pushed the cart, sometimes talking to himself, was very frightening. The man was referred to as "Walking Horse" by many people. One of his relatives, **Wayne Cogdill**, gives us a view into the man's situation. It is as follows:

Everyone was afraid of Walking Horse as kids. He looked scary, certainly didn't act normal, couldn't speak clearly. He pushed that cart up and down the alleys of Borger gathering bits of metal to sell for scrap and bottles to return for deposit. Remember those days? With all these things present, it was easy to accept the stories that would scare us, and so we did. He was surely the kind of person no one would prefer in their family, and, of course, must be an embarrassment.

So let me tell you a part of the story of my grandmother, Linda McPherson. She was the daughter of German immigrants, wheat farmers and a fine cabinetmaker. She had at least three brothers and three sisters, and grew up in Kansas. Her family was there during the time of the great meningitis outbreak in the early 1900's. One baby sister died from the disease, and one sister and two brothers survived the disease, but were both physically and mentally affected by the extremely high fever that came with it. Their speech was affected, and none ever learned to read or write. Medical help wasn't available then, like now, so people took what happened and tried to make the best of it.

Hard times and the depression came along, and my grandmother and her family wound up in Borger. She worked as a maid, her dad worked as a carpenter, taking care of the brothers and sister, as well as her two children, one of which is my father. Linda later worked for years at Borger Laundry over a steam press, later still at Jim's Grocery in the meat market, and even later, well into her seventies, at Borger High as a custodian. Throughout her life she helped care for her sister and two brothers because one brother could only work as a laborer (ditch digger, the real kind, with shovel) and the other was unemployable. The welfare system didn't exist then, as it does now, and families bore the burden of caring for such people. She later had another son, and buried a husband, dead from cancer at too young an age. The snowstorm of 1957 that everyone remembers started the day we drove home from the cemetery at my grandfather's funeral. Linda had all these responsibilities, plus caring for her own family.

The brother who was most severely affected by the meningitis couldn't speak very well, had difficulty with those "activities of daily living" that we know about from caring for our parents. She tried to keep him clean and shaven, but those things are sometimes hard to take care of when you have a job or two to go to, and a family of your own to care for. He lived with his brother and sister in a little shack of a house out by Rock Creek. He was physically strong, had a great interest in music, and played the harmonica. He had enough mental capacity and awareness to be able to gather junk and sell it, and also, enough awareness to know when people made fun of him and treated him badly enough to make him angry. He never married, never got arrested, and of course never attended school. Since there were no places for warehousing such a person then, he became a ward of the State on a couple of occasions at Vernon; not because he was violent or mentally ill, but because there just wasn't another place in the system to take up the slack and care for someone like him.

I was, of course, ashamed to acknowledge the familial relationship. My grandmother never made a big deal out of that. I didn't think much about it until he died late in her life, still under the care of her and one of her sisters. I saw that, to her, he wasn't an embarrassment, HE WAS HER BIG BROTHER. While then blind, deaf and wheelchair bound, he was still a part of family, just as I was. She mourned him as a brother, and not with relief to finally be rid of her burden.

My grandmother's maiden name was Walkenhorst. Her big brother was named Roy Walkenhorst. Of course, in a place like postwar Borger, a German surname on a fellow like Roy is going to get corrupted to something like Walking Horse. The things told about him were mostly untrue, or at least based upon a misunderstanding of his real condition, nature and history. He wasn't homeless, he wasn't a "bum". He also wasn't a monster. He wasn't born retarded, or genetically made wrong. He was just the product of the kind of poverty we didn't know was poverty and the lack of medical progress when life happened to him, as life happens to all of us.

So, if we want to conjure up our "bogeyman" for our kids from our younger days, just remember that there are things we don't know about people. Before you personalize your "bogeyman", read To Kill A Mockingbird. I wish I had read and thought more about it before I hurt my grandmother's feelings. This may be way too preachy, especially from a lapsed Druid. Of course, and for that I apologize, but you wanted to know about Walking Horse, and I thought I would tell you who the man really was.

Frieda Lanham Pickett, Class of 61
Wayne, this is beautifully written prose which evokes understanding, empathy and realization of unmeaning bias. I have a new view of what your family went through and a new admiration for the strong characters of those that settled in Borger. No wonder we, the children, developed our strong, independent characters. Wish I had known this when I was a child. I might

have been motivated to say a "kind word" to him, rather than run away as fast as I could!

Otis Phillips '64:
THANK YOU, WAYNE, FOR TELLING US ABOUT WALKING HORSE. WITH YOUR PERMISSION I WOULD LIKE TO ADD THIS TO YOUR STORY. AT CHRISTMAS TIME MY FAMILY HAD A TRADITION. NEAR CHRISTMAS AND SOMETIMES ON CHRISTMAS EVE AFTER ALL OF THE TRAFFIC HAD GONE HOME DAD WOULD DRIVE US TO MAIN STREET JUST TO VIEW THE CHRISTMAS LIGHTS AND DECORATIONS. THAT WAS OUR FANTASY TIME AND DAD ALWAYS MADE THAT TIME VERY SPECIAL. ONCE HE MADE ALL OF US GET OUT OF THE CAR. REASONS UNKNOWN THAT NIGHT HE WANTED ALL OF US TO WALK MAIN STREET. THAT NIGHT WE WERE MET BY A MAN THAT GAVE ALL OF US A CANDY BAR AND WISHED US MERRY CHRISTMAS IN A VERY SPECIAL WAY. I HAD FORGOTTEN ABOUT THIS EVENT BUT AT THE SAME TIME IT IS AN EVENT IN YOUR LIFE YOU WILL NEVER FORGET. MY FATHER SOMEHOW HAD A RELATIONSHIP WITH THIS MAN THAT I HAD NO PRIVY TO, EXCEPT THAT I KNOW THEY ALWAYS WAVED AND ALWAYS SPOKE WHEN THEY MET. THAT WASN'T OFTEN BUT I REMEMBER IT HAPPENING. MY FATHER THAT NIGHT REMINDED US HOW IMPORTANT GIVING IS AND ESPECIALLY WHO IT WAS THAT WAS GIVING. NOW, MY FATHER PROBABLY GAVE HIM THE CANDY AND ASKED HIM TO GIVE IT TO US JUST MY FATHER'S WAY OF TEACHING US ABOUT SOMETHING GOOD. I REMEMBER THE MAN BEING CALLED "WALKING HORSE". YOU KNOW, ONE THING I CAN TELL YOU IS THAT MY DAUGHTER AND SON BOTH KNOW THIS STORY AND THEY KNOW WHAT GIVING IS. I HOPE THEY TELL THEIR CHILDREN THIS STORY. Thank you.

Dan McGee (BHS '65)
Wow! You are right! It is a sad AND beautiful story. This could easily be a "Made for TV Movie". Or at the very least a wonderful short story - with a very pointed (& painful to many of us) message. Thank you Wayne, so very much, for "setting the record straight".
This should be Required Reading for us all. Not to mention our kids and theirs.

Bob Stephens
You can't judge a book by looking at the cover......forgive us all of our chiding or pointing at people....although I never recall this man...we all sometimes made "fun" of people....and never should....i.e. Larry Dean Simmons....Oh GOD forgive us and I wish we could personally ask those individuals to forgive me and others...i.e.: Walter Cloute at Sam Houston

Iris Wood '64
I just read the heart wrenching story from Wayne Cogdill. I never knew of Walking Horse while I was growing up in Borger. I was such a sheltered little girl growing up. I don't think I ever was faced with reality until I met and married my husband and left Borger and my sheltering family. I am a

nurse and have seen some tragedy and heart breaking things in families. That in itself has matured me. I am sure I also would have been afraid of Walking Horse as a little girl, but I think I would really like to get to know him now if it were possible. In my profession I have worked with severe physically handicap people as well as mentally challenged children. I have nursed the dying in hospice and seen the elderly get older and sicker. Until you are blessed to be a part of caring for someone like these special ones I don't think you can ever understand how much they have to offer and how each one can bless a life beyond words. I think Wayne's grandmother was the blessed one even if it does not look like it to the world system. I am sure she became greater and wiser than any of us. I just want to thank Wayne for sharing the story with all of us because hopefully it will make us stop and think how blessed we are, and most of all inspire us to bless someone else. Thank you Wayne....I wish I had known Walking Horse.

Danny Stephens
I remember "Walking Horse" coming in to Safeway Foods Store in Megert Shopping Center. I worked at Safeway with Johnny Baker and Ken Roark during my high school years. Walking Horse came in often when Safeway had promotional games, bingo, etc. He would buy a bar of soap, get his game piece, then sit down on the window ledge at the front of the store take a pocket knife and whittle the bar of soap into small pieces, carefully dropping each piece into a small paper bag. When the soap was gone, he folded up the bag and put it into his bib overalls and would leave. He repeated this process several times per week. I don't remember him having a beard but I do recall his bib overalls, usually clean and pressed and he always wore a baseball cap turned slightly off center.

Mary Lynne Bishop Tiner '64
I guess there's always a "story behind the story" that not everyone knows. I'm glad that Wayne enlightened us on this. "Walking Horse" sounds more like he was a person that made his way under very severe circumstances (with a very loving family) instead of someone to be feared or ridiculed.

Vera Jo (Aull) Springer '64
Wayne, this is absolutely beautiful, right from your heart. By sharing, you have enriched us all.

Nancy Roediger '60

Wayne's e-mail has made its way to me. I greatly appreciate his articulate, image-filled, tender story about "Walking Horse" and about his grandmother. His narrative about his grandmother conveys what an unusually strong, determined, fine and courageous woman she was and her determination to earn a living doing whatever was necessary so that she could take care of her family. His uncle's story is heart-breaking, yet he accepted the adversity that came his way. The human spirit which allows people to work hard and to cope and overcome adversity under the worst of circumstances is present in Wayne's story about his family. Also, the capacity of human cruelty toward others, out of ignorance or meanness, is also present in this beautifully crafted narrative. The extremes of the human condition are captured in so few words.

Teen Town, American Legion Hall and Club Dances

by Frieda Lanham Pickett '61

Teen Town was built following a bond issue to provide money for a community recreation center with a new swimming pool. The swimming pool in the past was at Huber Park and I suppose it was in need of repair and City Leaders thought it best to use the space for something else and move the swimming pool to a place where a modern facility could be built. I searched for a story on who was the City Manager or who initiated the bond issue but only found this story in the Borger News Herald, June 17, 1955.

"A summer Teen Town program sponsored by the City Parks and Recreation department plans for teens to meet Friday 8 to 11PM at the park under supervision of Mary Janeway and E.L. Dickerson. Cappy Stamps will serve as Teen Town mayor. Commissioners are Patty Barksdale, Dickie Propes, Chief Boyd, David Swinford, Pat Conner, Stanley Latman, John Paine, Sue Sharpe, Judy Blackburn, Kay Mahon, Jenny Reynolds, Nina Sue King, Jack McGlaun, Sandra Baxter, Leslie Hargis, Teddy Tanner, and Kay Lois Schrimsher. Activities are social dancing, square dancing, treasure hunts, scavenger hunts, parties, and picnics."

All these people were in the two classes ahead of me. They were Juniors and Seniors when I was a Sophomore at BHS. I never knew they had input from the school representatives. However this shows they did. The beautiful facility that was built and well attended by area children, has been replaced recently, with the new building located in Johnson Park, at the same location (2009).

We went to Teen Town when I was in Junior High school to dance to records. There was a food stand with soda, chips, candy and hot foods, like hot dogs. I never bought any of that as I only had enough money to pay the admission. On rare occasions, when I would get a job babysitting (50 cents an hour) I might have enough money to get a coke. I didn't feel too miserable about it, as not many other kids had enough money to buy food either. We had great times at Teen Town. My favorite dance partner was Durwood Williams. I met him at Weatherly Elementary school, at a dance in their cafeteria. Not many of the girls could dance at that age, and mainly stood on the side watching others dance. I watched "American Bandstand" on TV, though, and could see how to do some of the jitterbug steps. I cannot remember if Durwood asked me to dance or I asked him, but we found we could dance together pretty well. As a result he asked me to dance a lot and we became pretty good dancers. Each Friday I watched for him to come in so I could dance. It was really fun and something I looked forward to.

When one entered Teen Town there were pool tables and foosball tables. Possibly there were other games to play but I did not know how to play any of these games, so I never stopped here. I went directly to the large area for dancing. To the left one could exit the dancing area onto a large walkway overlooking the swimming pool. If one went to Teen Town during the day you could watch the kids playing and swimming in the pool. There were several life guards and they sat up on high seats, so they could overlook the swimmers. I went swimming on occasion, but we were members of the Borger Country Club by then, and mother generally took us swimming there…because it was free. I believe our membership was paid for by my step father's job, the Borger News Herald, as a benefit. They did not provide health insurance, I don't think. Good thing we were healthy as I had three sisters!

Teen Town was a place for socialization. We would meet girls we knew and talked about many topics of interest to girls. At this time there was only one Junior High School in Borger, so many of the girls I had seen in school, although there was not much time to talk to each other in school. Classes were disciplined well, so you couldn't chat during class and we only got 30 minutes for lunch, so almost all your time was taken by standing in line, waiting to be served and eating. We only had 5 minutes between classes, so Teen Town was where we found out what each other were doing. The building was modern, clean and well cared for. I can say Teen Town was a godsend to Borger parents as it kept us off the streets and kept us from getting into trouble. It also acted as a good babysitter, I suppose. Both my older sister and I went to Teen Town. We were two years apart.

Local groups could rent out the Teen Town building for parties and our local high school clubs rented the facility for Spring Festival Dances. We would decorate the place with decorations according to a theme and it would generally take two full days with about 30 of us working. I don't know how it got organized, but it always worked out. A committee would decide on a theme. My junior year the theme was "Quiet Village" and one of the girls got a grass covered hut to use as a decoration. We made colored flowers with crepe paper, folded Kleenex into fans and fluffed out the layers, making flowers that resembled camellias or large carnations. Others drew or painted posters or newspaper print and put them on the walls. When we finished it was just beautiful. I was so impressed by this event and the decorations, I can't remember what our decorations were for the SF when I was a senior! At the dances we invited dates for dancing and had booklets to write in names of guys to dance with. We asked the guys or they asked us, whatever worked, and a little of both I remember. The first and last dance was always for your date, but you didn't dance with

your date the other dances. I always filled my book up as I didn't like to watch others dancing, and stand by myself. We would also have some sweet foods and punch at the dances. Borger had a small town atmosphere with "big town" ideas! It was a great place to grow up in and a great place to be from.
When I saw AMERICAN GRAFFITI in the 70's I thought how strange it was that the story could have been in Borger, TX. It was based on a town in California. The scene where the "hoods" were standing on the sidewalk watch the TV in the electronics store was JUST LIKE BORGER. We had a store that had their TVs showing and people would watch through the window (Bergens). Dragging Main Street was just like we did it in Borger. The drag races outside the city...just like Borger! Going out into the "hills" outside town, very dark...just like Borger! It was good to know that we were so much like the kids there, enjoying the same type of "hijinks" (as my mother would say)! My most memorable recollection is all the trips and dances/events sponsored by the social clubs. We would earn money all year to pay for the end of year "Senior Club Trip"! We would get a bus from the Greyhound and they would drive us to "somewhere". I remember going to Colorado Springs! They were a big part of my enjoyment. We decorated the dances so beautifully. I was always surprised what people came up with in the decorations. Wasn't Teen Town great? The city fathers in Borger were very thoughtful and wise to provide tax dollars to build that facility for the kids. We had good, great music, dance floor, food, only 25 cents admission! We had the best atmosphere to grow up in and had so much fun, every weekend! People in Borger were very good hearted and friendly.

Bo Diddley came to Teen Town in 1964
Bobby Amador "64" mentioned Bo Diddley's gig at Teentown. I definitely remember this night. We had no idea at the time how important Bo Diddley was to become in later years, at least in music history genre. He started playing at a young age in the late 30's as a boy beating on a string attached to a broom, a Mississippi Delta juke joint music analogy to the current bass guitar. He later graduated to playing blues on a regular guitar thru the 40's and 50's, still in mostly black venues until he was heard by some promoter and asked to make a demo record, one which we all heard on the radio...remember Wolfman Jack on XERF Del Rio played Diddley stuff before his Teentown gig.
Diddley developed a distinct guitar beat signature we all may remember if we listen to his songs. This Diddly "beat" appears in many songs written by many writers and guitar players still today, even though many don't know why they play the beat, or where it came from. I have read comments by Keith Richards - Rolling Stones, Eric Clapton and others that they listened to Diddley stuff while learning to

play. They know the shoulders they stand on as pickers and Diddley was one of these guitar players.

American Legion Hall by **Nancy Shermer Grimes '61**

The American Legion Hall was located at the opposite end of the Borger Hotel Parking Lot. The dance floor was downstairs and upstairs was a bar where veterans went for socialization and drinking alcohol. The dances at the American Legion were instrumental in making Borger the premier dancing town of the Panhandle. You could go anywhere and watch people dance and recognize the unique style of the kids from Borger. There must have been a dance every Friday and Saturday nights. During Basketball season on Tuesday night we sometimes had a dance. Consequently we never lacked a place to go, and it was always fun. Dancing to songs like the Skyliner's "Since I Don't Have You" might have been the inspiration for the saying "THEY COULD DANCE ALL NIGHT LONG ON AN EIGHT INCH TILE." And there were some who did! My first recollection of learning to jitterbug was at a party on the patio at Frieda Lanham's house. The fact that rock and roll had just emerged made it the perfect music for the perfect dance. Even today people from other places ask me "Where did you learn to dance like you do?"

Club Dances at the American Legion Hall

By Frieda Lanham Pickett '61

The club dances were also a significant memory of growing up in Borger. They provided a way to socialize (under supervision as parents "chaperoned" or watched us to make sure we behaved ourselves). We ignored them mostly.... And danced to our heart's content. The dances cost around 50 cents to a dollar, I think, and we danced to records. Someone would volunteer to monitor the record player and pick out the tunes. We had some really good dancers in Borger... Jimmy Williams, his brother Durwood, Gary Grimes, Larry Fletcher, Tommy Gilbert, Jeff Levine, gosh...there were many we would watch jitterbug with special moves! The dances I remember were in the American Legion Hall, at the opposite end of the parking lot, behind the Borger Hotel. Plenty of parking and no drinking was allowed (although some would try to break this rule). The clubs would sponsor a dance most Saturdays, sometimes both Fridays and Saturdays. The high school group came to the club dances. The Jr High kids went to Teen Town, another good place to socialize, and inexpensive.

The clubs in the 1950s were Hi Double Dozen, Delta Rho, and Semper Fidelis. The clubs had about 30 members and an adult as a sponsor. The new members were voted on and invited to join by current club members. During the first few months we called them "pledges". Sometimes two clubs would invite the same girl, so she would have to decide which club to accept. The clubs had dances at Christmas and a Spring Formal, coming together to share expenses of the decorations and food for the dance. We would have a committee to identify a theme and decide what decorations to make, then assign each club member a job, telling her what to make. I remember making kleenex roses, about 50 or 60 of them. At the Spring Formal we had little booklets and would write the names of guys to dance with after we asked them if they would dance with us. We took dates to these special dances. This provided some fun and social events.

The pledging time was a time when we would make the new members do crazy things. I don't know how people came up with the things, but one member made one of the pledges, Carol Sellers (beautiful girl with platinum blonde hair), put soap and raw eggs in her hair. She was a mess! When I was a pledge Nancy Hill made me and several other pledges come to her house and do "Spring cleaning". We washed baseboards, walls, swept, wiped...I never knew a house could be cleaned so thoroughly. I never did it again....terrible experience. Once Nancy (she had a truck to drive) took the pledges out to the Whittenburg Ranch. Several people were out there, mostly guys. We had no flashlights, so used the moonlight to see things. The house was locked so couldn't get in, but we got into the fruit cellar and looked around. We didn't vandalize anything or break anything, just walked around and talked to the boys, then got in the truck and drove back to Borger. These were great times, simple times, and I felt it was much fun to be with the people.

Ch. 7 Post's Drive In and Other Drive Inns

When I was in high school the place in Borger where kids could meet up with other kids to see what was going on and meet up was at the local drive inns. Our favorite was Post's. It was owned by Marie Post until the McCord family (McCord's Grocery) purchased the business. We would look forward to driving around Posts, see who was there, and if we saw someone we wanted to talk to, stop and walk over to their car. We would also just park there, order some food or drink and watch to see who was circling. Sometimes boys would come over to our car and that was something we looked forward to. A typical night was to park at Post's for awhile, then start the car, drive up McGee to Main street, "drag Main" and see who was there, go to the other drive inns (Jet, Cone & Burger), circle and see who was there, then back to Post's. It was great! Everyone liked to do this. One of the funniest things that happened at Post's was when Mike Crouch and Terry Patchin did the "bloody leg" thing. But he has to tell you about it....

Mike Crouch (58) "The Bloody Leg"

I remember the Hitching Post, or "Post's" as we called it then....and of course many girls and other social interaction!

One night Terry Patchin (57) and I were bored....we put Terry in the backend of my 51 Chevy and put ketchup on his leg and left his leg sticking out with the trunk open (he was holding the trunk down with a rope)....we drove around Posts several times to the hoots and cheers of our friends and other onlookers....then we drove up and down Main a few times.....some of the drunks coming out of the bars in the 400-600 block of Main also were cheering and laughing.

We had a great old time for about 3 hrs then finally got bored and went home......where a Police car was waiting in my driveway with a my dad and a cop standing beside it! I looked for a hole to crawl into, but since none was available, I proceeded to my fate. My dad said some disapproving things which I cannot remember, then I went inside.....my room was adjacent to the garage and after I went in I heard my dad and the policeman having a great laugh as the cop told my dad of the various people's reactions and reports they had received at Police HQ. John Wilkinson's dad was Police chief and my baseball coach for summer league.....Chief W was not amused (at least in my presence).

I was on restriction for a week (my parents were not overly harsh) - Terry however was grounded for a month and couldn't talk to me for that time......his Mom was convinced I was a bad influence...actually the truth was we were a bad influence on each other. You never knew what to expect at POST's.

Jet Drive Inn by Frieda Lanham Pickett

The Jet was located on the highway to Fritch. It was a great place that would mix any drink you wanted (nonalcoholic, of course). I used to order a "cherry Dr. Pepper". It was great! They would serve a "vanilla coke", which is normal now, but an unusual drink to find in the late 50's, early 60's. Lots of guys from Stinnett went to the Jet for some reason. I dated Wayne Ferguson from Stinnett for a while. He had a truck-car with the name CHERRY PIE. I have no idea what that meant! Anyway, I started going to the Jet Drive Inn with him. They seemed to have a good business. There were lots of cars there.

The routine was this: drive down Main Street to see who was out, turn onto McGee (?) and drive down to Post's, circle around without parking to see who was there, if you saw someone you wanted to talk to stop or honk and tell them you would be back; drive up the four lane highway to the crossroads and turn onto the Fritch Highway and go to the Jet Drive Inn, circle around it to see who was there, stop or not and go back to the Post's. If no one was at Post's continue down the street, across Main Street out to the Pampa highway and turn left on the way to Phillips. When you got to the Cone & Burger (parents with children often went there to eat, or senior citizens) drive around the place to see who was there. Then on to Phillips to see who was out driving around there, Sutphens was on the left. Then you went back to Borger and to Main Street and started all over again. Good thing gasoline was between 19 and 25 cents a gallon back then!! Oh it was wonderful! Those girls who had cars were great friends to have. It wasn't unusual to see 4 or 5 girls in one car, waiting at Post's for some guys to come over and "talk to them". It was considered really "cool" to have a guy come over to your car and lean against the window (or to get inside) to talk. This was the bomb! The biggest saying at that time was "**I can't believe that** (whatever) ....!" One started almost every sentence with "I can't believe...". I'm sure Mrs. Arthur and Mrs. Vogel just cringed! They needn't have worried, as their students did eventually learn how to put together intelligent conversation!

Dusty Sosbee Lovell '65 "Mooning" at Post's
Gosh...This has brought back so many memories! I remember Bobb Cobb, Baird, and others circling **The Post** mooning everyone. I remember when I was a Sophomore in Senor Lopez's class, the topic of conversation was the draft into the Vietnam war. The guys were worrying about being drafted, as were the girls.

Danny Stephens '62
Ahhh - the Hitching Post - cherry limes, vanilla cokes, burgers, fries, circling all through the day and night to see who was there; circling, circling, circling (followed by "dragging" Main); honking; fights; but most of all, PRETTY GIRLS. I have more memories at that place than any other single place in town, I suspect. My favorite activity.

Ch. 8 Exchange Students in Borger in 60s

In my class of '61 our exchange student was Gudren, a girl from a Scandanavian country. Magnar Brekke came the next year, from Norway. He has kept in contact with Borger students in school when he was at BHS. Here is his story taken from his diary.

Magnar Brekke: Those were the days - Borger 1961-62.

On first arriving in the US: two snapshots:
Having just left an air-conditioned country on an air-conditioned airplane I stumbled into the sizzling saturated heat of the Idlewild tarmac in New York and complained to the immigration officer. Response: "So you don't like the heat? Well, just you wait - of all the fifty states, you picked the worst of them! TEXAS!"

A week later I had decided the dry Texas Panhandle sun was so much more pleasant, and convinced that the bright summer's day was such a rare occasion I put on my swimming trunks and spread myself on the front lawn across a white sheet from my bedroom. The driver in the first car to pass by pulled up his breaks sharply and yelled: "Has there been an accident?"

The Land
Waking up my first day in Borger (we had arrived about 2 o'clock in the morning after driving from Chicago) I remember thinking, "Hey, someone forgot to turn off the gas ...." But it is amazing how quickly the distinct Borger smell began to feel quite natural (after all, it was "natural gas"!), as did the brown, wind-swept landscape dotted with tumbling tumbleweed and other exotic desert vegetation. It was so utterly different from my cool, moist, green (and often wind-swept) landscape of Norway's west coast that it triggered a life-long fascination with organic and human "life at the edge" notions where survival is not a sure thing.

One day while riding in someone's car just outside Borger I had to ask the driver to stop and let me get out to take a photograph. "Oh? Anything worth taking a picture of here?" He did not even notice a (to me) stunning geological feature at the roadside, a distinctly layered piece of sedimentary rock sandwiched at an oblique angle between sections of the reddish clay of the hill that the road had been cut through. A few months later I had stopped noticing, too ... whereas the eternal plume of black dust rising from the carbon black plant to the west never became too familiar. I was allowed to tour the plant with the "Explorer Scouts" and was well aware of its fundamental value for the livelihood of many Borger residents, but I could never grow to like it... especially not when the wind was westerly and I had forgotten to close my bedroom window.

That reminds me of the football game which was cut short while everyone rushed into their cars and drove home from the Bulldog Stadium just a little too late to escape the violent dust storm on our heels. On the floor just inside each screen window lay a softly rounded heap of fine-grained sand – plus an almost unnoticeable layer of the same material spread through the rest of the house. It took me a day or two before I would confidently bite my teeth together again, and not hear that gnashing sound – perhaps a tiny little reminder of what residents of this region had to endure during the Dustbowl years.

Another similar episode is also well covered in my diary: the windy Saturday we were putting shingles on the new garage roof and discovered in the distance a rising wall of fire and smoke. A prairie wildfire was approaching from the southwest, and appeared to be making good headway in the strong gusts of wind riding on its back. Shingles were quickly exchanged for garden hoses, and pretty soon we, and most other residents, were busy hosing down roofs and siding across the neighborhood. Many agonizing hours later the danger seemed greatly diminished, apparently due to a combination of organized firefighting and the west wind subsiding towards evening. Quite a scare!

People and Places

Such was the physical, geographical backdrop of my very memorable experience as an AFS exchange student, but the main players on that stage were of course the people I met and associated with, in various ways through the year. The two most important factors that made my stay so enjoyable and, from my point of view, so successful, were of course my host family, Marion and Elton Brown Jr. with their son Elton III. They, on the one hand, and the high school/city community on the other, both received me with warmth and generosity as their guest for a year.

"Mom" and "Dad", as I quickly came to call my AFS parents, made me feel really at home in America from Day One – and even before that, when they called me long distance to Norway as soon as our contract was official – and spared no effort during the year to include me in their family circle. They came straight to the AFS headquarters in New York to pick me up and had in the space of a few short days introduced me to a good sampling of their own relatives living in Virginia and Washington DC. This included, also, my two American "sisters" and their husbands. To top it all they had arranged for me to meet two prominent Texas politicians in Washington, Senator John Tower in his office on Capitol Hill and Vice President Lyndon B. Johnson in the West Wing of the White House – a virtual crash course in American civics! This was immediately followed by "American Geography 101" as the four of us drove across the heart of the Midwest to Chicago, and then followed Route 66 across the Mississippi and into the Texas Panhandle. What an introduction to the United States!

This introduction was followed by other trips: during Easter we toured a good cross-section of Texas down to Houston-Galveston, with a visit to the Alamo thrown in for good measure. After graduation they took me on the Grand Tour of the West: across the deserts via Sequoia National Park to San Francisco, then along the California and Oregon coast to the World's Fair in Seattle, followed by a large sweep taking in Yellowstone and the Rocky Mountains before heading back home through thunderstorms and tornado sightings in Kansas-Oklahoma. Wow! When a few weeks later I learned to sing Woody Guthrie's "This Land is Your Land" I could claim with conviction: I have seen it all! I never went on to study American politics or geography at the university, but I have nevertheless taught such courses for a number of years, based on sheer enthusiasm for the subject (and thousands of slides) – and the Browns were my initial inspiration.

First encounter with the Natives
As for the role played by the Borger high school and city community, that also became one of almost overwhelming generosity. Many of my fellow students will still remember my first day at BHS – about a thousand of them were carrying a card on their shirt or blouse front with my picture on it, saying "Howdy Magnar!" and their own name just below, a brilliant idea from the Student Council for how to break the ice between a shy Norwegian youngster and what he otherwise might have perceived as a multi-headed monster of unknown, but very forthcoming, American high school kids. And the "kids" just took it from there, to introduce me head-on into various aspects of small-town American youth culture of the early sixties.

The centerpiece of this culture was, of course, the sacred institution called "dating". My own background culture had not prepared me for such a well-regulated and codified procedure for getting to know the opposite gender, but I was more than willing to learn and had no shortage of friendly instructors who gradually taught me the appropriate social graces, not without the occasional confusing and even embarrassing moments. When my lack of dancing skills became apparent, there were a small handful of volunteers who did their best to adjust my floor movements in the general direction of "Jitterbug", without noticeable success, however. The solution was eventually provided by Chubby Checker, who burst on the scene that year with "Let's twist again ...", and a dance that everyone could perform.

But there was one problem with dating: Under the rules of the AFS, exchange students were not allowed to drive a car (just as well, since I had no license at the time), and every young man will see the implication: how do you transport the two of you to and from the evening's venue? In some instances "double dating" would do the trick, but that was not always feasible or comfortable, and I am proud to report on a solution found by several young Borger ladies whose resourcefulness preceded "women's lib" by at least a generation: SHE would ask her dad to borrow the family car, and then SHE would pick up and deliver ME at the agreed location. That's how I was introduced to another great American institution, the drive-in movie theater, totally unknown in Scandinavia because our summer nights never get dark enough. Whenever I see Clark Gable's face I am instantly transported back to the Bunavista Drive-In Theater, the smell of popcorn and the humming noise of the external heater inside the car door. Gone with the Wind indeed!

The 4-Wheel Society
So many important things depended on driving: getting to school in the morning, home in the afternoon, shopping, leisure activities, visiting friends across town, to name a few – back where I came from, most of these would be undertaken by cycling or taking the bus. One afternoon I finished school quite early and decided not to wait to catch a ride with Elton. So I walked home, or tried to walk home I should say, since two problems immediately turned up: 1) there were no sidewalks along the route I had chosen, and 2) every so often a passing driver would roll down the window and ask politely if I was in need of assistance. So I did not repeat this experiment a second time. The gradual result of being much less physically active, combined with taking in two hot meals a day (as compared to one in Norway), were soon beginning to show, and by Christmas I had gained about 20 lbs. This could not be allowed to continue, of course, so I signed up for Track and Field for the spring term, and my weight gradually stabilized.

Another important car-related aspect of Borger youth culture took me a while to catch on to: the continuous driving around with "the guys" certain evenings, circling two important drive-in snack bars, punctuated now and then by going up and down Main Street. **The Hitching Post** was usually the starting point. We would drive up there and go around the circle of corralled automobiles with people waiting to be served or enjoying their ice cream or Dr. Pepper. All the while we intensely tried to determine who was there, who was going with whom, who was sitting in whose car, waving at some, or yelling or honking the horn before pulling out on the road and proceeding to **The Cone & Burger,** driving around the Clover Leaf, then down to **The Jet**, where the same ritual would be repeated. This would take us after a while back again to **Post's**, then straight ahead and a left turn into Main Street, where we might be cruising along for a few minutes before turning around and going back down to restart the cycle once again. Oh, it was wonderful....!

Occasionally we would actually pull up into a vacant slot and place orders for french fries or vanilla coke with ice, or whatever. Initially the whole exercise seemed pretty boring to me, since I knew none of the faces in the other cars or their names. But gradually, as my own circle of friends and acquaintances expanded and the social networks became more intricate (greatly assisted, I should say, by the sometimes quite descriptive commentary and discussion running inside our own car) I began to take a keen interest in the activity and even try to suggest where and when we should pull up or move on, as the case might be. In retrospect, I came to realize this was another highly concentrated introductory course, perhaps "Borger High School Sociology 101" which allowed me to nod in recognition as I, many years later, was watching pictures like "American Graffiti", "Grease" or "Saturday Night Fever".

On the whole I seem to remember only very moderate alcohol consumption among the groups I was running around with. Having beer cans in the trunk would get us in trouble with the Sheriff, I was told; on one occasion there was a drunken brawl outside the dance hall. The one element "missing" from my picture of teen age cultures in Borger is what later has come to dominate, and indeed ruin, so many venues for social gatherings: illegal drugs.

Coping with subcultures
Other social rituals gradually became familiar as my school year passed through its various cycles. The Tri-State Fair in Amarillo was great fun and an excellent opportunity for me to study the natives close-up. There was a memorable trip to the Student Council conference in San Antonio, which really opened my eyes to the specific organizational and leadership training such activities gave rise to. The basketball team took me along more or less as their "mascot" to a regional tournament in Andrews and initiated me into their impressive efforts in building team spirit, and I traveled with the track team to Graham, where I discovered what "water balloons" were all about. In many ways the choir formed my central social grouping, opening up many valuable links of friendship across social thresholds which I vaguely perceived were present in the student body as a whole. Perhaps the high point was reached as we formed quartets and spent an evening just before Christmas wading through the snow drifts to sing carols outside people's windows, being then opened in surprise and appreciation!

This being the first Christmas away from my homeland it was a little special, perhaps the only time I felt a pang of homesickness, as we were riding around on Christmas Eve admiring and photographing the gorgeous decorations people had put up on their houses. It felt just like any other evening, the contrast being that it would be the time of the big solemn celebration in Norway. But Christmas Day with the Browns completely made up for it! Early in the spring people started asking me "Who are you taking to the Prom?", so I realized I needed to be brought up to speed on the social responsibilities surrounding graduation and all that. Soon my vocabulary had become enriched by such exotic items as corsage, cummerbund, tuxedo etc., and it did lead up to a very memorable evening, with a beautiful "official" picture to show for it (in fact, when I showed it to my friends on returning to Norway some of them were not sure I had not become married while over there!)

In the wider context I was really impressed by the active role which the city community assumed in ensuring the wellbeing of their exchange student. My Norwegian parents had put up the agreed sum for spending-money which the AFS dutifully dispensed in the form of a monthly check, but the Borger chapter insisted on matching that – by 150 per cent, which provided a comfortable margin for snack bar visits and movies etc. without being extravagant. In addition they made sure my closet held enough items of the current style in button-down shirts, slacks, white sports socks and black shoes, without my having to spend my own funds. Other citizens really pitched in too: I got free haircuts at the Borger Hotel Barber Shop, absolutely essential for maintaining the flat crew cut (bolstered by liberal amounts of Vaseline) which the young male fashion dictated at the time (just take a look at the Annual portraits!), free medical check-ups from the Browns' family doctor, and free dental treatment – which turned into a major contribution, since the local dentist insisted on doing a complete overhaul of the somewhat shoddy dental work he saw as I opened my mouth the first time.

The spring term marked the beginning of my club season, i.e. following up invitations from about three and a half dozen civic clubs, church groups, schools and various associations to come and talk to them about Norway. Through the year I had been preparing for this somewhat intimidating task by taking speech-classes at BHS, my American "sister" Joelle had typed up my manuscript on stacks of 3'x5' index cards when she visited during Christmas, and the slides of Norway I brought with me had been carefully arranged. Now came the moment of truth: delivering the goods. Again I was amazed by the positive and very encouraging reception I received all around, and as I gained experience and perspective (especially from the questions asked by the audience) I began to feel more relaxed about giving talks. Not totally relaxed, though, as there were quite a few delicious lunches which I found to be less than enjoyable, because I would be the next speaker! I gradually managed to tailor my spiel to fit the interests of my audience, but on one occasion I faced an almost impossible challenge: One Wednesday in March I spoke to the Men's Club of Phillips Methodist Church – no problem, good audience, fine atmosphere. Next week's invitation was to a meeting of Phillips Lions' Club, an audience consisting of, er, exactly the same guys I had addressed the week before! They helped me out and were extremely inventive in thinking up some new questions to ask the flustered speaker. So, all in all, it turned out reasonably OK, as did the entire speaking circuit.

Perhaps the audience I remember most distinctly was at Booker T. Washington Grade School, where a large group of shy, shining dark faces read out their carefully prepared questions about Norwegian geography, the Gulf stream, the Northern Lights, and relationships of the Sami minority people to our majority culture, on my part a very enlightening afternoon. Another unforgettable moment came when Steve, Student Council President and accompanying driver for the day, managed to sabotage my slide show before an audience of gray-haired ladies by slipping in a picture of a scantily clad young woman in a most inappropriate context. It did not exactly bring the house down, but it did teach me the meaning of the idiom "pull someone's leg".

In retrospect

Such were some of the glimpses culled from the rereading of a young man's diary, kept during a formative year in his life. Looking into the rear view mirror 45 years later, what has been the enduring impact on me as a person, over and beyond all the fun and excitement of being the center of positive attention from a whole community? My AFS year in Borger, Texas, has without doubt been the most important year in my life, bringing me into close contact with a rich variety of individuals, families and their interactions, various groups representing so many dimensions of life in small-town America, organized institutions like church and school, as well as political bodies from City Council up to (and including!) the US Senate and the White House. It has no doubt determined the main thrust of my higher education, professional training and lifelong career as a professor of English in Norway and probably influenced a host of minor decisions and priorities along that path. And no doubt the personal dimension running through all of this – I do not relate to Americans as an abstract category but consider them as real people, persons more or less like myself, operating in circumstances that are familiar to me, voicing views and expressing convictions that I recognize, without necessarily agreeing with or sharing them. That personal dimension stems from growing up, for a brief but significant interlude in my life, in Borger, Texas.

In many ways my reader will think I have painted a very idyllic picture of America as I wish to remember her – the age innocence just before the onslaught of political assassinations, the Viet Nam war protests, the student revolution, drug abuse, the oil crisis, Watergate, not to mention more recent horrors. And some have looked in vain for the critical assessment of certain aspects of life in the US. I have not found this to be the time or place, nor the duty of a highly privileged guest. Although I must admit to feeling increasingly alienated by some of the ways in which American politics have unfolded in this century, America has enough detractors, and I much prefer America's failures over the successes of some other regimes that I am familiar with.

But through and beyond all of this – and I have lived altogether seven years in four different locations in the US – I feel that what began in Borger has given me a unique chance to form my own opinion of what makes Americans tick, of what America is all about. And I freely admit it is a highly subjective and emotional picture. With all the above "philosophizing", it can't be denied that I can be brought to my knees by the sight of a bright red 1957 Chevrolet, and all the memories that implies, just like the one Butch took us out in!

Ch. 9 Borger Movie Theaters

This is going WAY BACK, but seems like I remember we had 4 movie theaters: the Morley, the Rig, the Rex and the Crown (it was the oldest, your shoes stuck to the floor as you were moving from the aisle to your seat!) I believe I saw a mouse running down the aisle once. The silent pictures were played at the Crown. Just a few doors down, same side of the street was the REX, a newer, nicer theater. The 3D movies played at the REX. The RIG theater was across the street and down a block.

It costs 9 cents to see a movie at the Morley in late 40s and mother would give me a dime to go to the Morley. I would get the "two for a penny" banana BIKE candy with change. I always wished I could have coke and popcorn, it smelled so good. So when I was older and working at Dean's Dept. store, I bought myself a coke and popcorn! I remember it well! I also went to see Hopalong Cassady and Tom Mix movies (probably misspelled these) at the RIG when I was a child on Saturday mornings. They were called "serials". "Sheena Queen of the Jungle" came to Borger and appeared at the Morley in the 50s.

Joey Woods '61

There were 4 movies in the 50s: The Morley of course is still at 701 N. Main. The Rex was at 523 N.Main & the Crown was at 517 N. Main according to Claude Kuroki who graduated in 54'. The Rig was at 616 N. Main.

Danny Stephens '62

Wham-bam and wow! All four of those names ring some kind of bell with me. I probably started going to movies with my parents when I was about six or so, which would have been right around 1950. Of course I remember the Morley (who wouldn't?) – I sat in the audience many times with sweaty hands while I stole sideways looks at my date to see how she/we was/were doing; I remember taking fifteen+ minutes to put my arm around a "girl" for the first time there. I remember the Rex, too, if it was on the same side of the street as the Morley. I saw those same old serials that have been mentioned here a few times, and that's where some of the best horror shows were put on ... especially on Halloween (?? – or was that the Morley).

As far as the other two, though, I have a slightly garbled recollection – or maybe it's more of a question –I remember hearing stories about the Crown, but it seems to me that the "Crown" was only an earlier incarnation of the "Rig", which I don't even believe was ever actually open while I was going to movies. Seems like the old Rig was next to the old pool hall. Or at least within a building or two. Now I COULD tell some stories about that old pool hall. There were some pretty good (at least to me) high school "players" who shot "snooker" and "eight ball" night and day in that place. The last time I was in Borger there was a museum right where I thought the old pool hall used to be located. I'll ask my dad, who sometimes doesn't remember where he parked his car, but can talk for hours about things that took place sixty years or more ago.

Bobby Amador '64

Does anyone else remember the old run down movie theater called the "Rig" that was located on Main Street? You could go on Saturday for 10 cents. This theater had two balconies as I recall, the top one was for colored folks. They would show cliff hangers serials and you would have to go every week for about four weeks to see a complete movie. It was around "53-'55 when it finally closed down, I think.

Joyce Griffin Trigg '64

The "Rig Theater"---when I was a little girl (5-7yrs old), my momma told me that was a naughty place. They showed those bad movies; but once in awhile they showed Roy Rogers & Dale Evans movies. I only went there a couple of times.

Ed Vidaurri '65

If you remember the RIG and "House on Haunted Hill" then you must recall all the other "B" horror movies of the same era "I was a teen age werewolf", "them", "the attack of the 50 ft woman", "the day the earth stood still", 'the blob", "invasion of the body snatchers", and the most horrifying of all, "love me tender" with Elvis, we saw them all at the RIG. Do you remember standing in line for hours at the MORLEY to buy tickets for Walt Disney's "old yeller"? and how the line went all the way down the block? There was another movie house up the street from the RIG, the REX, it was on the same side of Main Street as the MORLEY.

Alice Rittenhouse Scully '64

I went to the Rig regularly with my brother I remember Creature from the Black Lagoon for one good movie also went to wrestling matches on the north end with my dad

Pug Davis "Movies and Drive Inn Theaters"

About the movies, Borger had Drive-In Movies, too, a popular one on the Fritch highway. One of the two drive-ins had a trench around it. Did anyone know that? There was a fence, too, which was easy to pass under or over, but if you were running along toward the fence and it was dark (it would be dark, of course) you might just fall into the trench and you and your friend, maybe Susan Harris, would be laughing and crawling out of the trench. It wasn't very deep. The car with your other friends might have left to enter the drive-in and you had to keep moving...and find the car on the inside. This is a true story. At one time they would have "Dollar a Car Night" and no one had to cheat then.

Gordon Garst '65

How many remember when there were THREE drive-in movie theaters. The Tri-City was on the east side of the RR tracks close to where SFA was built. (it had closed by this time and a trailer park built on the property.) Also, it seems like either the Bunavista or the Plains had those big search lights that scanned the sky every night.

Sharon Kaye Johnson Nichols '61

I also remember going to the 3-D Movies at the Rex. The one that frightened me the most was "HOUSE OF WAX". I remember dodging a ball that was "seemingly" aimed right at you, and trying to move out of the way of the big bucket of wax. I had nightmares for weeks.
I remember seeing a couple of movies in the "cafeteria-auditorium" of the old school that was WEST WARD, then it was changed over to Jr. High. The Movie was called "The Littlest Angel".

Ch. 10 – Buna Vista Apartments and Huber Camp
By Judy Hugg

Our house was a mighty, mighty, mighty, long house. Our summers were long, our stories safely sad or funny, and the times too short.

During World War II the Phillips Petroleum Co. built barracks type housing for the refinery workers in the Texas panhandle. These long connected apartments, all were built of wood and tarpaper with asbestos siding. The Phillips Petroleum Company supplied paint (if you liked white, which they would tint pink, green or blue) and they paid for the water, gas and electricity. We didn't have a telephone, until we moved into town. If Mom wanted me, she just opened the door and yelled. Apartments were designed with two bedrooms, bath, kitchen and living room. Small, bare & basic the family needed to "squeeze" together. Front porches were shared in pairs but each unit took care of their own yards. Our cabinet size radio sat in the connecting hall between the rooms. I would lie on the floor with the Sunday Paper & listen to the radio read me the funnies. Everyone just stepped around and over me.

There were 8 family units to a row plus the washroom. The rows were named using letters of the alphabet. There was an apartment row for every letter of the alphabet and then double letters and then triple letters. Many families planted Elm trees to give the yard some color and shade. A sidewalk ran the entire length of the apartments. At each end of the long, sidewalk was an iron bin with a constant gas fire for burning the trash. We melted crayons on that hot trash bin, we called it art, "graffiti" was a word yet to be invented. If I melted the crayon in just the right hot spot I could touch body parts to the melted crayon and "transfer" the wax, colors and designs to myself. Took A LOT of scratching to get it off before going home.

The apartments were crowded with kids and **Halloween** was the best! This was the day of the BIG candy bars? Mom would give us pillowcases and my brother and I would go house to house with our soap bar. "Trick or Treat! Smell my feet! Give me something good to eat!" We yelled at every door. The pillowcases would get so heavy we took them home to empty, then, we were on the run for more treats! Some disagreement happened one Halloween. Usually all was quiet, this night Little Johnny Tucker threw a piece of concrete at the back of my head and hit me right where my braids were plaited. My Momma *made* me go to his momma, Roberta, and show her my blood running down the part in my hair and down my neck. The rule was that every girl had to learn to stand up for herself. "Hit them back" was the next step (that's what the Daddies said to do) or "Go tell their Mom" (that's what the Moms said to do). So, it was fight or negotiate-depending on what parent, saw you first. Johnny and I went silently to school together through all 12 grades but that Halloween separated us.

We had our own elementary school at Bunavista. My favorite school meal was beef stew and half a peanut butter sandwich; half a pimento cheese spread sandwich, peanut butter cookie and milk. All other days I packed. We learned to save the waxed paper from our sandwiches and using our "horse hoof school glue ", we made glue fingernails on the wax paper and then when dried, peel them off, **lick** them and try to get them to stay on our fingers.

Soon after the apartments and the school, there were big churches and summer Bible School was the excitement. We couldn't wait to get our COOL-AID and cookies and do arts and crafts. One year the "craft" was an *artistic* wall hanging. We were asked to bring a big old phonograph record (78) to church and we painted them with wall paint (yep, pink and blue and green) and glued a Jesus picture in the middle to hang on the wall. Well, MY MOM had a drawer full of those old black records. I picked up a couple off the top and took them to church-never asked her of course. They were OLD weren't they? Well, when my Momma couldn't find her copy of *San Antonio Rose or Harbor Lights*? WHOOPS!

Summer meant Drive-in Theatres. Mostly the movies were cowboy movies at a dollar a carload. Lots of swings, teeter-totters, slides, climbing rigs, sand boxes, fast food, the Texas sky above us & golden western sunset in our eyes, our parents around us, Bugs Bunny Cartoons, friends, staying up and playing till the movie came on, life was good. Phillips also showed outdoor movies on occasion as a treat for the families of the workers.

Mudbug fishing and July 4th

Sometime before teenage days when appearances still didn't count, we would go into the meat section of the grocery, talk the butcher out of a nickel's worth of sliced bacon or liver—which we took to the "run off creek". The rule was, go without the boys. They had their way and we had ours. Bits of meat were tied to a string, pitched in the water to drag out crawdads gripping the strips of raw meat with their pinchers. Exercising the crawdads was our secret past time. None of us was willing to take them home, so usually we just dumped them back to exercise another day. The rule was Eeeeuuuuooo on mudbugs.

Fourth of July, Poppa always bought lots of fireworks. We were creative in our blowing up stuff and knew JUST what the real rules were, as far as how far we could go, with our "crackers". If we even THOUGHT about tossing one at little brother—we could have been spanked, and preached at, spanked and preached at, forever. Did grownups follow their own rules? Poppa would let go of one of those howling, running, screeching, bullets called a 'chaser' anytime he could get in the middle of a crowd of relatives. Of course the women hollered and the men laughed. Throwing a firecracker? Not us! There were other RULES: We didn't step on cracks (Break your Momma's Back) or look cross-eyed too often (Your eyes might stay that way) and we didn't pop our knuckles (That gives you GORILLA hands) or cheat playing anything because there wasn't nothing worse than to be called: A CHEATER. We said, Yes and No, M'am and respected our elders (at least while they were looking at us).

The worst thing you could get caught doing was lying-especially to an adult. Liar! Liar! Pants on Fire! This had real meaning in our lives, as most of our parents did not despise using the rod for punishment. Momma usually did the spanking. A few well-aimed swipes at the back of my legs left me dancing in air and Mom preaching to the marionette. The preaching lasted a lot longer than the switching. The almost worst thing you could do was to go into your Dad's-Holy of Holies (his dresser drawer) to raid his private 4th of July, cherry bomb, fire cracker, stash. Sneak out a cherry bomb and light it up and quickly toss it into the little, glass mailbox hung on the side of the front door jam. A thing like that was not easily hidden or lied about. Switch and preach, switch and preach.

The long multiple rows of apartment barracks were moneymaking territory for the food venders, especially the snow cone man. For five cents you could get one big round dip with every flavor of syrup. What was important is that you had every one of the flavors. The guy would (almost) give you a free cone, if you would just pick "ONE" flavor and get out of his face! Of course, in due course the paper cones leaked and you had to **lick** them, lick your fingers and lick your arms up to the elbow. Pop never skimped on any food for anyone at anytime. It was the one constant fact, food, in my life was never regulated or denied. Momma said she knew what it was like to be really hungry and Poppa knew the feeling too. Pop loved popcorn. Mom would pop an entire can of JOLLY TIME Popcorn and fill up an aluminum wash pan with the corn, then pour over melted butter with popcorn salt. We ate it all. I would scrape my fingers over the bottom of the pan to scoop up the salt filled butter and **lick** my fingers. We did a lot of licking in Bunavista.

Poppa's birthday meant canned oysters, fried crisp. Once, I bit into a pearl, canned, breaded and fried. Good thing my teeth were strong. Pop said it looked like a dried up *booger*. Truth is we would eat just about anything when we got home from school. Mom said that the bark on the tree wasn't safe from us. I ate cold fried liver dipped in mustard like some people today eat cold pizza.

We Shared Everything.

We shared our stories, our toys, our parents, our food, our clothes and our pets (even to the fleas), our diseases (measles, chicken pox, whooping cough and pink eye). We gave up our beds when relatives came in the night and needed to sleep. Momma would come in and get a strong handful of our jammies, yank us up and walk us to the blankets on the floor and let go of the jammies. In the morning we woke up in the floor, cold and with cricks in our neck, but happy that we had "company" come in the night.

There was a long sidewalk in front of the apartments. Charlotte and I shared one pair of skates between us, we learned to balance and skate with one skate each, on the long sidewalk. When her skates wore out, we got another pair and we wore those out, with each of us wearing one skate at a time. Some of my friends and I decided that we were a'gonna walk to the little grocery store up the long hill. We had enough "pop" bottles to sell or trade for candy. So, we took off walking, in summer, along the blacktop hwy, hopping along from grass spots to weed spots along the right-of-way. The thing we discovered VERY early was that the grass didn't grow on the grated and graveled side road. So, our trek was like 3 drops of water in a hot skillet! We bounced around-arms flailing wildly, hollering and laughing and finally decided to run-for-it and to cross the highway-with its sticky, tar, melted, blacktop. Finally, with blistered feet and squeals of relief we landed in the grocery store's cool shade on the wooden porch. It was Clementine Time. The three of us talked the store clerk out of some empty candy boxes. Charlotte Gayle had the little feet and she bargained for the narrow candy box but I had larger feet and went for the Butterfinger box and don't remember what Linda Kay choose for her shoe" style" box, but armed with some string courtesy of the thoughtful clerk—we took some time sitting on the porch and tied the boxes to our feet and took off in a crab type shuffle, cross the highway and find our way home, cardboard skiing. Well, the string didn't work and soon broke apart, so we were forced to "slide" our way home. As the wear and tear on the cardboard soon left us, we were "scooting" along with bits and pieces. Momma scrubbed my feet with "coal oil" that night before she let me put my feet in the clean bed. Her only comment was, "For crying out loud, where were your shoes?" Do you think I was going to tell?

Christmas at Home

Santa ALWAYS came during the night to our house and left (2 of) Momma's stockings filled with goodies. Somehow, I never made the connection about Santa's stockings being mom's nylons, until the year that she used her old "decorated ones" with the black seam up the back, lacy heels with rhinestones and black lacy tops. That was when I paid attention and figured it out. I suppose the Christmas that I got the bike was just the best! I was 11 and it was a full size cruiser with white rim tires, white leather spring loaded, seat & white handle bar trim. The bike had a wide "pamper" seat in the back for an extra rider and came with an electric horn, electric head lights, front basket and a front spring, wheel, suspension. It was a MONARCH brand and it was the biggest and brightest and most classy bike in the neighborhood. Poppa helped me outside with it and turned me loose to ride my way to glory with my headlights beaming. When it came to a good ride? My Pop had it covered.

Explosions, Loud And Quiet

I have memories of the explosions in the gasoline refinery and being afraid for Poppa as he was at work in the refinery. The fuel storage tanks blew their tops-straight up into the air. I don't know how the fires started or how many men were burned or lost but I remember standing on my front porch with my mom and my brother. We saw everything, the flames, watched the blazing lids of the tanks flying, away, landing in the fields. One fire is the one I remember the most. All the neighbors who saw the flames and heard the explosions knew what was happening so they loaded pets and kids and took to the highway. We had a brand new Chrysler sitting in the front of our apartment-but we couldn't leave. Pop never let Mom keep the extra keys. It was his car and he didn't like women drivers. Pop was not hurt, but not allowed to leave the plant until all the men could be counted and found. Many were badly burned. All were scared. Pop took his car keys to the plant guard gate. Pop asked him to go to our apartment and give Mom the keys so that, "She can take MY new CAR to safety, I don't want it burned!!"

Momma saw the man coming and we all went to the door. He took off his hard hat and told Momma exactly what Poppa said, handing her the car keys. He looked directly at her and she looked directly back at him saying nothing. I looked up at him and I looked up at her and knew something important was being said. Mom's face was sad and mad and the iron was in her spine and she didn't blink, just took the keys and said, "Thank You for your help". She took us to the car, unlocked it and loaded us up and drove us into town to my Uncle and Aunt's house. We listened to the radio and watched the smoke and just waited on Poppa to call. Momma drove to pick him up at the refinery. They were gone a long time. Poppa was really quiet when they came in to the house. After that she always had a set of keys, no matter what.

Ed Vidaurri '65

Those apartments that Phillips had in Buena Vista is where I met many of my long time friends, including "Bugs" as we used to call David Padilla in those days. Phillips used to spray DDT to kill mosquitoes out in the apartment area. We would all gather around and follow the truck doing the spraying. The fog was so thick you could not see where you were going. It's a miracle we are not all dead or ill from inhaling all that poison. I recall when notice came down from Phillips that they were going to close all the apartments and everyone would have to move out. That is when we had to move into the "city". Does anyone remember Coach Stone and football at Buena Vista Elementary?

Patsy Eason Phillips '64

Judy mentioned the apartments in Buna Vista. They walls were so thin, we used to hear the man next door snoring! Patsy Sams lived next to us. She and I would knock on the walls when we wanted to talk. I guess that was the equivalent of having phones in your own room! Our back doors all had wooden stoops. The fences between the yards were not the nice fences. They were the wiring used to make rabbit cages. We could all sit out and talk to each other.
We did not have garbage pick-up. There were large incinerators between rows of apartments. They were always smoldering. We used to write on them with crayons and the Avon sample lipsticks samples. We all played in the area between the apartments. A lot of football games were played there. There was a large ant bed there. I tried to stamp it out. The ants won!

Joyce Griffin Trigg '64 – Halloween in Buna Vista

Hope all the fifties kids (our childhood days) and the sixties' kids (our teenage years) remember the special times we had on "HALLOWEEN". Bunavista was the place to be!!! I loved the 3-4 yrs I got to go "trick or treating " with my aunt Margie. Anyway, I remember one time Aunt Margie was dressed up and a couple of people got on to her and would not give her any candy---they could see her wedding rings.!!!Ha Ha! She was soooo much fun! The kids in the fifties and sixties that had so much fun!! I still have all my black lace, skeletons, witches and candles up and they will be up for a week or more. I love "Halloween".

Growing Up in BunaVista

By Carol McVay Bowers '61

I HAVE SO MANY WONDERFUL MEMORIES THAT I DO NOT KNOW WHERE TO BEGIN.

I REMEMBER BUNAVISTA. THE NAME MEANT BEAUTIFUL VIEW. AS WE ALL KNOW IT WAS A DESOLATE VIEW BUT THE VIEW WAS NOT THE LANDSCAPE IT WAS THE BEAUTIFUL PEOPLE THAT LIVED IN THAT PLACE. I REMEMBER MY DEAR FRIENDS BARBARA THOMPSON, LAUNITA WALKER, VERNA RUTH WILSON, CHARLOTTE MIER, WINNIE WHEELIS, LINDA WILSON, AND MANY OTHERS. I REMEMBER MY MOM PUTTING ME IN THE BATH TUB AND SCRUBBING THE CARBON BLACK OFF MY KNEES AND HANDS.

I REMEMBER THE MORNING I WOKE UP TO THE SOUND OF A BIG NOISE. THE PLANT WHERE MY DAD WORKED WAS EXPLODING AND WE HAD TO RUN FOR OUR LIVES. SOME OF MY DAD'S FRIENDS WERE KILLED IN THE BLAST.

I REMEMBER THE SUMMERS WE SPENT AT YPO PLAYING PING PONG AND JUST PLAYING GAMES TOGETHER. JUST OUTSIDE OF YPO AND BUNAVISTA ELEMENTARY SCHOOL THERE WAS THIS BIG PIPELINE THAT CROSSED A BIG RAVINE. THE OLDER KIDS ALWAYS DARED US TO WALK ACROSS IT. ONE DAY (I GUESS I WAS ABOUT 8 YEARS OLD) I GOT MY NERVE UP AND STARTED ACROSS THE PIPE AND PANICKED. I SAT DOWN AND STARED TO CRY. I COULD NOT MOVE. MY BEST FRIEND BARBARA THOMPSON WALKED OUT AND HELPED ME UP AND SAID "STOP BEING SUCH A BIG BABY.YOU CAN DO THIS". SHE HELPED ME ACROSS AND WE ARE STILL BEST FRIENDS HELPING EACH OTHER ACROSS THE GREAT RAVINES IN OUR LIVES

ONE DAY WHEN I WAS WALKING HOME FROM SCHOOL (ABOUT 5TH GRADE) DUDE MCCLAIN AND DONNIE ANDERSON CHASED ME DOWN KISSED ME AND THREW MY BOOKS IN THE GUTTER (SO MUCH FOR FIRST LOVE EXPERIENCES). MY DAD WENT TO THIER HOMES AND GAVE THEM A GOOD TALKING TO. HE WAS A DEACON IN THE CHURCH AND EVERYONE WAS AFRAID OF HIM (INCLUDING ME).HE SCARED THEM TO DEATH.

BARBARA THOMPSON AND I STARTED SINGING TOGETHER IN CHURCH AND SCHOOL WHEN WE WERE ABOUT FIVE YEARS OLD. WE HAVE A PICTURE OF US ON STAGE SINGING (A HUNTING WE WILL GO) MANY OF OUR BUNAVISTA FRIENDS ARE IN THE PICTURE.

I WAS SO SCARED WHEN I ENTERED JR HIGH IN BORGER. I WAS COMING TO THE BIG CITY. THANKS TO NEW FRIENDS LIKE FRIEDA LANHAM, BARBARA FERRILL, ANN SCHMITZ, JACKIE TRADER, AND NANCY SHERMER, I SOON FELT LIKE I BELONGED.

MY FIRST DOUBLE DATE WAS WITH RAY ADKINS. BABARA THOMPSON AND RED JENKINS WERE WITH US. I REMEMBER GOING TO THE BUNAVISTA DRIVE INN. ONE NIGHT WE WANTED TO SAVE MONEY SO THEY PUT ME AND BARBARA IN THE TRUNK. I HAVE SUFFERED FROM CLOSTROPHOBIA EVER SINCE.

LINDA WILSON, BARBARA AND I STARTED A SINGING GROUP IN JR HIGH SCHOOL. REMEMBER THE HARMONETTES AND THOSE AWFUL BLACK AND WHITE OUTFITS? WE LOOKED LIKE THE SINGING NUNS. IF WE'D HAD SEXIER OUTFITS WE MIGHT HAVE MADE IT BIGTIME!! LET'S SEE, SUE GUTHRIE, VICKI SELFRIDGE, and NANCY SHERMER JOINED OUR SINGING GROUP. IN HIGH SCHOOL SUE GUTHRIE MOVED AND FRIEDA LANHAM TOOK HER PLACE. I REMEMBER MANY LONG HOURS OF PRACTICE TRYING TO SOUND LIKE THE CHARRELL'S SINGING (WILL YOU STILL LOVE ME TOMORROW?). ONE NIGHT AT MY HOUSE MY DAD RAN OFF A BUNCH OF THE BOYFRIENDS WHEN WE WERE PRACTICING.

I MUST SPEAK OF MARVIN HARVEY. HE REALLY WAS MY FIRST BOY FRIEND. HE TOOK ME TO MY FIRST DANCE IN JR. HIGH. HIS YOUNGER BROTHER JOHNNY DIED OF POLIO DURING THE EPIDEMIC WHEN WE WERE ABOUT THIRD GRADE. WE ALL LOVED JOHNNY SO MUCH. IT WAS MY FIRST EXPERIENCE WITH THE DEATH OF A FRIEND. I WILL ALWAYS LOVE AND REMEMBER JOHNNY AND MARVIN AS TWO OF MY BEST FRIENDS EVER. I DATED LOTS OF THE GUYS IN HIGH SCHOOL AND I LOVED THEM ALL, EVEN THE ONES I NEVER DATED!! THE GUYS AT BHS WERE THE GREATEST, HUMOROUS, FRIENDLY, COURTEOUS AND, MOST OF THE TIME, THOUGHTFUL.

I LOVED ALL THE FRIDAY AND SAT. DANCES, EVEN THOUGH I HAD TO SNEAK OUT OF THE HOUSE TO GO TO JUST ABOUT EVERYTHING (THANKS TO DAD THE DEACON). I THANK GOD HE WAS A HEAVY SLEEPER. I JUST REMEMBER YOU ALL WITH SO MUCH LOVE. IT IS STRANGE HOW IN THE FEW SHORT YEARS OF HIGH SCHOOL, WE MAKE THE BEST FRIENDS OF OUR LIVES.

Great story about early Borger

Interview of Rosa Spann, early Borger resident by Patsy Eason Phillips '64

Recently I was able to spend some time with my aunt, Rosa Spann, and her sister, my mother. I asked them about coming to Borger and their first impressions. Remember now, Aunt Rosa will be 101 in September; Mother will be 95 in November. In unison, they said one word, *"Dirty!"*
"Daddy had finished his time in the army, he had children, and the war was winding down so he got out a little early. His cousin Paul Sherrill told him there were jobs in Borger. I asked why there were openings with so many getting out of the army." Mother said the men who had worked for Phillips during the war were exempt from being drafted since Phillips was considered important for the war effort. With the war winding down, they were free to

move elsewhere without fear of being drafted! So anyone who was unhappy or wanted greener pastures, felt safe to leave.
Rosa continued, "Mother and Daddy were able to get a company trailer in Bunavista to live in; definitely not the best accommodations. They then moved to a two-bedroom apartment on P-6. I remembered the wash house that was next to our apartment." Mother said everyone had their own washer (wringer type). When they wanted to wash, they moved the washer over to the water hose. There were big tubs to rinse the clothes in. The water was changed after two or three loads (I guess depending on how bad the carbon black had been!). When washing was finished, the washers were rolled back against the wall. Since not everyone had a washer, they were never sure if their washer was used by others.
"Daddy asked the principal of Weatherly if there were any job openings for teachers. Daddy told the principal about Mother's sister, Rosa Spann. The principal called Rosa and asked her to come out." Rosa's pay was doubled! Mother and Rosa Lee rode in on the bus. As they got close to Borger, there was a horrible black cloud. Aunt Rosa got really concerned about a tornado; however, no one else seemed concerned. She didn't say anything, just pulled Rosa Lee closer and put a coat over her to protect her. The closer they got, the blacker the cloud got! Rosa said everyone kept talking and she thought they were crazy for not being worried! She later became very familiar with that black cloud!
Rosa was able to get a house in Borger after three weeks. There were some shotgun houses being built close to Weatherly school. All the houses were spoken for, but the builder felt a teacher needed a house more than another family! So Rosa got a house that had already been promised to someone else. She said it caused quite a "stink." It wasn't built well, as the house had no insulation. Also the doors froze shut and the windows frosted over!
"Every once in a while the principal would tell the teachers to go home and bring buckets and old clothes. The kids would get to play all day while the teachers took turns watching them and cleaning the classrooms of the carbon black."
Mother and Rosa were laughing about everything that happened. Even with the cold and carbon black, they both loved Borger and would like to move back!

Ch. 11 Camps around Borger -- Huber Camp (by Judy Hugg)

Actually, the Huber camp was built by Huber Oil as an office and residences for the managers, owners and people that worked in the offices. It was much the same as the Bunavista housing. In Bunavista, the Phillips Oil Co. built single unit homes for their engineers and managers, and the lower down on the totem pole, the smaller your housing. All free though and utilities paid.

By the time that my folks moved into Huber Camp, most of the people higher up the employment ladder had moved into newer housing or retired/moved or stayed. There was a very nice home with a sun room across the street from our little house and the elderly couple who lived there (next to the Takewells) were very gracious and well educated and I was most impressed that they had a separate room just to sit and talk and read. My real name which I never knew until I was somewhere around 16 was Judith Lavonia Hugg and I was known as Little Judy in the neighborhood.

Our house was two bedroom and small and had not been remodeled. We thought it was heaven but actually it was old fashioned, run down. Some, people would call it "a farm house". There seemed to be sections of larger homes that were well kept and just across the street would be smaller and older homes. My memory is that Huber Camp became open to other settlement as the older generation of employees moved on to other things. There was an even older Huber Camp that was about 5 miles south on the Panhandle Hwy and at one time it had been a flourishing company village, but by 1955 it was all but abandoned and most of the housing moved.

There was a freight train track that ran 'whonkerjawed' to the Huber Camp and followed on across the trestle over by Huber Park and 'switched' making it possible to go to Phillips Camp (which was North of Borger) and also went through the Carbon Black Plant and off toward Amarillo. Phillips Petroleum Co. and Huber Oil both were working during WWII and also hired many women to replace the men who went to war. My mom, Dovie Hugg worked as a B-Operator in Plains Plant and did the same job as my step-father, James McKown and my future father-in- law, Mark Grimes. When the war ended the men kept their jobs but the women (called by history: "Rosie the Riveters") were "laid off."

The graded dirt streets were coated with heavy oil every few summers to help keep down the dust, even-out the ruts and eventually were blacktopped as the "Camp" became incorporated into the City of Borger.

Many of the Huber Camp residents had, or still have, good water wells and there were many complaints about the salt water coming from the city when it started using Lake Meredith water.

There was a public swimming pool at Huber Park and it was always the place of choice in the summertime. The park had mulberry trees that gave fruit. A person had to eat the mulberries at night or risk getting a mouth full of ants! Of course at night you didn't know how many you ate! One of the special delights was the city "Watermelon Feasts", at which time families went to the park and were served free watermelon. There were swings and other equipment to play on, while the adults visited and socialized.

The Phillips Camp, North of Borger had schools, even through High School, a hospital and necessary stores and management. They even had a yearly fair, called: Tri-City Fair. I won my first best of show award for a painting at that Fair.

Bunavista had elementary schools but kids were bused into Borger for Jr. High and High School. Bunavista also had some stores, a grocery and a small medical clinic. Huber had an elementary and now is closed but it is where they built the Community Center in Huber Camp close to Cedar Street. After high school I went to the art class instructor at the Huber Community Center and asked if I had to qualify for the painting classes by being "old?" She said for $5.00 I could join. So, I did and painted there for three years right after graduation.

The oil companies all had men who were members in the "Union." Among the workers, your pop was either in the union or not. Black and white and no middle ground. Borger had a "Union" grocery store and dry goods store located between Main Street and Turner Ave. somewhere up close to Barney's Pharmacy. The Union employees could go there and buy meat from the meat department, canned goods, vegetables, dishes, sewing supplies, soap and necessary things.

In 1958 there was a Union "Strike" and it put people off work for months. It was graduation year for my husband, Mel Grimes and a lean year it was. All the high school kids who could find work, did so. Mel worked as a child delivering newspapers and as a teen, at a couple of stores downtown. When he grew muscles, he did some carpentry with his father to buy his car and pay for upkeep and gas.

Huber Camp and Huber Oil still were the one and the same up even into the late 50's with executives moving in and then out again. The old iron natural gas incinerators were replaced by garbage trucks and dumpsters for the employees but the people who weren't "Huber" had to dispose of their own trash. I remember when the city took over this job and gave everyone shiny, metal, trash cans with lids. People had to get creative and build HEAVY holders for the cans and heavy chains for the lids or when the Texas wind blew in March! Well, your unsecured garbage can, could be seen bouncing toward Pampa in a few minutes!

Girls could find out where the boys lived by looking at the laundry outside on the clothes line! Momma squeezed my brother's Levi jeans, tightly, into metal frame, blue-jean stretchers...one stretcher for each leg. That way we didn't have to iron them. Boy! Did they have a good crease! Boys could find the gals by checking out 'on line display' of fresh laundry, too. (I'll leave that up to your imagination. Women would know who did a good wash (the right way) by the way the clothes were hung up on the line. Also, the way they were taken down, taught a big lesson to the young or busy wife when she had to contend with Carbon Black blowing over.

My mom would let us go outside and play all day and it was better if we DIDN'T show up back in the house wearing a roller skate as Poppa slept shift work and on his graveyard shift did NOT appreciate being blasted awake by the sound of metal wheels on the hardwood floor--my neighbor was Charlotte Meier and Johnny Tucker and Linda Pratt, Bennie Tennie, and Talmer Huff, and we had our ball games, and wars. If we needed to use the bathroom? We used the friend's house where their Poppa was away at work-we shared that, too.

We lived in our imagination and the Company 'dump' at the Plains plant was open "fodder" for anything we could find, drag home and make into games and toys. Telling stories while sitting on the welded-pipe-fences built around the water "plug" was our evening tradition. There in a group therapy session, we worked out how we felt about the "boys", school, teachers, parents, what to wear to school-black shoes or white? All the really important things, like zits and "periods"-who got them, why?

Wood, Joey (Linscott) and Pat Minton:

My earliest memories of life in Huber camp is around 1949 or 50. We lived on 1st street (Wisconsin now), right across the alley from Whitey & Pauline Warren. The Smith's (Dwight & Sharon) & their folks lived next door to the east of us. Buster Clanton & his folks lived just up the street. Dennis Miles, Diane Neely, Wanda Maddox are a few more I remember living on 1st as well. I can still remember that winter watching my dad walk up to Huber Avenue to catch a ride to the Plant. The snow was like a blanket, up over knee high.
We lived there until we moved to 1206 Indiana St. (the old 3rd Street) in 1956. "When Huber Camp was annexed into the Borger city limits 1st, 2nd, & 3rd Streets already existed in Borger so the streets were changed to Wisconsin, Minnesota, & Indiana respectively."

We lived next door the Durant's. Jimmy was our age. The Sander's lived on the other side Wendell & Colleen & their folks. The Gipson's lived across the street... Truitt, Kenneth & James & their folks. George Moore & his family were next door to them. The two Families of Roden's, Ed & Orrie, Jake & Eileen & Dobbin & his wife Sue's folks , Marj & Bob Shelton with Royce & Waunell, Johhny Hanes, his wife & Audrey. The West's, Ray Lee was our age. The Rhouten's were Edna & Neva.

We moved down to 1219 in 1959. When we moved out of 1206 The Petty's moved in. Rooster & Myrble, Sammy, Lenna & Glenda. I still remember Rooster calling my Dad a week or so after we had moved & asking him for a key to the house at 1206. Dad got a sheepish look on his face & said we never got one when we moved into the house in '50. We never owned a key the whole time we lived there. It was a different era back then neighbors looked out for each other. We never thought anything about someone in the neighborhood walking in & borrowing something they needed until they could repay us & they did the same for us. It was a wonderful atmosphere to grow up in. You couldn't get into too much trouble back in those days because anything you did got reported back to your folks PDQ.

If you got into trouble in School, you were in a LOT more trouble when you got home. I actually recall one of my teacher's calling Mom & telling her she was going to give me an F for a Six weeks grade when I'd actually made a C. Mom told her to go ahead if she felt like that was what I needed. She did & gave me an ultimatum. She said she would flunk me if I didn't make an A the final six weeks. I put my nose to the grindstone & had a 94 average for the final six weeks. That was in the sixth grade. I really don't think I learned anything else in English till I had her again in the 12th. It was a hard time but a GOOD time. I wish we could go back & do it again knowing what we know today.

Joey Woods '61

I was a Huber brat & lived in company houses all of my school days. Many of the things Judy recalls were a BIG part of my childhood as well. Especially the Wash House, since we lived right next door to it. The year we graduated, enough people in camp had obtained washing machines in their houses that the company decided to close it down for lack of use. Ralph, my step-dad bought the lot & had a brand-new brick house built on the lot.

Albert Shirley '64
Who remembers the Huber Camp in Bunavista (Production) just up the road from the pipe yard ?(where Bob Foland lived) The names were very colorful Big J Jordan and Iowa(my brother-in-laws Dad and Mom) , Rabbit and Edith Grubbs (Betty Sue's Dad and Mom), Rooster and Merble Petty (Sammy's Dad and Mom), Buck and Linnie Whitsen (Dalford's Dad Mom) , The Farris, The Wetsels, The Grogans, The Holcombs, and The Bales, most of whom lived on Carbon Street. South of the camp is where the Millers lived (Delbert and Burdet and the paint horse Punk). The first telephone I can remember was black with no dial, my phone number was 3627-J.

Huber Camp (my world) in 1953 my family moved to 1203 First Street aka Wisconsin street in Huber Camp. Typical company house 2 bed room, 1 bath, living room, hall kitchen, and dining room. All houses in the beginning were the same, all cookie cut. The house at 1201 Wisconsin was an executive house Huber allowed the transient executives, chemists, and oil and gas men to live there as long as they were in Borger. Residences included Dick and Marie Strohmeyer, Larry and Dianne Riggins, the Scarfs, the McDaniels and many more. The house at 1200 Wisconsin was home to the McBrides, the Big J Jordans, the Millers (Burdet , Judy , Ronnie , Moo (Rodney) and Sissie), 1202 Wisconsin the Clantons (Howard, Pauleen, Buster and Garry), 1203 the Shirleys, 1204 the Maddox Tommy Jo, Colleen, Linda, Wanda Jo, and Larry Bob, 1205 Wisconsin the Powells JC (little J) , Willene, and Ronnie J, 1206 Wisconsin the Lambersons , 1207 Wisconsin the Tooms Johnny, Minnie, Troy and Kent, 1208 The McGlaughins Billie and Clara. Other names no numbers the Starks Pat, Pam Peggy, Jimmy and ect., The Cantrells et aux, The Chambless-Chief, Inez, Don and Sharon, The Jacksons-Willie, The Penningtons-Donna, The Lawyers-Donny, The Miles, The Hines-Urma, The Johns-Mickey , the Uptons, The Treats, and some I cannot remember Others in the Camp , Hutto-Larry, Tubbs, Petty-Sammy, Roden, Routen, Johnson-Charles, Shelton (professional paper carrier), Courtney (Kathleen <3),Gibson-Truitt Laffiett Jr , Kenneth ,Poston-Larry , Spake, Aull -George Ann and Vera Jo, Lister Linda, Estes, Linda, Wright-Johnny, Brown-Elton , Wilson-Clara, Shirley Kay, Fowlers, Hale-Susie

School carnivals and Halloween at Huber Camp

by Mary Lynne Bishop Tiner '64

School carnivals? We always had neat Halloween carnivals at Huber School – dunking for apples (it wasn't considered unsanitary or unhealthful back then – don't think anyone ever got sick), games and treats. The "Huber kids" were a pretty tight knit group – there were only four grades (1st thru 4th) at Huber and only one class of each grade. We got to work in the cafeteria and would get a little cup of ice cream after we'd done the dishes and cleaned up the kitchen – that was always fun. I always thought it was especially neat to get to work in the cafeteria with Albert Shirley (we called him Abie back then). It was considered an honor to get to work in the kitchen - I believe the cook's name was Mrs. Snyder. She was really a neat person.

Halloween? Our next door neighbor was Mrs. Skoog (Mr. Skoog the choir teacher's mother) – we always went to her house first to trick or treat. She either gave us oranges with peppermint straws or popcorn balls. We'd go to all the United Carbon houses on Hemlock, down Lee Street and work our way back to Hemlock and then on to Huber camp. Our parents didn't worry about where we were or that we'd get into trouble – they knew everyone else's parents and knew they'd get a call if we did anything wrong or if we were in trouble.

Girl Scout Brownie troop? Pat Stark Reaves reminded me the other day of our Huber Brownie/Girl Scout troop – George Ann and Vera Jo's mom, Peggy Aull and Kathie Courtney's mom, Ruth Courtney were our leaders. We met in the Aull's garage after school. They tried to teach us to sew one time for a merit badge – I think "tried" is the operative word there. We spent most of that afternoon laughing at Wanda Maddox. For some reason she couldn't say "thread" the needle – it always came out "fred" the needle. It would send us into gales of laughter. We always had fun – someone said they had a picture of us from an old Borger paper. I'd love to have a copy of that. If I remember correctly, our Brownie troop included Sammye Petty, Frances Badgett, Kathie Courtney, Betty Bowman, George Ann and Vera Jo Aull, Kay Johnston, Kay Shirley, Wanda Maddox, Linda Anderson, Pat Stark and myself. Hope I didn't leave anyone out.

Pat Stark Reaves, 64
Thanks for the memories of Huber Camp. I remember the snow drift to the top of William Jackson's house. Nola and Jessie Jackson sponsored Teen Town for a few years. Her laugh was always so infectious.

Mary Lynne Bishop Tiner '64
I remember all the people you mentioned in Huber Camp - what a great bunch of people. My sister, Julie, corrected me on the name of our cook at Huber School. It

was indeed Mrs. Smirl, not Mrs. Snyder. What a wonderful lady! Just for grins, on a really clear night, KOMA and WLS came in loud and clear in Houston. It made me seriously homesick when I'd hear a dedication for someone in Borger on KOMA. That happened relatively frequently 1962-64. We could also get WLS in Atlanta, GA but WSB (an Atlanta station) drowned out KOMA.

Sandy McCarty Tooms '61
I also lived in Huber Premier Camp on Carbon Street--last house on the right. Can't remember the house number, but my phone number was 2675J. I know we had a party line.

Other Camps Around Borger and Spring Creek School

The oil companies often placed workers in the outskirts of Borger to watch over their equipment. These included 'TexRoy, Dial, Phillips Camp and Plemons.

Tex Roy Camp and Spring Creek School - Skellytown, TX

By Jean (Reich) Stewart

It is a pleasure to go back on memory lane and recall the wonderful days of growing up at TexRoy Camp, as well as going to Spring Creek School.

To Paint A Picture of Tex Roy Camp in the Panhandle of Texas

As you travel either way north or south between Pampa Texas and Borger, Texas you will find half way either way a small spot on the east side of HWY 152 a camp they call Tex Roy. This camp was built to house the workers who maintained Phillips Petroleum booster plant, approximately 18 miles north of Pampa and 18 miles south of Borger. You would turn east on intersection 280 go east about ¼ mile then turn south to the entrance of this camp. Either direction you drove you would top a hill in this flat land and see a green spot with the layout of the homes neat and clean in the middle of nowhere. There was a small grocery store and I thank gas station on the corner of HWY 152 and intersection 280 within walking distance of the camp.

This camp consisted of eight (8) big houses to your right as you turn into the camp and seven (7) small houses on the west side of the camp. The big houses had a living room, kitchen, two bedrooms and a bath in-between, and a small room called a built in back porch and an open front porch. The houses were set up as two houses, then a four car garage; then four houses a set of four car garages, then two houses. The dirt road curved down along the small shotgun houses toward the plant. The small houses were called Shotgun homes which had a living room, kitchen with a small bath (shower, stool, sink) to the side, and a small room on the back. No Porch's just a straight shot through the house about the size of a 10' X 59' trailer. A set of seven garages set at the south end of these houses. Each set of homes had a chain link fence all down in front of the homes with gates to each house and the same all across the back of the homes. There were no fences between any of the homes. Across the back fence wild grape vines grew and each home had a large tree growing between each home snuggled in it's shade during the hot dry summers. Just south of the houses set the booster plant where the workers pulled their shifts, they could walk to work, it was that close. In the middle of the camp was a tennis court with a high chain link fence and just open prairie all around as far as you can see. The camp set about ¼ mile off the main highway 152.

Parents move in

In 1938 or '39 my parents; Bill and Alberta (Bert to most) Reich moved there with their oldest daughter Deanna into one of the shotgun houses. I was born in 1940 and we lived in this house until I was about 9 or 10 years old. We then moved into one of the big houses and my little sister was born when I was 13, her name was Tawahana. My mother was thrilled to move out of the cramped shotgun house into something bigger. Our neighbors and friends were Tom Gross, wife and son (Butch); Mr. & Mrs.Wynager and family; Mr. & Mrs. Messenger, son Wayne and his big brother; Mr. & Mrs. Brewer, son Eugene; both of the Ross brothers and families, Big Ross had two sons, Little Ross had I think four daughters; we called them big and little because one lived in a big house and the other lived in one of the shotgun houses. Also there were the Williamsons-daughter Doris, Coopers, Scroggins (Curley and Opal) Patsy and her brother. All neighbors living there from the time Mother and Dad moved there. Many others moved in and out from time to time over the years.
During the depression the camp pulled together with each family taking turns going into town to buy flour, sugar, and gas, with rationed stamps and whatever else anyone needed. When they got back they would gather together and distribute the goods. No one went hungry and they used the flour sacks or feed sacks purchased to make our clothes. We had cows in the fields that would stray our way, chickens (who ever could afford to raise them), and wild game to eat. I can remember going rabbit and quail hunting with my dad, and fishing at a lake not far from there. I want to call it the Clemmons Lake. I just know it seemed like we drove for miles and miles to get there. The neighbors would pack up and all of us would go fishing and share evenly our catch.

COMMUNITY GARDEN

After we moved into the big house my father bought a small plow and plowed up about an acre in the middle of the camp built an irrigation ditch and the community bought seed to plant. Everyone that wanted to helped with this large garden, weeding, irrigating, and harvesting. My father taught me how to drive the tractor and he built a small trailer to pull at harvest time. It was hard work, hot; and to reap the harvest was very rewarding even for us kids. The women would gather together at each other's home and can the harvest. At the end it would all be divided amongst those who worked the garden. Those who did not do their full share got a small portion, no one was left out. There was trust, team work and friendship completely in this community. At the end of a hard day's work the families would gather together and play Dominos or cards until the wee hours of the morning and then go back to work.

GAMES WE WOULD PLAY

When we were not in school we would play cowboy and Indians and our bicycles were beautiful horses. The bad guys we caught were put in jail (which we used the wild grapevines as the jail), or make believe houses, or secret hiding places. We would raid the peanut butter and crackers to eat and yet we knew our parents knew where they could find us. Then someone got the bright idea to dig tunnels in the sandy soil and we would take candles to light our way. We pretended to be digging mines and finding treasures until the tunnels began to cave in and our parents found out... that ended our excavating.

OUR FIRST STORM CELLAR

Curly Scroggins had been traveling a lot one year and one day he came home using crutches. He had been caught in a tornado somewhere and got a broken leg so when he came home he dug a storm cellar for everyone's safety. (I have a piece of petrified rock from that dig to this day.) Before that we would sit out on our porch and watch funnel clouds form four or five at a time. And when it got really scary we would get in the car go to the intersection and watch to see which way they were traveling; we would go in the opposite direction. After Curly got his built then Mr. Brewer dug another storm cellar to help keep others safe. I do not remember if any other cellars were dug after that. We were fortunate that no tornado's or twisters touched down to do any amount of damage during my time there.

MY FATHER, BILL

I remember the many things my father did for other people, as well as for us. At one time he refurbished guitars for musical companies. He set up his shop in the garage and would have guitars hanging from the ceiling to dry from the fresh varnish to dry. I would sit for hours watching him sand, varnish and polish them to show their beauty. Many of the kids would sit and watch him with me.

He had two barrels buried in the back yard, one for worms and the other for minnows, which he sold for fish bait. We would go down to the creeks around there and seine minnows all day, bring them back and put them in the barrel to grow big enough to sell, then dig worms to replace those that he sold. He also built rabbit hutches all along the back yard to raise fryer rabbits to butcher and sell to Jim's Grocery Store in Borger. We would buy rabbit feed in cloth sacks so that mother could make our dresses for school. It was a wonderful life back then.

MOVING AWAY FROM TEX ROY CAMP

We had to move away in 1955, I had just started high school in Borger and my father got promoted to the big plant in Phillips, Texas. It was a sad day for all of us. Many of our neighbors had already moved to Phillips and we would be joining them, but not as close neighbors. They were scattered all through Phillips, but we all still stayed in contact, no matter what. I was 15 at the time and life changed drastically moving to a bigger school, and so many people there one could not remember who was who. The closeness I had known with classmates was forever gone.

Gary Martin Class of 59
Texroy Camp was on the Pampa Highway 152 & the intersection of 280 on the NE side. There used to be a Phillip Compressor Plant there. The Scroggins & the Ross Families lived there in the 60's.There were some other families, but I do not remember their names.
In 1961, I think, there was a gas pipeline leak behind the camp. Fumes gathered around the houses during the day. It ignited probably by the incinerator used to burn trash. Several of the houses were burned and Mrs. Ross and another lady were severely burned and I know at least one of them passed away from the injuries. There should be records in the archives of the Borger News Herald. There were many camps in the Spring Creek Area. My family lived in three different camps while we were growing up. I started first grade there. We moved to Borger, then back in 1954. We left when the oil companies sold us the houses to be moved to town. I remember where most of the camps were, but it is hard to explain on paper to one that hasn't been in the area.
Dee Chisum:
I have some friends that have lived in Texroy for many years. My friend Linda Hensley and her husband lived there. His family included his mother, father and sister and himself. His parents are gone now, but he is still there. There are several families that live there now. It has grown in the last few years. Thought you might like to know this. I am Cecil Chisum's widow. He also went to Spring Creek School, Cecil lived in the Kerr McGee camp. There is a picture at the school that shows the graduating class and people who see it, would swear was our youngest son. They looked so much alike, it was unbelievable. I am really enjoying all these memories, Cecil brought me here in 66. I thought he had brought me to the most God forsaken place on earth. But after all these years I have come to embrace it in my heart. It is HOME. I still live in the house we bought in 67 in Hughes Pitts. It was an old home and we found a letter that was written from a fellow in the service to his parents in the early 40's. I think I still have the letter somewhere.

Spring Creek School
In 1958 and when I was in the Tenth Grade at Borger High School kids from the Borger Junior High and from Spring Creek School came together for school. The girls from Spring Creek could play basketball and girls from Borger did not play basketball. It was strange watching them shoot baskets (they were pretty good, too!) on days when the weather was bad and we had to stay in the gym after lunch. Here are some memories of the Spring Creek area kids, which include the communities of SkyTex camp, TexRoy camp and Skellytown. One contributor recalls having "party lines" on our

telephones. We had party lines in Borger for awhile, too. When you had a "party line" more than one person could hear the conversation. One was supposed to NOT listen to conversations of others, but some people were "curious" and instead of being a *peeping Tom* they had a *peeping ear!*

Gary Martin (SCS Class of 59) had this to say about growing up in the Spring Creek area:
Thanks for your interest in the Spring Creek Community. It was a great place to grow up in. We always had a great basketball team. There were not enough for football. The school had very small classes, larger classes may have 12-15 students in them, some as small as 5. All of the school board lived in the community, so only the best teachers were hired. It was truly a family. You knew if you got in trouble at school or out anywhere, your parents knew before you got home, then you were sure in double trouble. We rode our bicycles from camp to camp to play in the summers. Everyone looked out for all the children in the community.
The oil companies built the house and camps so that the employees could live onsite. This housing was included in the salary agreements. This was before there was electricity available in high voltage to run the pumping equipment. Most of the oil pumping units were run by natural gas motors. If a motor quit running, they lost production. The Lease Operators/Pumper's and the field workers lived on the property being produced so they were available 24 hrs. if equipment failed, they could get it running quickly. The roads from Borger to the camps were mostly dirt roads. A lot of the camps were set up in the 40's & 50's.
In the early to mid 60's the oil companies started running electricity to the fields. They installed electrical motors and timers to start and stop the equipment, so, it wasn't necessary to have people close by. Other events leading to the phasing out of these type camps was that oil production was not as large as it once was. In addition, the small independent oil companies were being taken over by larger companies that consolidated the different operations into a producing unit that did not require as many people to operate it (thereby, jobs were eliminated). Usually the camps were called by the oil company's name, and/or the land owner, to differentiate if there were several camps from the same company in the area. [aka: The Skelly Watkins Plant Camp].

Phillips Camp by Lindsey Yell

We lived in the Phillips Camp on FM 280 North East of Spring Creek School about 3 miles, when I started first grade. My Father soon transferred to a different job with Phillips that was not in the area. Following that, we moved to Borger. I attended Coronado Elementary 2nd &3rd grade. In 1954 my Dad started a job as a pumper with Drilling & Exploration Oil Co. The

company built us a brand new 2 bedroom house in their **Watkins Camp**, just northwest of the Skelly-Watkins Gas Plant, about 1/2 mile. There were three houses and a material storage yard in this camp. The Field Superintendent lived there also. We got to go back to school at Spring Creek School. We lived there 2 years, then moved to the Haile Lease which was just east of Byars Corner, off of Jim's Lake Road. The county maintenance barn is at Byars Corner. I graduated from SCS in 1959. It then had one 8th grade class. We had a wonderful time growing up there. SCS maintained bus routes that picked us up close to home. We rode the bus from SCS to Stephen F. Austin Jr. High for 9th grade, Then to Borger High School after that. If you played sports in Jr. High and high school, you had to get home after practice yourself.
In the early sixties Drilling & Exploration was acquired by Sinclair Oil and Gas. They sold our family the house for a few hundred dollars with the stipulation that it be moved, or a personal lease agreement made with the land owner to leave it there. We moved it to Pampa, where it is today. Spring Creek School ISD location is and always has been +- 6 miles East of Borger on FM 2171. It had students from TX 152 to the Canadian River, and most of SE Hutchinson County. It now has classes 1-6th grade. Students from the Borger area are bused locally to and from Borger to Spring Creek School, also. It has never been in Skellytown which is in Carson County. Some postal routes in the area are serviced from Skellytown, so the mailing address reflects a Skellytown postal address. I have added a link to Google Maps for an aerial view of the SCS area. You can spot a lot of the camps that still have a few houses in them. You can move the map to different views with the mouse. Google shows the mailing address as Skellytown. It had a Borger rural postal service when we lived there. The SCS District area is pinpointed on Google at Byars Corner, which is several miles north & east of the actual school location.
There was a store in the area, the Hale Center store if you wanted to call it a store. It was about 8 x 10 feet in size and stocked with little more than candy, cokes, chips, and popsicles. I remember no groceries or canned goods but there were probably some. Many families had gardens, ours did. Many had chickens and livestock, we did. My mother canned produce, and froze some items. Our refrigerator was powered by gas and not electricity. We milked cows, raised hogs and chickens, slaughtered them for meat. It was an inelegant, but a practical life style. The house we lived in was a very small clap board 4 room mansion of about 700 sq feet. I remember it as being cold and drafty. It was a lease house. The employers of the time rented you the house on the oil lease where you lived. They got 24 hr/day coverage of their equipment from you.
The social life of the families revolved around the Hale Baptist Church and Spring Creek. In addition, many families would go to each other's houses and play card games. There might be four families together, the parents in

playing cards or dominos and the children outside running about playing red rover or hide and seek. There were seldom any alcoholic beverages that I remember, probably because they were expensive.

We almost never had any personal money as a child. I kept a dime in my pocket as a security item. Most of the time when my parents went to town, Pampa or Borger, the older children were left at home. I do not remember seeing Borger or Pampa until I was 5. I am sure this is not the case but that is my memory. My mother was a good seamstress and many of my shirts were made from the cloth of feed sacks. Animal feed was purchased in 100 pound sacks and the cloth of the sacks had a pattern and was a cotton fabric. Most of my sisters' clothes were also made this way.

As a child, almost all of my activities as a child outside of school were solitary. I ran the hills and canyons involved in my made up world of the moment. I remember my sisters listening to the radio shows that came on, "The shadow" etc. When we got a phone, VI8-2219, it was a party line. Our ring was a long and a short. The girls usually only allowed it to ring one time. The remarkable thing concerning all of the children I remember in the camp is how successful many became in later life.

Rita Davenport O'Donald Noel '66

I spent half of my childhood at Spring Creek with my grandparents, JF and Lorene Crow. They lived "next door" to the Maloneys or the Jollys - I also remember the Terry's. My mother, along with siblings, went to school at Spring Creek. My cousins and I played in those hills, never once seeing rattlers while exploring among the rocks and "cliffs. My mom's large family would gather out there for Sunday dinner which always ended up with the boys and men playing music. We kids would stick around for a while to listen but boredom would soon kick in because we had bigger things to do. What we loved the most was a big red cylinder gas pump with a hand pump. The top quarter of the pump was glass so you could see gas when you pumped the handle. It reminded me of a lighthouse. That was so fascinating to us!!! Pawpaw was a pumper and he often times would take me with him to turn on all of the "big horsies" called pumpjacks. He let me ride the smaller ones. We would always end up at the little store there on the big curve for candy. In the summer evenings, we would go to the rodeo somewhere out there at the area. Just a bunch of men folk getting together to calf rope, ride bulls, etc. I went back about 4 years ago (before the big fire) and was able to find their home place (sans houses) but it was a bit difficult to get to and, of course, the store is long gone. Ah, but what memories........

THE DIAL by Pug Davis '64

Treeless, laden with cactus and yucca; a dried up, eventually damned up river, gave some relief from the flat giving the impression of hills and valleys.

Hidden in the flat, was an oil camp we called "The Dial". My grandparents, all four of them, lived at the Dial. Everyone knew everyone else in this magic community in the country, barren and beautiful. The people who lived at Dial Camp came from many places. Some of them came from other oil camps like Stekoll and Gewitt and Burnett. There were two camps at the Dial. There was *rich camp* where my grandparents lived and about a half mile away, there was *poor camp* where I lived with my parents before we moved into town. Rich camp had a tar-covered road and you could ride a bicycle on it. There were houses on both sides of the road at rich camp. It is hard to know which camp was more fun. There were lots of friends at both camps. Because I was younger than all the other children at poor camp, I did not start school when they did. Every morning, I watched them climb up into a big yellow bus and go away. The afternoons took me to my sandbox where I played until they returned later in the day in that yellow bus. Sometimes one or two would come to play. These friends were busy with other things as I would be some day. Mike Quimby lived next door at poor camp. His mother, Mickie, was my mother's best friend. Mike and I played in our wagons. Everyone in poor camp played across the road in our community sandbox which was actually a big hole dug for who knows what. We took advantage of the situation and jumped into and crawled out of this wonderful pit. There was a tennis court at rich camp. I don't recall anyone ever playing tennis there, but there was a basketball goal at one end and the boys in camp bounced and shot and sunk a few. The tennis court was also a good place to ride a bicycle, because the surface was smooth and you could turn and lean and do daring things you wouldn't try anywhere else. My mother's parents and my father's parents both lived at rich camp and they would have lived side by side, but the Fowler's house was in between. I played with my uncle, my dad's youngest sibling, who was only four years older. I liked his games better than anyone else's games. At his suggestion, we played office and he was always the boss. When I could choose, we played cars, which was my favorite childhood game. The making of roads and fences and water holes was my main creative activity. At rich camp, I stayed mostly with my mother's parents. My mother's mother, whom I called Bibi, would turn over my granddaddy's chair so that the front of the arms was on the floor and the back of the chair became the roof of my hideaway. A sheet or bedspread was thrown over the top and I had complete privacy if I wanted. To this day, if I think of a safe place in my life, it is that one. It is there I would choose to go for peace. Some of the women at the Dial worked. Bibi worked in town and she did ironing at home. Both grandmothers crocheted. I tried several times to learn. Couldn't do it. My father's mother also did ironing and some quilting. Several of the women did quilting and it was exciting to see those huge conglomerates of fabric pieces hanging horizontally with some kind of wooden supports tied by rope to something overhead. I used to search for familiar patterns. There might be a piece from some dress or shirt that one of us had worn. Mrs. Fowler had chickens and I always went away when it was time for her to "ring their necks". The Fowlers had some garden things and so did my granddaddy. Different people grew different things and shared with others. It seems that everyone grew black-eyed peas. There were so many black-eyed peas that the major activity of every woman and child (boys included) in camp was shelling peas. I hated shelling peas. Fortunately, pea-shelling time didn't last too long. Grace Williams was a seamstress and made clothes for me and for my mother. I was uncomfortable standing still while Grace stuck pins here and there, but the dresses were always pretty and we were pleased with her work. We saved scraps for quilts and I always held hopes for perpetuating a favorite design. Yes, I liked looking at the dresses but I did not like wearing them. Jeans were more suitable for the traditional activities of oil camp children. Ruth Germany had a cherry tree in her back yard. My uncle and some of the other boys in rich camp climbed tall ladders to get to those little red treasures. Some of the cherries fell to the ground. We knew the rules about cherry picking. One, you never ate one until it was washed; and two, you always shared. That is, you always put any cherries you found into the bag or the bucket with the other cherries. We all cheated. All the children broke the cherry rules and munched a few. No one ever got sick. I don't remember any gardens or fruit trees at poor camp. Poor camp had houses on one side of the road which was made of dirt and rocks. No tar on top. The dirt was hard enough for tricycles, wagons, and for brave bicyclists.

There were cattle guards at the Dial. I remember only four. One was at the end of the road at poor camp and one was at the end of the tar road at rich camp. To go to the office where my granddaddy worked, you had to cross another cattle guard, and to get from there to the community hall or the store, you had to cross still another. Crossing by foot was easy. Crossing on a bicycle looked hard. Back then, I walked a lot. Not just to the office or the store but out into the canyons and to the creeks. The best hikes were those done alone. Walking from one gathering of cottonwoods to another was an event for me. A "found" walking stick and an old army canteen strapped around me from shoulder to waist, were my only tools. Alone and free, a half mile maybe, my hikes. Above ground, the only vertical structures were oil wells. The wells, before they became those big bobbing mosquito-like things, were taller. Artesian wells. Lots of dirty men and rusty pipe. Up and down. Big and black. And the smell of crude oil was like the most exquisite perfume. God's perfume. Black and pure from this earth, richer than blood, just as vital. My daddy was a roustabout. His daddy was a pumper and my daddy's uncle drove a truck. All the men I knew who worked for Gulf were dirty and had oil on their overalls. All except for my granddaddy, who worked in the office. He had clean khakis and he always wore a hat. The other man who was clean was Curly Parker. He was not related, but he worked in the office with my granddaddy. Once, I sat at

Curly Parker's desk and beneath the large piece of glass which covered the entire desk, was a picture of naked women in hard hats. They were working on a rig. All naked and pushing some big wheel around. I told my granddaddy that it wasn't a very nice picture. He agreed with me. Hiding a smile, he went into another room. The next time I was there at the office, I noticed the picture was gone.
When I went to the office with my granddaddy, I wanted to hide when the roustabouts came, even though my daddy was one. If no one but me and my granddaddy were at the office, I could play on the typewriter. When the workers came, I could listen to the pumpers and their own particular jargon about "the Byers and the Dial number two" (lots of numbers and strange names). All the men there liked me and I felt that I fit right in. Once in a while, I would hear a joke and be able to tell it to a captive audience of oil men. One time, I told a dirty joke and everyone laughed and everyone there told everyone else who wasn't there about my joke. When I knew that it wasn't very nice, I was embarrassed, but it was a good experience and, given the opportunity, I might have done it again. Besides the houses at Dial Camp, there were four other buildings that I remember. There was the big office where my granddaddy worked and the warehouse filled with lots of rusting pipes (that counted as one building). Across from the warehouse was a small building covered by wavy sheet metal. The roustabouts changed clothes inside the small building. I never saw the inside of the corrugated building. There was the Community Hall used for meetings and parties. A barbed wire fence surrounded the Community Hall but you could get in easily through the revolving gate. We all tried to use it as a merry-go-round, but it was too small and too hard to push. Finally, there was the general store--The Dial Store. In the middle of the store was a pot-bellied stove, and on cold days there were Gulfmen sitting on strong, wooden milk boxes positioned into a double semi-circle around the stove. The men talked about the weather. There was a post office in the store. Our post office box number was 101. There was candy, potato chips, cokes and banana fudgesicles. If I had any money, I liked to spend it on chips instead of candy. One day, I noticed several people gathering up things in the store. They would get food things and house things, and sometimes lots of things. At the counter, there was no exchange of money. These shoppers told Clea Sims to charge it or put it on their bills. I learn easily by example and I learned early about charge accounts. Seems that potato chips were often not enough for my snack, so I would get a coke and nonchalantly tell Clea to "put it on the bill". Sometimes, I would even have dessert. Yes, Clea put banana fudgesicles on the bill, too. Gee Sims, who was Clea's brother, drove one of the buses from Plemons. I was lucky to be assigned to Gee's bus because it went over a road with a gully. All of us on the bus knew when the gully was coming and we would all yell for Gee to go fast... he did. The back of the bus would go flying into the air and we would scream and laugh and our

stomachs would fly up right along with the bus. The buses raced to see who could get to the store first. One good thing about getting there first was that you won the race. The best thing was that you didn't have to stand in line very long, for the candy or chips. The first television I ever saw was at Gee Sims' house. His wife, Katy, let the children go to her house after school to watch Crusader Rabbit. There was one channel then, Channel Four. Crusader Rabbit came on at four o'clock. If we were there early, **we just watched the test pattern**. On some nights, everyone in camp went to watch TV. Everyone liked Name that Tune. Everyone tried to name that tune before the contestant on the show named it. Some people did. One night, I was there with everyone watching Name that Tune when my favorite song came on and I yelled out the title. It was *The Wedding of the Painted Doll*. I'd heard it in school and I knew all the words. I was very excited to know that those fancy TV people knew my favorite song. When I yelled it out, everyone looked at me funny and then looked back at the TV. The contestant did not know the name of the tune and the host announced the title...The Wedding of the Painted Doll. In Summer, the bookmobile came weekly to the Dial. Because I was always at Bibi's, I checked out books there. I suppose the bookmobile went to poor camp too. You could check out as many books as you wanted. I usually got three or four. Those, I read faithfully, usually in the heat of the afternoon when it was too hot to play cars. I sometimes read in the bedroom, in my granddaddy's big four poster bed. If it was very, very hot, I would sit in my granddaddy's now upright chair, cross my legs and read there. That was the coolest place in the house because the swamp cooler blew right that way. If Granddaddy came home, I would give him his chair. Granddaddy sat in his chair in the evenings and there was an ottoman for his feet. Then, we played "barber". I would sit up on the wide back of the chair and put my feet on the wide arms. Granddaddy's hair was thin and straight and he wore it combed straight back. You could never see his hair because he always wore a hat, but I had the privilege of not only seeing his hair, but of combing and brushing it. There were all sorts of fancy hairdos I invented. Now, I can only remember the turtle which was created by a constant swirling of the brush.

Learning to ride a bicycle was a difficult but not a dangerous process. My uncle would hold the back bumper of my little blue Schwinn while I got situated and ready to peddle. Off we'd go, me peddling and my uncle holding me up. The day I finally did it alone, I was so proud that I turned around to see if my uncle was watching. I crashed. I learned to not look back. It was a while before I could glide along with the others but that time came. I could peddle real hard and then coast. Coasting was an up town thing. My goal was to ride to the office, but I wasn't ready for the cattle guard. I watched others cross it in different ways. If no one was watching, I would get off my bike and push it across those metal bars. On rare occasions, I noticed someone might have seen me, so I pretended to check the chain or one of

the pedals. Checking it out was appropriate because no one could possibly do bicycle maintenance on the cattle guard. Regular maintenance was important because of all the wear and tear from cattle guard crossings. When the dismount went unnoticed, I would simply get back on that blue Schwinn and ride to the office.
Another of the four cattle guards was entrenched between the office and the general store. This was the most famous of all the metal barricades at camp. Famous because it was between the two most important structures at the camp and because it was so out in the open that cheating would have been close to impossible. No, it would have been impossible. There were four ways to get across this famous cattle guard or across any of them. You were judged by the others by the way you did it. Or better, by the way you chose to try to do it. There were always a lot of us around there and someone would always suggest going to the store. There was the challenge. We learned early to make our decisions based on how we could get it done and how that would look. I still make a lot of decisions using the same criteria. The first way to get across a cattle guard was to back up a little and see what was ahead. Backing up also gave you some space and a chance to get some momentum. Then you peddled as hard as you could to get going real fast. If you were very brave and somewhat stupid, you choose to go right across the big round metal things. You couldn't peddle if you crossed this way and you had to hold the handlebars so that they were always straight. Most of the boys tried it this way and some were successful. Some crashed. Some of them were hurt but would never admit it. Another way to cross was to get a little speed and carefully cross on the small flat bars which held the big round ones together. More skill than courage was required, but one would be admired for this choice. The easiest way to cross while still upon the seat of the bicycle, or standing on the peddles, was to go to the edge of the cattle guard and cross on the dirt. The only thing you had to know was that if you crossed on the right side, your right peddle had to be up. If it was down, it would hit the vertical structure beside the cattle guard. This was painful for your toes and you would probably crash. In the same way, if you crossed on the left, the left peddle had to be up. It was very important to coordinate this. Plan it and do it right. The last way to cross was to get off the bicycle and push. This was seldom done in the company of others. I never did it at the main cattle guard and would never admit to doing it ever. I tried crossing in every way I knew and I became quite skilled at taking the connecting bars. Straight and sweet. I guess we all had our own ways, but I do think everyone got off and pushed sometimes and never admitted it, just like me. It felt like cheating. Like doing it the safe, easy way wasn't good enough. Today, I'd get off and push and not be embarrassed, but I do miss the daring and the risk which was a part of those other choices.

I miss the feeling of community. There was probably gossip there but I never heard any of it. I still could not watch that chicken thing but I would love to search for familiar patterns in big quilts and make some roads and fences for toy cars. Standing still to be fitted for new clothes would go better and even a little pea shelling would be refreshing. Going back there now to look at what is left is like going to the ruins of some place that holds the history of ancient times. The roads are still there and the foundations of the houses which were moved away, stand in place. The office and other buildings are standing like props held up for a theater production about the old West. The memories of it feel crisp and sweet, but are possibly arranged to suit what we thought it was. The cattle guards, though showing more rust than before, rest unchanged. They rest as historical markers but keep their challenge. The challenge is to keep the memories and to speak them.

PLEMONS, TEXAS, COUNTY SEAT by Pug Davis '64

Leftover from what was once the county seat, Plemons had become only a place to go to school. The story was that one night, some people from Stinnett broke into the Plemon's courthouse and stole the official papers of Hutchinson County. Then somehow, Stinnett became the county seat. Slowly, Plemons became a school and a part of history. Both my parents graduated from what was once Plemons High School. They met at the school when they were fifth graders. I went there, to that school, which lost high school status but kept the first eight grades. The same school building was used for my generation mascot of "the Plemons Indians." Our colors were orange and black. The Phillips Blackhawks had the same colors. If you earned a letter "P" on your orange and black jacket at Plemons, you could still wear that jacket if you went to high school at Phillips and feel you fit in.

Daily, from town, Mrs. Borum, who was my first and my second grade teacher, drove a black '56 Ford transporting me and two of her own children. The school and the empty stone buildings which were once a bank, post office and courthouse, were embodied in a recess of land, like that which held what was left of the Canadian River. In such recesses were mesquite and cottonwood and an occasional skinny creek. There were horned toads, lizards and rattlesnakes. To get to Plemons from town, you had to travel the back way through Phillips. Phillips was another part of those golden times. My mother worked at the hospital in Phillips. She was a nurse, an R.N. I knew Phillips well. I have always known the back roads. The shortest distance between two points is probably the back way.

On the road, every weekday, we passed through Phillips with all its huge pieces of refinery equipment dazzling in the morning sun. There was the steam place, or the fog place. Some mornings, Mrs. Borum would turn on the headlights of that '56 Ford and we would drive very slowly through a section of the refinery that had dense fog. I still don't know what caused that, probably some kind of condensation. The experience was like being in the clouds and I never really wanted to know what it was all about. Still don't.

From Phillips we traveled down a steep hill. This road was a tar road like the one at the Dial. The Dial was the oil camp where many of the Plemons' students lived and where all the men worked for Gulf. Past the hill at Phillips, there was a big pool. Surely it was some kind of oil or some chemical compound. To me, it was the lake. After the lake, we crossed the river. We took the old bridge, wide enough for only one vehicle. If we got to the middle and met another car or truck, either we would back up all the way to the end of the bridge or the other vehicle would do the backing. There were invisible markers, known only to those who traveled there. Most travelers knew where the boundaries were and who should do the backing up. I did not learn about those boundaries. I was busy looking for any water left in the Canadian River. Mostly, I looked down upon bushes and red mud.

Because we traveled down into a canyon, we were surrounded by what seemed to be hills. After all, when you are in a canyon, the regular ground appears hilly. I thought that I went to school in the mountains. Up and down and around, not too fast. A turn to the right put us on a red dirt road called caliche. After the infrequent rains, the road would be slushy and sometimes we would slide a bit. When that dried, there were big ruts in the road from the trucks of the ranchers and oilmen, from the one school bus that took that road, and from Mrs. Borum's car. Riding the ruts was fun, but probably not for Mrs. Borum.

Along the caliche road each day, we came to another bridge. This one was an old wooden bridge. Not too long, but strong I guess. One year we had a real flood. The two buses and the two cars got to school, in spite of the strong morning rain. The rain continued and word came that the little bridge was "down". I know that this was a problem for the adult world, but for me, it was exciting. We might be trapped. The girls might get to have a slumber party at Mrs. Kirkwood's. Her house was on the property. The vehicles were definitely trapped. We continued to read and study and play and then, when it was time to go home, we all marched, or better yet, plodded through the red mud, across the cattle guard, and to the place where the bridge was...or wasn't. Across the way, there were all the Gulf men in their trucks and I saw my daddy there in his roustabout clothes. I was too little to get across the creek so Johnny Carter, an eighth grader, picked me up and put me on his shoulders to take me across to the invincible Gulf men with trucks.

For a while after the flood, we took what we called "the detour". This was a skinny, slushy, two-rutted trail through the pasture. Soon, the bridge was repaired and was as good as new. Or as good as it was before it went down. Between that bridge and the school building, after the cattle guard, there was a big open space. Mrs. Borum parked on the side of the building where the first and second grade rooms and the boy's bathroom were located. We parked under the windmill and by the basement door. Mr. and Mrs. Grimes parked their '56 Ford there, too. Theirs was a two-toned Ford, black on the bottom and on the top with white in the middle between the three layered chrome and the windows. A Galaxy.

Scary stories about snakes and tornados were going around but the only thing that really scared me was when I had to change the goldfish bowl. There were two goldfish in one of those little round bowls. The kind of bowl that was two circles upright and a circle on the bottom to hold the thing up and an open circle on the top. The girls had to carry that bowl of water with the fish in it all the way to the other end of the building because the girl's restroom was there. We would also have to carry a net to catch the fish and a container to put water and fish in while we cleaned the bowl. It even seems hard if I think about it now. I like fish ok. If you got a drink in the drinking fountain and looked at that round silver thing with holes in it, you could see fish eyes. I always did see fish eyes when I got a drink. Sometimes, at drinking fountains, I still see the fish eyes.

Outside, there was a big Saint-Bernard dog named Buster. I think that I was originally afraid of him, he was so big...bigger than any first or second grader. And he ran very fast. It was at the swings one day that I finally saw that Buster was as gentle as he was big. My fear passed.

The Whittenbergs owned most all the land around there. There was someone in that family that we all called "John Jake". I don't know if that was his real name or not. Everyone said that he was crazy and everyone told awful stories about him. There was this big, old house out in the middle of nowhere and that was supposed to be where John Jake lived. If I spent the night with someone on a weekend, I got to ride the bus. When the bus passed by that old house, everyone would ouh and awh. I thought it was a pretty house. It was white and had a red tile roof and it did not look old. Sometimes, John Jake would "get loose". The Sheriff's posse would be out looking for him, and there would be helicopters out, too. They say that John Jake always traveled with the wind at his back, like the cows do. Sometimes at school, you could hear the helicopters.

There were PTA meetings at Plemons. One year, or maybe more than one, my mother was president so we always had to go. The parents were always in the gym which was filled with folding chairs. The students went to several different places, depending upon their grade level. The year that we always went to PTA, I had to go the room next to the boy's restroom. It was the room where we had music in the day. We would dance to the *Golliwog Cakewalk* or gallop to *The William Tell Overture*. In the music room, during PTA, we watched movies while our parents and teachers solved all the problems that we knew nothing about. We were watching *Frances the Talking Mule* one time, and there was a disturbance in the back. Did someone break the rule and go to the bathroom during the film? Was someone sick? Just as the noise subsided, the film sputtered and stopped and the lights went on. It is really hard to see when the lights come on suddenly like that, but we all turned, squinting, toward the back of the room.

Mrs. Borum was at the door with her hand by the light switch. Then I noticed the man sitting on a chair in the back row. He was a round man with a very red face. He had on dirty clothes and a hat which sat crooked on his head. There were murmurs amongst us and maybe a gasp or two. Mrs. Borum told Kenneth Bynum to go get Mr. Beasley. She told us that we had a visitor and that he was welcome. She said to just wait and we could see the rest of the film in a minute. At this, the round man smiled. I liked him. In a minute, Mr. Beasley and several other people came into the room and they asked the round man to go with them. He did. He looked sad to leave but he did not resist. We watched the rest of the film. When we were on our way back into town, I asked my parents who that round man was. It was John Jake Whittenberg, my daddy told me. I did not think that he looked mean or scary at all. I was glad to have seen him and I was glad that he showed up there instead of somewhere out on the prairie with the cows. My mother explained many things to me. She explained about John Jake and why everyone made fun of him. When she told me things, she told them with great compassion and concern for the person she talked about. I learned that John Jake was not as smart as everyone else; that his body grew but his mind did not. He did not know any better than to run away. My mother told me that I should never make fun of anyone who was not very smart.

On Monday, back at school, everyone was talking about John Jake. I tried to explain what I'd learned and told the others not to make fun of him. Some of them said ok and some of them just went away to play with someone else and to continue to talk about it. Things just kind of go like that.

The music room was filled with memories from the first four years...John Jake, the Golliwag Cakewalk, and learning to gallop. In the fifth grade, we had classes at the other end of the building. We were close to the girl's restroom. Cleaning the fish bowl would be easy now. But the upper grades didn't do that. I learned that the music room was the math room in the morning. It was a nightmare as I sat there not understanding fractions, but a dream in the afternoon for music. I cannot sing or play an instrument. I really tried though, probably to the great displeasure of those around me. When an English speaking person is speaking to someone who does not speak English, the speaker starts yelling, thinking that if it is louder, it will be understood. This was my approach to singing. Maybe, if I did it louder, it would sound better. We were trying to learn a song called Largo. I did not like trying to sing but I did like the way those Latin words sounded. My favorite part of music was the music that Mrs. Johnston played. I liked Tchaikovsky and Debussy, but I did not like Dvarok. Dennis Wheaton and I were saying one day that we did not like Dvarok. We were saying that to each other. Mrs. Johnston got on to us for talking. She did not know that we were talking about the music. She probably thought that we were talking about John Jake or something.

In fifth grade, I was in Picture Memory. There, we learned about famous paintings. We learned to look at a picture and identify it by the title, the artist, and the country where the artist had lived. I liked Renoir and most of the other French ones. We learned this during Art time. If we were not doing Picture Memory, we were learning Art. I loved this. We learned what value and intensity meant and the difference between them. I could do one point and two point perspective and knew the color wheel well...primary and secondary and complementary. Mrs. Johnston taught us Art in the upper grades. She also taught us science and I did not like her as much during science. She was different. My uncle eventually married her niece.

Mrs. Borum had to tape my paper to the desk one time in first grade so I would stop turning it funny ways and making only vertical lines. I did quit doing that. I never did quit capitalizing the word Art. I thought it deserved it. By the upper grades, I'd learned to catch myself if I started staring out the window. In the lower grades, the teachers told my mother that I was slow to do my work and that I didn't pay attention to what I was doing; but that I had such potential. If only I would apply myself. Today, they would say that I did not stay on task. I read slowly, but I was thorough. I knew all the answers to the part that I had time to read.

Poetry was something to read. We would have to memorize and recite poems. Some of it I liked. I really liked English. Mrs. Cox taught us English and I loved diagramming sentences. I learned everything about the parts of speech and about punctuation. We knew by third grade where to put a semicolon and how to write a proper letter. Mrs. Grimes taught us English in the upper grades and there was more reading and paper writing...more of that than sentence making and diagramming. Then, unlike now, I always tried to use complete sentences. We had to try to understand the poems that we used to just read. We were more excited about Mrs. Grimes having a baby than about poetry or literature.

Arithmetic was a good thing. Mrs. Kirkwood taught us in the third and fourth grades. It was not really until the upper grades when we called it math and the advent of fractions and percentages that I had trouble with. My only C at Plemons was one six weeks in math in 7th grade.

Even though I liked maps and I learned the capitols to all the states, I did not like geography. I did not like reading about Eskimos eating whale blubber and I did not care how tall the mountains were. I stared out of windows again and once when Mr. Grimes called on me to read, I had no clue where we were. He probably knew that. I told him that Dennis Wheaton read too fast and I couldn't keep up. Lies are often much worse than the truth. What do you do if you study geography? Travel? I was unable to connect geography with the local red mud and my important surroundings. How could I know that all the things I loved in my heart were the things people had studied in their heads...having been led, hopefully, by their hearts. Who has studied orange as artist and who as scientist...knowing why

West Texas gives the most beautiful sunsets of orange and purple. Who has studied the minds of people like John Jake and who has studied how to make them better?

I did not learn everything that I need to know in kindergarten. Plemons had no kindergarten. But the beginnings of all which is a part of me is a part of that time and place...even fractions and percentages, recipes and income tax. I continue to stare out of windows looking for beginnings and endings. I find none. I find, instead, the continuity of permanence and change. I can look at the past or the present and know that if there is a flood, there will be heroes with big shoulders and big trucks or there will be women who will throw slumber parties.

Ch. 12 The Borger Gassers - **Tom Lindsey, Class of 1960**

I have memories of the old Borger Gassers that I would like to share. The Gassers were a class C club in the West Texas-New Mexico League. Towns in the league that I remember were: Borger Gassers, Pampa Oilers, Lamesa Lobos, Lubbock Hubbers, Abilene Blue Sox, Albuquerque Dukes, Clovis Pioneers, and the Amarillo Gold Sox. These were the teams in the fifties; there were other teams over the years, i.e. Wichita Falls, Big Spring, Midland, Wink, Odessa, Monahans, Hobbs, and Roswell to name a few.

Some of the Gasser players that I remember best were: Gordon Nell (first baseman and a top hitter), Windy Eldridge (right fielder), Eddie Carnett (center fielder and general mgr. for a while)), Lloyd Brown (infielder and playing manager), Nim Free (second baseman who settled in Borger and passed away a couple of years ago). Nim was an avid golfer and played for many years at the Huber Golf Course; now named the Borger Country Club. Goose Goff was a Gasser (black catcher), Larry Gilchrist and his brother Verdon Gilchrist both played. Larry later became the manager and was one of my customers on my paper route. We both lived on Yows Street and on Saturdays when I would collect the $.25 cents for the week, he would never pay me with money. Instead, he would give me a baseball or a broken bat, etc. which I would much rather have than money. The bats were nailed and taped and were as good as new to me. I can name many more players, but these are the ones I remember as the better players.

It was a real treat for me to go to the games and chase foul balls and get to talk to the players. There was a tradition in the West Texas-New Mexico League of fans poking dollar bills through the screened in backstop to any player hitting a home run.

J.M. Huber Corporation was very instrumental in forming the Gassers. Huber had a semi-pro team, the Huber Carbons, which was very successful. Some of the Huber players were Choppy Spencer Sr., Al Summers, Lefty Blair, Buzz Ross, Carl Brown, and Wade Wilson, to name a few. Many of the players stayed in Borger and worked for Huber after baseball. Huber Corp. built the ballpark in the 1930's that we know as Huber Park. The city of Borger owns it and it is still used today. The Borger Gassers were formed and joined the West-Texas New Mexico League in 1940. Some of the Carbon players played for the Gassers and they won the league in 1940. The league was started in 1937 and lasted until 1956 or 1957. I have many fond memories of the Borger Gassers and the West Texas-New Mexico League. I'm sure that is what sparked my interest and career in baseball

Truitt Gipson '65
Go to Goggle and type in Borger Gassers and you'll find additional information about the league. Abraham Latman owned the Gassers of the early 50's. I remember Neal Latman and Stanley, Abraham's sons. Neal and I taught Red Cross Swimming lessons at Huber Swimming pool. I believe Neal is in Amarillo. Mr. Latman owned Borger Pipe and Metal and late in life received his law degree and practiced in Borger.

I played golf in the Huber Golf league with Nim Free. He was a natural athlete and excelled in anything he tried. I thought Clyde Hutto played for the Gassers in the 50's. Clyde still lives in Borger, retired from Huber

Wayne Renfroe: 62

There are two things that I remember about the Borger Gassers. We lived in Phillips at the time. There was this one time when I went to the concession stand and got back more change than I should have. I can't remember if my dad made me take it back or not. Then there was the time a game was called because of a terrible rain/hail storm. As we were running for our car, another car moved forward, and there on the ground was a baseball that had rolled underneath from a pop foul. When we finally got home, most of the windows of our house were broken out from the hail. We had to sleep at the neighbors that night.

Part Three

SPORTS, MEMORIES AND GRADUATES

Ch. 13 Sports in Borger

Football in Borger During the Late 50s and 60s

By Frieda Lanham Pickett '61

I've asked several of the boys who played sports at Borger High to submit their memories of participating in sports during Junior High and High School. As a girl, I participated as a "fan, a supporter of their efforts". It was an activity which students, who were not athletes, frequently participated in. I remember going to see Harlem Globetrotters and basketball games at the new gym at Borger Junior High (6th and McGee). Enthusiasm was high for sports in Borger. When I got into high school we went to the football games every Friday or Saturday night. The games began soon after we started school in September. The evenings were cool, as was the case in the Texas Panhandle. It might be over 100 degrees F during the day, but it always cooled off in the evenings. Borger leaders supported the teams and in 1958 reserved a special train to carry Bulldog fans to Lubbock for a game. The story was in the Oct. 26, 1958, Borger News Herald and informed fans that the Borger Chamber of Commerce athletic committee made arrangements for a 600 passenger special train to take fans from Borger to Lubbock with the Monterrey Plainsmen at Texas Tech's Jones Stadium. The Santa Fe Special could be boarded in Borger at 3 PM, returning immediately following the game from a siding near the stadium. Round trip fare was $5.45 per person with tickets purchased at Chamber office, Borger Hotel. An hour following confirmation of the arrangements with Santa Fe, more than 30 tickets had been sold. Ed Lewis was president of the Borger Chamber and Mayor Jerrie Keith signed a resolution proclaiming that Borger citizens should show wholehearted support of the Bulldogs and go on the special train. Halloween was the same night as the ballgame that year and the mayor urged citizens to celebrate Halloween on Thursday so they could go to the game on Friday.

After Gene Mayfield and his coaching team came to Borger and our team started a nice winning streak, many parents and local businessmen came to the games. Students sat on one side of the stadium and our parents sat on the opposite site, next to the "opposing team supporters". My guess is that that there was not space on our side, as the band sat with us. The Borger band had many members. We had a good band and twirlers. In the 50s there was a twirler who did acrobatics as part of her routine, very impressive.

The high school clubs sold mums to make money during football and basketball season. If one of us girls was dating a player, he often would buy a mum for his girlfriend. The flowers were just a few dollars and Mrs. Kieckbusch at a local flower shop prepared the mums. We members of the clubs were supposed to sell five mums each week. You had some "regular customers" among the adult males you knew, but only a few, not five. So, one week I complained to my step-father asking him "How can I do better selling these mums?" He told me I should call one of my former customers and say "I'm calling to get your order for a mum for this week's game. Do you want one mum or two?" That only worked for one week.

There had been mediocre clubs before Mayfield came and some years not even that good. There had been the promise of a few great teams but for whatever reason championship stats didn't develop. Then, there was a coaching change in 1958. Mayfield and his coaching team came to Borger bringing an era of football success our town had not known. It started the first season when the Bulldogs won their first district title, taking the 3-AAAA crown with a perfect 7-0 record. It was the first time a club had ever gone undefeated in the tough league. People in Borger were ecstatic and wondered how long it would last! In 1959 hopes were dashed when the Bulldogs lost two games (Tascosa, Monterey) in the race, ending with a 7-2-1 record. After this, things changed and the won/lost stats never reached this level again. Changes included the success in motivation of the young athletes and in the style of play. Of course, behind every successful football coaching staff there are a staff of competent assistants. These are the men who seldom draw the praise, but who work even longer hours than their bosses to help build winning football teams. Assistants handle jobs such as chores of taping injuries, act as scouts, watch opponent films while their own clubs are playing elsewhere, and often are not present at most of the games played. They work long hours grading films and going over the reports they compile on the opposition to be played the next week. It is their job to make sure every move the opponent makes is communicated to their team. The staff at BHS included Gene McCandlies, Roy Lee Dunn, and Leldon Hensley. Behind the scenes they are largely responsible for the strategy behind each victory their team scores and will score in playoffs to come.

In 1960 Borger won the District title for the second time. Corky Dawson was our quarterback and we thought he was awesome as a leader of our great team. My senior year was the 1960-61 season and I'll never forget it. We started the season by traveling by school bus to play Snyder, a non-district game. We beat them 22 to 0. The next week we played another non-district game with the Dumas Demons and beat them 21 to 0. The next week our team traveled to Duncan OK (a nondistrict game) and massacred the Demons 47 to 0. Our district play began with a close victory over Palo Duro Dons 21 to 14. We were on a roll but were caught by the Tascosa Rebels and lost 0 to 7. We redeemed ourselves the next week with another massacre over the poor Plainview Bulldogs (well, maybe we should call them the bullpups) with a 66 to 6 victory. The next week we played Lubbock Westerners and won 19 to 0. And the week after that beat Monterey Plainsmen 27 to 7. November saw us with a decisive win over the Amarillo Sandies (a long time rival) of 20 to 6. The second weekend in November was an idle week giving the players time to take girlfriends for an actual date!! The rest was short as the next week we had to travel to Pampa where we showed them our stuff with a 41 to 0 victory. Although the next week we lost 0 to 14, in 1961 Borger had it's third District crown. We chartered buses to go to the Bi-district game with Wichita Falls and their awesome quarterback. It was my senior year and my friend and classmate, Larry Dyke, was our quarterback. We were very proud of him. We went with high hopes and yelled our lungs out encouraging our team. We lost the game 0 to 14 and came home with sadness, although we felt our "boys" had done a good job ending the season with a 9-2-0 record. It was just fate, we guessed. One of our players, John LaGrone, made all-state that season.

Then in 1962 Mayfield's magic worked again and Borger went undefeated, winning the District crown for the fourth time, and the second unbeaten record in school history. It was this year, the 1962 season, that the United Press International polls placed Borger at the #10 spot. The team steadily climbed the polls chalking up victory after victory, until they were #3 on the rating scale. They remained in this spot for three weeks while beating Plainview and Lubbock gaining a real foothold on the 3-AAAA title. Then on November 2nd the bottom dropped out on the #1 and #2 ranked teams (Wichita Falls, Port Arthur) as they were beaten by Irving and Beaumont South Park. This elevated Borger to the top spot and for three weeks held its rating by whipping Monterey and Amarillo before an open date. When the ratings ended this year Borger was No. 1, claimed the district 3-AAAA title and scheduled to win the first state title in history of the school. Borger beat Irving 27 to 7 in the bi-district race and beat San Angelo 21 to 13 in the quarter finals, then beat Lufkin 28 to 6 in the semifinals but lost 26 to 30 to San Antonio Brackenridge in the state finals. It was estimated that 10,000 people attended the game in Abilene. **Lee Johnson** played one of the finest games in his life, with 156 yards rushing in 20 carries. Borger's defense was so solid that Breckinridge was limited to only 14 yards rushing. The difference in the score was due to injuries on the Borger team. Backs **Jerry Wilson, A.C. Tillman and Fred Linton** were hurt and quarterback **Dean Alexander** was out for the season with Wayne Rape moved to the quarterback position. Borger had to play without four defensive starters. Borger's first score was a safety in the 1st quarter when LaGrone and Coffer raced through the line to nail Castillo for a yard loss in the end zone. What a delight!!

Some of the outstanding athletes that year included **A.C. Tillman, halfback; Lee Johnson, Wayne Rape, David Walton, Joe Coffer, Bill McKinney, Dean Alexander (quarterback) and Jerry Wilson.** All the players on the 1962 Borger team were accomplished but much credit was given to the Borger linemen**, John LaGrone (#67) and Melvin Gibbs, Center (#52).** They were called "the awesome twosome". The Borger Sports editor at the time wrote a story about interviews of other coaches of Panhandle teams saying that "there aren't two interior linemen anywhere in Texas better qualified for all-state honors". They competed with each other for Lineman of the Year award that season, one working on offense and one on defense. **John LaGrone** was named all-state and went on to SMU on scholarship.

The 1963 season was close with Borger having 6 wins, 1 loss and 1 tie. Tascosa was the District Champ with a 7-0-1 record, the tie score of 14 to 14 with Borger. Tascosa went almost all the way to state, losing to Garland in the semi-finals. The 1964 season found Borger again in 2nd place behind Tascosa with a 7-1-0 record. Tascosa went to semi-finals, again losing to Garland. After this season Mayfield and his staff left Borger and took the coaching positions at Odessa Permian.
Mayfield left Borger and accepted a position as coach at Odessa Permian high school in 1965. He led them to the 4-AAAA state championship that year, his first year coaching that team, a feat matched by only four other coaches in Texas high school football. He stayed at Odessa until accepting a head coach position at West Texas State University – Canyon TX, his alma mater. Mayfield's "reserved and gentle nature" delivered a calm and respectful manner when directing his players. One word that is mentioned by his players to describe him is *integrity*. Players and coaches through the years have shared with family members his ability to inspire and change their lives by leading them to meet their potential, which brought them success on the field and in their adult lives. The evidence for this is that when Coach Mayfield was inducted into the Texas High School Football Hall of Fame in 2005 over 50 members of his teams, both from Borger and from Odessa, traveled to Austin for the ceremony, along with several of us girls who remembered the coach with awe. We felt it was a fitting honor, as he was a legend in our minds. I went to celebrate with him and to see some of the players I remembered. I took a bottle of water with a Borger Bulldogs label which I found at a water store in Borger. I purchased it and kept it as a souvenir. When I gave it to him he smiled broadly and seemed genuinely glad to get it. Coach Mayfield died of complications from Alzheimer's disease in Lubbock TX on October 2, 2009.

CONGRATULATING COACH GENE MAYFIELD ON HIS INDUCTION TO THE TEXAS HIGH SCHOOL FOOTBALL HALL OF FAME -- (House of Representatives - April 27, 2005)

(Mr. CONAWAY asked and was given permission to address the House for 1 minute and to revise and extend his remarks.)

Mr. CONAWAY. Mr. Speaker, I rise tonight to congratulate Coach Gene Mayfield on his induction into the Texas High School Hall of Fame. On May 7, 2005, Coach Mayfield will be inducted into the Texas High School Hall of Fame.

Coach Mayfield was a master at turning mediocre football programs into State title contenders. A graduate of Quitaque High School, Mayfield played quarterback for Coach Frank Kimbrough at West Texas State University. In 1950, Mayfield led his team to a Border Conference Championship and a win over the University of Cincinnati in the 1951 Sun Bowl. After serving as Kimbrough's assistant for two seasons, Mayfield accepted the job at Littlefield

High School, where his teams advanced to the Texas State semi-final games in 1954 and 1956.

Coach Mayfield began rebuilding the football program at Borger High School in 1958 with a district title in his first season. His 1962 squad was undefeated until losing the Texas State championship game to San Antonio Brackenridge 30 to 26.

In 1965, the ``Father of Mojo'' took over an Odessa Permian team picked to finish last in the district. The Panthers went on to win the Texas State championship, beating San Antonio Lee 11 to 6. Mayfield's teams also advanced to the title game in 1968 and 1970.

Mayfield left Odessa Permian and took the West Texas State University job in 1971. He finished his coaching career at Levelland High School.

Coach Mayfield posted a career high school record of 156 wins, 35 losses and 4 ties. While his teams were very successful, Coach Mayfield's greatest accomplishment was the influence he had on the lives of the young men he coached. He instilled in all of us the value of hard work, responsibility, discipline, and being prepared. Coach Mayfield left a lasting impression on everyone he coached. I credit much of my personal success to his influence on my life during these years since 1965. Congratulations, Coach Mayfield, on a life well led.

Coach Mayfield's induction into the Texas High School Football Hall of Fame Saturday May 7, 2005, Submitted by **Susan Parker Miller Class of 64**

We had a good group from Borger to honor Coach Mayfield. It was a pleasure to see him and hear him speak so humbly of his years as a Texas HS Football coach. For those of you that are not aware his record stands as 156 wins, 35 losses and 4 ties. He is also a member of the Panhandle Sports Hall of Fame and the Texas High School Coaches Association Hall of Honor.

After the induction a group of us visited and the men in attendance all agree he had a profound effect on their lives. They were proud to have been associated with Coach Mayfield.

A list of those in attendance is as follows:

Coach Leldon Hensley, Billy Kidd and his wife Carolyn Plumley, Phillip Parker and his wife Gwen Poole, Melvin Gibbs, Bert Barron, Wayne Ray, John Lagrone, Patti Kelly Collins, Jim Shaw and his wife Debbie, Buddy (Merle) Harrington, Jerry Wilson, Dean Alexander, Clifford Stover and his wife Pam, Gordon Beamguard, Lee Johnson, Mike Harrington, Larry Reed, Barbara Sargent, Jim Blair and his wife Nel, Jerry and Betty Collins, Frieda Lanham Pickett and her husband Russell, and yours truly.

Memories of players and coaches: Gene Mayfield Years at BHS

From Borger News Herald Interviews

Coach Jeep Webb recalled his time working for Mayfield with great fondness saying, "Coach Mayfield expected us to carry ourselves in a professional manner from expecting us to wear a shirt and tie in the classroom to the way we interacted with the kids. We were expected not to grab or holler but instead to treat the boys as young men by talking to them in a normal tone. After practice we were not allowed to go hang out in the office but were expected to stay with the kids. One thing we were required to do was if we had gotten on or had said something negative to any of the players during practice, we were to try to find something encouraging to say to that kid before he left. The approach he had did greatly influence me throughout my career in the way I would interact with the kids". Webb recalled, "I remember when we scrimmaged against the seniors in the spring of 1958 we lost 26-6 and really felt like we had a lot of work to do. But the kids did a great job that summer buying into what Mayfield wanted to do." Webb added, "In 1958 after we lost the first game of the season to Snyder, Mayfield would not allow music or anything like that to be allowed on the bus trips to games, but instead gave each player a slip of paper with that player's responsibilities to think about for the game." The approach paid off as the team went on to win the district title that season, which included a win over Amarillo High, a team who had dominated the Bulldogs for many years.

This personal concern for the player's self-confidence impacted his players as former player Pete Loftis, who played on the varsity team two years under Mayfield, recalled in a Borger newspaper article, "Coach had a way in communicating to where you felt like what you were doing was always contributing to the team and you felt like you could do anything on the football field."

Bob Berry, who played under Mayfield his junior year, said, "You always knew what he expected out of you as a player and did a great job in treating all his players the same."

John LaGrone, an All-State standout for the Bulldogs under Mayfield, added, "when he talked you knew he was trying to teach you something and did a great job in making sure we understood what we were expected to do for him out on the field." Webb and LaGrone are both quick to point out that prior to Mayfield's arrival, the Borger football program had minimal success and were picked to finish last in the district in his first year in 1958. Lagrone said, "Mayfield had a great way of turning underachievers into overachievers. It's said of former Alabama Head Coach Paul "Bear" Bryant that he could take his players and beat you but he could also take your players and find a way to beat his players. Mayfield was able to do the same thing."

Another area where Mayfield excelled as a coach was his attention to detail. Loftis said, "He was big on working on fundamentals and the off-season program. He would tell us that you cannot expect to get something out of nothing, so if we wanted to be better than Tascosa or the Lubbock schools we would have to put in a lot of work. But if we did what we were supposed to do in the way he told us, then we knew that everything would be ok."

LaGrone remembered in the newspaper piece, "We were always prepared to play when we were on that field. During the 1962 season we were set to play the final regular season game against Pampa on a Saturday, so Mayfield and several of the other coaches went to scout our first round playoff opponent that Friday night. During that night a heavy fog caused Mayfield and the coaches not to be able to get back in time for the game which led to a junior varsity and a middle school coach to lead the team during the game. But we were so prepared in what we were expected to do that we came out and were able to get the win."

Mayfield also allowed his assistants do their job, with Berry saying, "He would break the team into groups and let the assistants do their job working with us one-on-one while he walked around and watched what we were doing and then talk to the coaches and move on." Webb agreed with that statement saying, "He was well organized and would allow us to do our jobs. He would never correct us on the field or in front of the kids and would always talk to us in a way that was just like a normal conversation." When asked if Mayfield would be considered the best head coach the Bulldog program has had, all four men seemed to agree with that statement, with LaGrone saying, "Mayfield was the best coach I ever played for because he taught me not only a lot about fundamentals of football, but also about life." Loftis added, "He instilled a work ethic in players to where you didn't take shortcuts, which I believe is what made his teams successful."

BORGER FOOTBALL 1958

[I asked some of the guys who played football at BHS to share a couple of memories for the book. **Gordon Beamguard, BHS '60**, fullback, provides these memories.]

This event occurred during the 1958 Bi-District football game between BHS and the Wichita Falls Coyotes played in Borger, Texas. That year, Wichita Falls was ranked #1 in the state and Borger had just won the first District Championship Title in our school's history.

Jim 'Corky' Dawson was the quarterback and I was the fullback. The game was very hard fought with the half-time score, WF 6, BHS 0. In the third quarter, the Coyotes kept hitting me at the line of scrimmage and standing me straight up after gaining a yard or two. Corky started telling me in the huddle to lateral the ball back to him after I got hit. Corky claims that he told me twelve times before I finally got the picture. Wait just a minute! I think he only told me eleven times. Anyway, Corky called Slant [47] Left, again I got hammered at the line of scrimmage. As I was falling toward the ground, I managed to lateral the ball back to Dawson. Corky Dawson tore down the left side of the field dodging and weaving past several Coyote tacklers to go 55 yards for a touchdown. The extra point was missed. The score was tied at 6-6. We ultimately lost the game 12 to 6 although we were on the Coyote's one yard line when time ran out. Wichita

Falls went on to win the State Championship beating all of the remaining opponents by margins of 30+ points.

After the game, we were discussing Corky's long run. Corky asked me why he had to ask me so many times to lateral the ball back to him. My answer was, "Well, the coaches always told me that a fullback was nothing but a guard with his brains beat out". The coaches' statement was affirmed the next year. They moved Billy Ray Kidd from guard to fullback!

#2 story of memories

1959 – We were playing the Harvesters in Pampa. There was a long history of heated competition between the players and fans during Borger-Pampa games. That year was no exception. Pampa had a pretty good team but we were beating them without much trouble.

Pampa had some excellent players on their team that year. One of their biggest, most touted players was Benny Stout [appropriate name]. Benny Stout was a shoe-in for 1ST Team All-District and expected to make 1ST Team All-State.

Anyway, Merle 'Buddy' Harrington had gone one-on-one, head-to-head, with Benny Stout for about 3½ quarters. It was a bitter, bloody battle. By that time, Harrington was getting pretty tired and very frustrated with the monster Stout who was showing no mercy to any of us. On one particular play late in the game, Harrington was back about five yards off the line-of-scrimmage when he saw Stout get hit by a couple of our guys and fall straight forward, face-down, with both arms completely extended in front of his body. Buddy, not to miss an opportunity for a token of revenge, quickly dashed the five yards against the action of the play to 'accidentally' step/stomp on one of Benny Stout's out-stretched arms. Stout certainly knew what happened but he never saw who did it. The play, however, was vividly portrayed on film.

Back in Borger, we reviewed the game film at the field house. When that play came up, Coach Mayfield ran it over and over and over [at least 10 times] while the coaches and the rest of us were rolling in the floor, reeling from laughter! It was absolutely wonderful!

<u>FINAL SCORE</u>:

BORGER 28 - PAMPA 0   HARRINGTON 1 – STOUT 0

Borger Bulldog Football stories: by Merle (Buddy) Harrington

In the summer of my junior year, e.g. 1960, **Larry Dyke** was supposed to come by my house and pick me up in his old white 1951 Ford. I don't remember what we were going to do and it doesn't matter. I got tired of waiting on him and drove my ancient 1952 Ford over to his house and found him busy trying to change a flat tire on the front driver's side. You have to know, Larry knew nothing from nothing about cars.

He had managed to get the car up on the bumper jack and had removed the tire. When I drove up, he was having a problem trying to put the spare tire on. Fortunately, Ford engineers had planned for guys like Larry, and the fender was designed to keep you from installing the tire backwards as he was trying to do. I interceded and turned the tire around and helped him install the lug bolts. I told him to take if off the jack and proceeded into his house to wash my hands.

I heard the car door slam and Larry fired up the engine and proceeded to back the car off the jack! The force of the car coming down off the jack propelled it thru the redwood fence that was immediately in front of his car. I came running out to see what had happened and noticed the bumper jack impaled in the broken slats of his parent's fence.

You see, Larry didn't know there was a lever on the jack that allowed you safely let the car down by jacking it......I don't know how he explained the damaged fence to Dr. Dyke and Martha (his mom).

SECOND STORY

John McDaniels and I were team captains for our 1960 football game with Lubbock Monterey. The game was played in Texas Tech's large stadium and, as captains, John and I had the honor of leading the team out onto the field at the start of the game.

As you'll recall, the Borger cheerleaders lead the team onto the field and John and I followed them and sat down on the bench. We were busy clapping our hands and talking about how we were going to beat them when we noticed Monterey players coming out of the tunnel at the opposite end of the stadium and they were beginning to sit down on 'our bench'. We looked up to see our entire team across the field.

You see, John and I had mistakenly followed the Borger Cheerleaders to the wrong side of the field......I must say, that run across the field to join our teammates was the longest run I've ever made in my life. I was trying to think of some way of covering my number up but alas, they were too big....we were recognized!

We were humiliated and it must have been an omen as we ended up losing the game.........That's enough for now. I have other stories but they are so despicable, decorum prevents them from being repeated in public.

Coach Mayfield: the man behind the action, submitted by Dickie Meyer—BHS Class of '59, now living in Amarillo TX

I have only one regret about playing football for Gene Mayfield----I was a senior when he arrived, and only got to play for him one year. I had many meetings with him after my high school football experience was over in Borger High, as he asked Corky Dawson and me to scout football spring training games at various cities in the Panhandle. He was already planning way ahead for the next year.

Coach Mayfield was a very unique person, and had a very unusual coaching style. I can't remember him ever raising his voice or screaming at his players. I had a lot of coaches, and he was the only one who never hollered at me, or anybody else I can remember. He even gave us a little water to drink, and ice to suck on sometimes, during practice. Not like other coaches of that era, he made out schedules for our practices, and pretty much stuck to them. I remember him calling the team together a couple of times, and telling us that since we were not hustling and paying attention, he was ending the practice session. He sent us to the showers early. It worked...the next day we had a great practice.

Coach Mayfield introduced us to the dreaded 3-a-day practices at the beginning of the school year. All the other coaches only had the dreaded 2-a-day practices. Those of us who survived thought we were pretty damn tough, and perhaps we were. We did good!

Coach Mayfield introduced us to lightweight football shoes. All week long we practiced in old heavy clogger cleats, and on game-day, he put us in feather light shoes that made us feel like we could fly. After Corky Dawson and I graduated from BHS, we went to school together at West Texas State University. Coach Mayfield attended some of our games, and visited with us before and after the games. It made my day.

Coach Mayfield had lots of great players during my senior year in high school, and they were mostly seniors, but not all of them. Our senior football captains, who were elected by the players were:

Jim Harper------ went on to Texas A&M, attending on a football scholarship
Corky Dawson-----Went to WT, led the Buffs to a Sun Bowl victory, and served in Vietnam as an Army pilot.
Joe Kidd----- Went to college on a football scholarship and got a degree in Engineering.
I think my facts are accurate, but I have destroyed billions of brain cells since then? Other good guys that Coach Mayfield counted on to make a great team were:

Bobby Jack Spencer------ Kent Connelly-------Billy Rash--------Gordon Beamguard-------- Bobby Landis--------- Jerry Drake-------Buzzy

Baker--------Dennis Holt-------George Young-------Tyler Collins------- David Hogg-------Dale Keith------Cotton Lamb-------Phillip Parker----- -Issac Robinson-- (I think the 1st black player to graduate from Borger High)-----Gerald Schroeder----Phillip Harden---John Ward---- Jeffry Wilcox-----and probably many more.

We had so many great players, that you were afraid of getting hurt, as the coach would just run in another great player, and you might lose your job. It was a memorable year, in 1958-1959. During the summer before I was a Junior, we scrimmaged Littlefield in a preseason game. They kicked the hell out of us. We were bigger, stronger and faster. They won! The next summer, Gene Mayfield was our coach. That's when I found out about charisma and leadership, and how a coach can actually influence performance on the field. Some things cannot be described in words. It's kinda like auto racing---You gotta be there !

For his career, Mayfield posted an overall record of 178-71-8 that includes an impressive record of 62-13-2 during his time in Borger. Mayfield's time in Borger lasted a little under 10 years, but their no doubt that the impact he made in the football program and the community is still alive and well today.

Footnote from **Joe Kidd**:

I also remember the first time Coach Mayfield sent us to the showers for a bad practice. We were undefeated and had scored about 50 points per game and were feeling very cocky. After he called practice and walked off the field, I don't think anybody moved for about 5 minutes. We couldn't believe it, we should have been running sprints. He got our attention and we finished out a great year.

Gene's type of football was just like he always said when asked "How did you win with no big name players?" He said " Have you ever had a team when you had a player that if you had 11 just like him you would win? Well, I've got 22 just like that." That's how I remember the Borger Bulldogs Class of 58-59. I could talk for hours.

My Unforgettable Football Days - MARVIN G. CASEY, Class of '62

It was a cold day in the fall of 1961 and we, the Borger Bulldogs were leading the Pampa Harvesters 66 to 0 in a one-sided football game. I was playing left guard, which was right next to the center, Melvin Gibbs, (who is also my cousin) and was responsible for blocking the defensive inside linebacker.

In a weak moment I asked the opposing team's defensive player if he would like to tackle the quarterback. He excitedly responded "yes"! When Melvin Gibbs snapped the ball and the play started, I moved to one side letting the defensive player have free reign to smear our quarterback, Jimmy Brooks. Returning to the huddle, Jimmy Brooks asked "What the hell happened Marvin?" I explained how I would feel if I was that poor player that hadn't successfully made a tackle the whole game. For some reason, Jimmy did not appreciate my sympathy play.

Sunday (following the game) we were having our weekly chalk talk and reviewing films of the previous game and there was one other person who did not appreciate my sympathy play. Coach Gene Mayfield got to the spot in the film that showed my play and he replayed that scene over and over and over. In my already humiliated and embarrassed state I was shown no mercy as Mayfield asked "What happened Marvin?" I explained that "the guy had not made a tackle all day and I felt sorry for him and let him through. I made his day!!!" But that cute little incident ruined my Sunday at the field house. (It seems coach Mayfield did not have the same sympathetic feeling for the other guy.)

A Class Act: by **Billy Ray Kidd & Gordon Beamguard**

In 1959, Borger High School might have had the best football team in the district, but we had stumbled in an earlier game falling 22-21 to Lubbock Monterrey.

The final game of the 1959 season was played against the Amarillo Sandies in Borger. That year, the Sandies had won the District Championship by virtue of their win over Lubbock Monterrey. Borger High School's head coach was Gene Mayfield and the Amarillo Sandies were led by the legendary Coach O. A. 'Bum' Phillips. The Sandies were expected to beat Borger, but we had other ideas. At the end of the day, with the great direction of Borger coaches, Gene Mayfield, Leldon Hensley, Gene McCanlies, E. J. 'Jeep' Webb and Roy Lee Dunn, the Bulldogs had beaten the Sandies 22-8.

After the game, we were in the field house still shouting and yelling, reveling in our victory when Coach Phillips marched straight into our dressing room. Everyone was very surprised to see him. The room became quiet. At that time, it was unheard of for a losing or a winning coach to come into the opposing team's dressing room after a game. Coach Phillips proceeded to walk around inside the field house shaking hands and congratulating each of the Borger players. It was one of the finest acts of class and good sportsmanship that the Borger players ever witnessed.

Coach Phillips went on to become a famous head coach in the NFL for the Houston Oilers and later for the New Orleans Saints. Coach Phillips retired from coaching in 1985. Coach O. A. 'Bum' Phillips is definitely a class act.

REMEMBERING GENE MAYFIELD. By **Glenn Baxter**, BHS Class of '63

It was 1963 when I graduated from Borger High School as a shy young man. I remember Gene Mayfield, the mild mannered coach of the Borger Bulldogs football team. In my mind he fit the mold of a Tom Landry.

Mayfield was a quiet man and a man of integrity. He didn't need to lie, curse or brag to be a winner. He was a straight shooter who inspired a team of young men to be Class 4-A State Finalists. In my Borgan Annual he wrote, "Outside of often being tardy, I hardly knew you were in Study Hall. Seems like you were always busy. Come to think of it, I was tardy about as much as you. Best wishes for Happiness. Coach Mayfield." He probably never knew how his presence inspired a student in his study hall class.

I would thank Coach Mayfield today for the example he set for me and others. The shy kid with sweaty palms and shaky knees in front of a high school speech class grew up. Today, I'm seldom tardy and have learned to be outspoken in my convictions and beliefs.

Throughout my life there have been other Coach Mayfields. I recall a private meeting with Trammell Crow dealing with a corporate brochure we were producing. I asked him how he would describe his company in one sentence. He replied, "Son, we are nothing but a back woods Camelot." Mr. Crow was referring to "Camelot" as related to John Kennedy. Funny thing was that few people knew about Trammell Crow at that time, The Trammell Crow Company owned more real estate property worldwide than any other developer. Trammel Crow was a quiet man like Coach Mayfield.

I'll never forget the embarrassing moment in a board room trying to present a multimedia slide presentation. We had convinced our client, Justin Industries to purchase a new $3,000 projector. My staff spent months producing this presentation to meet a deadline for stock analysts in New York City. We made a practice run by playing the presentation beforehand in our offices.

We set up the presentation in the client's board room. John Justin (Chairman of the Board) and 4 other corporate officers entered the room and took their positions at the table. I pressed the play button and nothing happened. When I looked at the expressions on faces surrounding me, I regressed to the kid with the sweaty hands and shaky knees. The President's temper was going ballistic. Mr. Justin calmly got out of his chair walked down the length of the table where I was standing and simply said "Just call and have a technician come here to fix the projector." Problem solved.

A proud memento I have today is an ad with a headline, "What Winners Wear". John Justin is sitting in a chair wearing a cowboy hat and Justin Boots. Surrounding him are George Strait, Randy White, Jim Shoulders, Dale Earnhart, and Nolan Ryan...all wearing Justin Boots. The ad is signed, "To my friend Glenn. Best regards. John Justin.

John Justin has passed on. He was a man like Coach Mayfield and Trammell Crow. They were all straight shooters. Their successes came from inspiring others around them through examples of honesty and integrity. Each one of them was a winner leading winning teams. Gene Mayfield died in Lubbock TX on October 2, 2009, of complications from Alzheimer's disease. He was 81 years, 8 months and 1 day old. It was a loss to the many men who knew him, were mentored by him and inspired by him. According to his obituary "His reserved and gentle nature delivered a calm and respectful manner when directing his players. Players and coaches through the years have shared with family members his ability to inspire and change their lives by leading them to meet their potential."

Other Coaches at BHS

Coach Jeep Webb [interview with Frieda Lanham Pickett, 2008]

I asked Coach Webb to write a historical account of when he came to Borger and why. We ended up talking at his home as I interviewed him. He still was living in Borger, right up the street from where I lived from the fourth grade through high school.

Coach Webb came to Borger in April 1958 with Coach Gene Mayfield and Gene McCandlis. Roy Lee Dunn was already in Borger and joined the coaching team. Coach Webb taught World History to sophomores at BHS. When asked how he came to be associated with Gene Mayfield, Coach Webb said he was at Littlefield with Mayfield when they got the invitation to come look at Borger. But the association was way before that... Mayfield was a graduate from West Texas State University playing at the quarterback position and Coach Webb played football for Mayfield as a graduate assistant. Coach Webb remembered that Borger had good football players in the early 50s, namely **Bubba Hilmon, Kenneth and Mark Clapp, Howard Pilcher, R.C. Dalton, Philip Wright, Lloyd Reynolds, J.D. Covington and Bobby Covington, Leon "Corky" Chapman and Roy Lee Dunn**. All these Borger people played at West Texas State University in Canyon.

Coach Webb described coming to Borger in the Spring of 1958 and looking over the players' abilities. They saw there were some good players to work with. The coach has a good sense of humor and it was displayed as he recalled a parent of a player who had been kicked off the team the previous season. The parent asked Coach Mayfield to allow his son to try out for the team. At the first scrimmages this parent stood up in the stands across from where the coaches were standing. He had a booming voice and the coaches listened as he yelled from the stands "Can these people teach football? Are we paying these guys?" The next week they stood on the other side of the field so they didn't have to listen to his "commentary". Coach Mayfield replaced Coach Willard when he came. Coach Willard had kicked several players, including John Ward, off the team for breaking rules... all of them were good players. **John Ward** was allowed to rejoin the Borger team and went on to get his degree at Colorado, doing so well in his adult life that he purchased his parents a new home in Borger. "This is the mark of a fine

young man with good values and respect for his parents." replied Coach Webb as he reflected on their decision and the young player.
When asked what he considered to be "a most memorable moment" he immediately said, "Well, for sure the 1958 District Championship we won! It was the first time Borger had won the district...ever!" He remembered the star quarterback, **Corky Dawson**, who led his team to this outstanding victory, although they lost in bi-district, it was a huge success for this new team of coaches. He recalled that Coach Mayfield ordered red blazers for coaches and players to wear on Fridays, to encourage team and school spirit. One of the low memories was when the team played Snyder, the first game of the season, and the coaches had to watch a great player, **Isaac Robinson**, be barred from staying in the motel with the other players and being forced to eat in the kitchen at the restaurant, due to the extreme prejudice against his race. They had to go all over Snyder to find him a place to sleep that night. Coach Webb said Isaac didn't seem to be bothered much by this rudeness, but the coaches had very heavy hearts as they could not protect this fine young man from the insults. He continued reliving these early years in Borger and mentioned that the next to last game that season they lost 6 – 0. **Buggs Fincher** was the bus driver and usually played a radio letting the boys listen to the latest Top Ten tunes of the day. Coach Mayfield said "No radio allowed so the boys can focus on what went wrong tonight!" The next week the team beat an Oklahoma team, then the first district game they beat Palo Duro 14 - 7. The season continued successfully as they beat Monterrey in the last seconds to win district. They went to Wichita Falls that year and lost 12 – 6 but winning the remaining games by 30+ points. Wichita Falls went on to win state that year. Coach Webb went on to describe that Borger went to state in football in 1962, losing to Breckenridge San Antonio. Although he was no longer at Borger during this time, he kept up with the team activities. He felt Borger would have won the championship if their star players were not hurt. The star BHS running back was out due to injuries (**A. C. Tilmon**) and couldn't play. They moved **Robin Harrington**, the JV back, up to take his spot. **David Dillingham** was an outstanding player, going to O. U. after graduation. **Wayne Rape** and **Joe Robinson** played on this state championship team with **Joe Cofer** playing the full back spot. This was over 40 years ago and Coach Webb could recall these players' names and the positions they played immediately...what a memory!
Coach Webb recalled that he stayed at Borger for two years, then went to Canyon High School to take the Head Coach/Athletic Director position. He stayed there five years and a highlight of that experience was that he started a girl's basketball program. Then he went to Pampa High School, coaching football and track. He was there one year and J.C. Knowles, Superintendent of BISD, called to lure him back to Borger. He replied that he had just gotten to Pampa and wasn't likely to make a change so soon, so Dr. Knowles asked him how much he was making. Coach Webb thought that was a strange question, but told him the amount. Dr. Knowles offered him $1,000.00 more...well, that was pretty good incentive! So in April 1967 Coach Webb came back to Borger, staying there until he retired in 1996. He taught

football and boy's track, adding girl's track, cross country track and girl's basketball programs. He rotated between Freshman coach and varsity coach, taking whatever needed to be managed in the school system. My sister, **Kim Lanham**, was a cheerleader when Coach Webb was at Borger during this time. She had great respect and admiration for him and still does to this day. One of Coach Webb's most inspiring moments was when one of his students, **Terry Bob Moore**, told him he felt Coach Webb was responsible for his achieving his degree and fostering his start in adult life. Terry Bob played football and ran track at Borger. He was Student Council President at BHS. When he went to a regional track meet he got into trouble. Dr. Knowles said he could not represent Borger at the upcoming state meet. Coach Webb knew there would be scouts at the state meet and how much it would mean to Terry Bob in securing a scholarship in college. The Coach met with Dr. Knowles almost every day the week before the names of Borger's runners had to be submitted to convince him to "forgive and give the youngster another chance." Well, Coach Webb was successful, Terry Bob went to State and got a scholarship at the University of Texas—Austin. Terry Bob later expressed his gratitude by starting a scholarship at BHS in Coach Webb's name. The Outstanding Athlete Award was established and named after Coach Webb. Coach Webb is now retired from faculty responsibilities, but still remains associated with BHS, driving a school bus. In fact, the day of this interview he was making final plans to drive the Borger Band to Austin for the state competition, leaving at 5 AM Sunday morning...what a commitment! Coach Webb also has maintained his association with organized sports. He is in charge of the Press Box at football games and keeps the clock for basketball games. He is an official in track and field events (officiating in an event in Hawaii recently), on the Jury of Appeals, a referee at Waylon College Conference - 3 A and 4 A, and participates in officiating at the A. A. U. Jr. championship decathlon. Last year he officiated at the Western Athletic Conference Championship in discus and javelin. He definitely is not sedentary in his retirement.

Coach Gene McCanlies

Students at BHS said Coach McCanlies had a strange habit of putting his middle finger on a misbehaving student's forehead and "thumping" him. I'm sure it motivated many to "get to work" and follow the rules in class. McCanlies and Gene Mayfield were coaches at McCanlies' alma mater in Littlefield in 1956 before moving to Borger in 1958. Weldon Hensley joined them. In an interview with the sports editor in Midland Odessa Coach McCanlies recalled the day they decided to make the move from Borger.

"Coach Mayfield had come to Permian in Midland a couple three times," McCanlies said. "He had been invited to look at both OHS and Permian, because both were open at the same time. He came back a time or two and said, 'Man, they've got some good looking athletes, but I still don't know.' He hadn't decided, but he took it, then the next thing we knew he turned it down. He said, 'No, I'm not going.' So Hensley and I went to the movies. When we got out of the movies, he called and said, 'Coaches, if y'all can do it, we're going to Odessa to Permian.' So we decided to go. In the spring of 1965, Mayfield was offered the job at Permian, and McCanlies/Weldon Hensley made the move south with him. McCanlies finished his coaching career there, having much success. He coached baseball, football and other sports, as needed.

Coach Jake Halter and Math Teacher Extraordinaire

Submitted by the family

A true rags to riches story, Jake was always grateful for his young start with discipline and education at the Presbyterian Children's Home in the Texas panhandle. Handsome, athletic, and smart, he won the hearts of many, as he excelled as Pampa High School's salutatorian and football star. He fell for Frances, twin, beauty, and dancer. They lived a great love story, and we all loved watching them dance. After serving in the Pacific campaign in World War II, Jake won a scholarship to the University of Tulsa in Oklahoma, lettered in 4 sports, and earned his Master's degree from the University of Texas. He began his coaching career in Claude, Texas, as the coach: football, boys' and girls' basketball and everything else. 1951 was the first year that girls' basketball came under UIL, and his girls were the first Class B state champions. He and that team were honored in 2001 at the state tournament in Austin.

His players and math students all loved and respected him, especially the ones from his years in Borger, who dedicated their school annual to him, and continued to stay in touch over the years, sharing their appreciation for his teaching of self-respect, an attitude of positive expectations from dedication and hard work, honor and duty. He wasn't much for sympathy; his players, students, children, and nephews remember his saying: "Come on, get up cowboy (or cowgirl), you're not hurt." He lived and taught excellence without excuses or whining. The young guns tried to beat him in tennis, and he would lure them in by making it a close game, and then always put away the win. After leaving Borger, Coach Halter taught in the Amarillo school system and ultimately left teaching, moving to Austin TX area.

Being a rugged individualist, he and Frances tried several ways to increase their income over the years, from partnering in a camper business to "trying" to sell resort real estate at Lago Vista on Lake Travis. He was extremely shy, his face turning bright red when speaking to a crowd, but with his shy smile and twinkling eyes, he would speak one-on-one to anyone and everyone. They became independent business owners, building a team of entrepreneurs, still coaching and teaching...only in a business setting, and in four years created a "walk-away" income that has afforded them a wonderful lifestyle of golf and tennis, living in Bentwater on Lake Conroe. They have made great friends here, who have been so thoughtful these last years; his tennis buddies including him and watching out for him up until just a few years ago when he quit playing. His church family and their business team and business leaders from all across the country have been so dear.

He loved his students and athletes, and his family and wife, Frances, appreciates you all. Coach Halter has now passed away but is remembered with much respect.

Coach Halter by Bill Zajicek

"Teacher, coach, and gentleman" were the words that described Coach Jake Halter by the Class of 1958-1959 when they dedicated their class annual (The Borgan) to him. He has been married to his college sweetheart, Frances, for many years. Jake attended Tulsa University where he lettered in four sports: football, basketball, baseball and track. He was an outstanding punter in that he averaged over 41 yards per punt. He also played in the backfield for the Tulsa Hurricanes. After his years of coaching, he became a successful businessman.

Although Coach Halter is known for his coaching, his main success may have been his algebra class. Making an A in Algebra II was sweeter than making a touchdown or game winning goal. I believe his algebra class stirred the minds of students, unaware of what they would later do in life. He made you think, which gave you confidence to overcome the challenges ahead. It was not uncommon for him to have students who were failing in class over to his home in the evening to go over the lesson. If one thought the basketball and football players had an advantage, they could not be more wrong. He taught like he coached: get the most out of the students and show no favoritism. I know in my case, he was one of the teachers who influenced me and gave me the foundation to be an engineer. Coach Halter had the respect and trust of his students. This was shown when he was traveling with the teams. He had a unique idea for stimulating interest in learning in that he appointed row captains who would see that those in their row would keep up with the lesson or homework, and provide tutoring as needed.

Coach Halter coached the basketball B team and had some unique methods for getting the team in shape. I remember running up and down the bleachers in the old gym. The bleachers were the type that were locked at the bottom, and after each game were folded back like an accordion. Anyway, while we were running up and down the bleachers, the locks gave way and the bleachers folded up leaving most of the players hanging by their arms and legs. No broken bones, but a lot of bruises!

In the summer months, we worked out in the field house behind the junior high school. I remember one practice where we not allowed any water during practice. I never understood what this accomplished, but we got around this by soaking our towels before practice began, and sucking the water from them during practice (ah! Ingenuity of little minds). Gordon Beamguard tells me that they did the same thing on the football team and remembers the time Coach Halter told Gordon, who was the starting fullback, that "a fullback was nothing but a guard with his brains beat out."

I remember one practice that followed a basketball game the night before in which we had missed a lot of lay-ups during the game. To make a point, Coach Halter had us line and shoot lay-ups. If you missed the shot, you immediately went over to the table where the coach was waiting with the paddle with the holes in it! As you might guess, our lay-ups got better quickly!!

Coach Halter's record speaks for itself. The B basketball team for the class of 1959 had a record of 21 wins and 5 losses with 2 wins over the arch-enemy, Pampa. This team was led by **Tracy Cox, John Kent, James Wilson, Don Seamster, and Frank Schaffer**. The B team of 1959 again reflected Coach Halter's coaching skills. They had a record of 14 wins and 2 losses. This team was led by Frank Schaffer, with help from **Jeff Levine**. As you can see, Coach Halter's teams didn't lose many games! I think the reason for his success was the effort he was able to get from his players and the discipline he required to excel in what you did.

A little more about **Frank Schaffer** . . . . he tells the story that before he even thought about playing basketball, he went by the gym to pick up a friend. He got Coach Halter's attention when he walked through the door since he was about 6'8" tall. The average height of the players then was under six foot. Under the coaching of Coach Halter and Coach Hanna, Frank developed his skills to the level that he went to West Texas State on a basketball scholarship for four years. Frank had to endure the dreaded paddle in practice, and he was often put up against a superior basketball player, **Warren Tipton**. As stated earlier, Frank met that challenge and became a good friend of Warren's. Frank tells how his class schedule was adjusted by Coach Halter and Coach Hanna so that he could practice at the end of the day. This resulted in Frank having to take English under Mrs. Vogel which was intimidating, but rewarding.

In one game even Coach Halter's skill as a coach would not produce a win. This was the game where we played the lowly community of Hedley. We showed up in our shiny Bulldog bus... the Hedley players came on tractors and in pickups. The stage in the auditorium was the basketball court. Out of bounds were the walls and the open space in front of the seats. Needless to say, we were not used to such tight conditions and lost to a team we would have easily beaten on our own home court. We left Hedley hurt and beaten, and a little better prepared for unique situations.

Coach Halter got the most out of his players because they respected him. This respect carried on after graduation. Coach Halter and his wife Frances attended several of the reunions over the years where they more than kept up on the dance floor! Also he and Frances attended one of Gordon Beamguard's famous "Borger Parties" here in Denver. You could see the respect shown for him when talking about the years at Borger High. He still is the gentleman whom we all respect, and his smile will always be remembered. Frieda Lanham Pickett tells of Coach Halter attending the 20th

BHS reunion of the Class of 1961, asking for a partner to enter the "jitterbug contest", Frieda volunteering to be his partner, and them winning with a tie, sharing the win with Phillip Hardin and his wife. Dick Weddington made the point that "Frieda wore high heels and Phil's wife danced barefooted! The coach outdanced everyone of us!"

Larry Dyke: Football memories by Buddy Harrington

I remember the incident when Larry was injured during practice. I was with Larry on the sideline after he walked off the field. Coach Jake Halter was a Christian Scientist and didn't believe in doctor's care, much less believe Larry was really hurt. Larry gutted it off the practice field and was later taken to the hospital for X-rays....and low and behold, he did have a break....I think it was his ankle, as opposed to his leg but not sure of that. He did end up with a knee high cast....

Our coach's were not too well versed in diagnosing injuries. I remember spring training of my sophomore year when I got my right middle finger caught in **David Boyer's** helmet. The finger was headed in a complete 45 degree from the rest of my fingers. I think it was Coach Webb who decided it was simply dislocated. He had another coach hold me and he proceeded to pull on it as I almost passed out.....talk about "hanging tough...".

The coach's decided it was more serious, and told me to go to the doctor to have it looked at. I was sent (with no help) to the field house and had to pull my jersey over my shoulder pads with only one good hand. Anyone who has ever played football knows how difficult that is, even without a broken finger. By the time I had showered and changed into street clothes my whole right hand was purple and swollen beyond recognition. I drove myself to the emergency room (with my left hand...and it was not dominant) at the hospital and had to patiently wait on Dr. Henry Hamra to show up, about an hour later. X-ray's revealed the finger was broken in three places. Dr. Hamra had a fit when I told them what the coach's did in their attempt to "pull it back into place". After the swelling went down a few days later, the famous 'fruit finger' cast was fitted to my right hand. It made it very easy for me to greet friend and foe alike over the next 8 weeks!!! My right middle finger still has a rather noticeable angle to it. How we ever survived our football years is beyond me!!!

Basketball and Golf

Playing Golf and Basketball at Borger High School

by Elgie Seamster

I would have to say that Borger High and Borger, itself, was a special place for me. The opportunity to play on the outdoor basketball courts and to caddie at the Huber golf club were a blessing, as were the many other benefits that come from living in a small town. One notable big benefit was that two major corporations provided so many opportunities for their employees and family members.

I grew up out at Bunavista, the Phillips plant town, so many of my Borger memories are connected to the guys that I grew up with there and who were my sports heroes. Lots of these guys were really good basketball players A few that I remember are the following: **Mac Carter, Jim Morgan, James Scott, Max Miller, Alvin Pausell, and Warren Tipton**. Most of these guys made All-State First Team in their day. Other older guys from Borger that were my heroes were **Jack and Don Kaplan, Gerald Myers, Red Hooper, and Keith Lane**. Coach Hanna always told me that Gerald Myers was the best player he ever coached. Gerald went on to become athletic director at Texas Tech.

Jack and Don Kaplan, both older than I, would let me tag along with them to play any outdoor sport. Don was a special person in that he would not only practice for hours, but would also always find the time to help me with my game. After he left Borger, he played on the Texas Tech golf team from 1954-1958. At Tech he was a part of the team that won Tech's first Southwest Conference title in 1958. He then went on to play on two Texas Cup teams. To this day I think **Don Kaplan** was the best golfer to ever come out of Borger. It was sad to see him pass away at the age of thirty-three from systemic lupus, an autoimmune disease. I think of him often and wish we could have had more time together. His brother, Jack, still lives in Borger, and we stay in touch.

In 1958, the year I was to graduate, we had four good golfers on our team: **Vance Moxom, Jerry Abbott, Don Seamster, and myself**, We went to the Texas State High School Finals in Austin, Texas and lost by two shots to Austin High School. The game was played on their home course. I was the individual medalist state champ at that tournament. In addition, all four of us received athletic scholarships for our college educations. ...not too shabby for the boys from Borger!

Now for a little more of the story about each of us.

1. **Vance Moxom** had a great talent, and to this day is a good golfer. Vance played basketball AND golf at Texas Tech University and became a golf professional in Cleveland, and in Florida.
2. **Jerry Abbott**, who lived two blocks from us, played golf at the University of Tulsa. He went on to play on the PGA Golf Tour with lots of success in the early seventies. Later, he went to work for Bo Wininger at the Desert Inn Hotel in Las Vegas.
3. My brother, **Don Seamster**, played basketball and golf at Hardin Simmons and then went to law school at University of Texas. He has lived in Abilene all his adult life and practices law there. We are very close and play golf together every chance we get.
4. I went to University of Houston my freshman year on an athletic scholarship for both basketball and golf. What I quickly learned at

Houston that year was that there just aren't enough hours in a day to play TWO sports and still have time to study and be able to graduate! Therefore, I accepted a golf scholarship from North Texas and graduated from NT in 1963.

We would never have had the success we had in golf without the help of Borger businessmen we caddied for, and also for golf professionals, including **Joe Houck at Huber Golf Club** and **J. T. Hammett at the Phillips Golf Course**, who spent hours helping us with our golf games. We are forevermore indebted to them and their generosity. I remember one day while I was a caddie for Mr. Bill Barton, he engaged me in a conversation and asked me if I wanted to be successful in life. Of course, I said that I did. He responded by telling me to always remember to say "Thanks, please, yes sir, May I help you? etc." I probably haven't always done it, but I often think about the wisdom behind it and will always be grateful to Mr. Barton for the best of advice.

Basketball was my winter sport of choice, and **Coach Tex Hanna** was my mentor, as well as my coach. He demanded seriousness and discipline and would not put up with any foolishness! As a sophomore in the 1955-56 season, I remember our first team meeting. His advice was the following: If you want to be a member in good standing with this team, you need to do these 4 things.

1. Be in church on Sunday morning.
2. Respect your parents.
3. Make your grades in school.
4. Be a leader and set good examples for your classmates.

He always made me feel as if I were a part of his own family. I knew I could always go to him for advice. Playing for him was a joy and he was truly a life-long dear friend to me.

Some of my fondest memories of Borger sports were not only the games, but the bus trips. We had really cool buses, not the normal, old yellow school buses! We had great "42" games, music, and of course, homework on the bus for those of us who didn't quite make straight "A's." I think we all looked forward to practice at 2:30 PM daily. (I know I did.) On holiday breaks I would go to Coach's house for the gym key and invite a few friends to play. It sure did beat the outside court! Can you imagine being allowed to use the school facilities for personal pleasure??? Of course, we cleaned up and left it just as we found it! Some of the boys who joined in were **Warren Tipton, Jackie Coffey, Vance Moxom, and my brother, Don**. We usually had 5 or 6 guys show up anytime the gym was opened.

One feature that made basketball fun was... winning! From the 1956 season through 1958 season we split wins with Pampa on home and home bases, but lost two play-off games. The one game at Pampa in 1958 hurt the most. We lost 60-58, missing two "one and one" free throw attempts in the final seconds of the game. It was a hard loss to accept. Although winning would not have changed by life, I still think about that game today. The 1960 Borger Team went to the state basketball finals, and my brother, Don, played on that team. It broke my heart when Borger lost in the last seconds of the game in Austin. Of course, again it was in Austin; and, of course, again it did not change anything in my life or my brother's life, BUT WE STILL BOTH REMEMBER!

Esther Bryan "Tex" Hanna

Submitted by family

Coach E.B. "Tex " Hanna coached boys in basketball and golf in Borger. He was inducted into the Panhandle Sports Hall of Fame in1959 as the golf coach division winner. He was very popular with the boys he coached and was a great motivator of young men. He was also very altruistic, helping those less fortunate than he in many ways. Coach Hanna grew up in the Borger school system, moving to Borger when he was 12 years old. His family was poor, like most people in Borger and he lived in a two-room, half dugout house, working in a local bakery, at a local grocery store and washing dishes in a café. Tex was washing dishes in a restaurant one day when the truant officer saw him and realized that Tex was not attending school. That was the end of Tex's full-time job as a dishwasher and the beginning of a lifetime career in education. Chances are that his hard life as a child is why he had so much empathy for others that were having trouble in their lives.
Upon graduating from Borger High School in 1934, Esther attended Amarillo College on a scholarship, where he played football under Windy Nicklaus. He later attended Altus Junior College and went to the University of Florida, where he played football as a Florida Gator for three years. He was what was known in those days as a "crashing fullback". This position resulted in his getting his nose broken numerous times resulting in the unique Tex Hanna nose. He graduated from Eastern New Mexico University and served as assistant coach there. Later, he received his master of education degree from West Texas State University.

After his marriage to Marjorie Dennis on July 6, 1941, they moved to Borger and Tex worked for the Borger Independent School District as a coach and teacher. Marge's twin sister married Firman Haynie, another school teacher and administrator in the Borger school district. This job did not last long as the military obligation found him serving overseas in the Battle of the Bulge and as a tank commander under General Patton's command. He served in the Army until March 1946, and then returned to Borger. He and Marge made their home in Borger and raised their three sons. Tex worked again for Borger ISD as an assistant football coach, golf coach and later the head basketball coach of the Borger Bulldogs.
During that time, the Bulldogs won or shared district six times and three times they advanced to state. In 1966, he became the assistant principal for Borger High School. He retired from BISD in 1984, but returned immediately

to serve as part-time attendance officer until 1998. During all those years, Tex Hanna spent endless hours encouraging and helping young people who needed a strong arm to lean on. He often took his own time and finances to help many disadvantaged families in this area making sure they had their children in school and that they did not have to do without utilities and the necessities of life. When necessary, he went to his friends or local organizations to get financial help for anyone who desperately needed it.

Coach Hanna not only worked hard, he played hard too. He spent countless hours on the golf course. His tee-off time on Sunday was 1 o'clock and the preacher had better not preach too late. He always bragged that in golf he could shoot his age and finally, as he grew older, he could shoot below his age.

He also loved playing dominoes and played them for many hours upon retirement. His pastimes brought him many friends. He was especially close to one group of friends that met each Friday and ate lunch together at Lorene's Mexican food restaurant. They called themselves the "Mafia," but were truly a group of good hearted, fun, loving, generous gentlemen.

The family of Tex Hanna dearly loved him. Family gatherings were always looked forward to with the anticipation of food, fun, jokes and good times to be had by all. Many times those gatherings included well loved aunts, uncles and cousins. For years, Marge and Tex, the three boys and their families worshiped together each Sunday taking an entire row on the north side of First Baptist Church.

Finally, life's journeys sent the families on different paths. Tex always said that once the family left home, he and Marge just sat and waited, listening for the car doors to slam announcing the arrival of some of the kids coming home for a visit. Those visits will always be cherished memories by all the Hanna family. There were three boys, and all three boys were good students, good looking and popular. They are Bryan, George and Randy.

The life of Tex Hanna yielded many accomplishments and awards. He was Basketball Coach of the Year in 1960, Texas School Administrator of the Year in 1977, and was inducted into the Panhandle Sports Hall of Fame, again in 1984. In 1983, the new Borger High School Gymnasium was dedicated to E.B. "Tex" Hanna. He was elected to serve on the board of directors for Cal Farley's Boys Ranch and for the Board administering Girlstown in January 1990. He was the longest serving basketball coach at Borger High School, having 414 wins and only 111 losses.

He was athletic director of American Legion Texas Boys' State for 45 years. He was honored with a resolution from the Texas House of Representatives for his contribution to Texas Boys' State in 1990. He was submitted for the "Seven Who Care" award in 1993 by Juanita Kitchens. In 1997, Borger

Chamber of Commerce named Tex *Citizen of the Year*. Coach Hanna died September 18, 2004, at 90 years of age and was buried in Amarillo.
Note from Frieda Lanham Pickett:
"Mrs. Marge Hannah was well known by kids in Borger in the 50s and 60s. She often was present at the ball games and she ran a kindergarten and day care from her home for over thirty years. Since her sister was married to Mr. Haynie, our principal at high school, and they had two daughters in the Borger schools (Prudence and Priscilla) we all knew them. Marge died January 30, 2009 in Amarillo, age 87."

My Greatest Memory Playing Basketball at BHS
By Jeff Levine '61

It was my Junior year at BHS and I made the first team in basketball. The MIDLAND HIGH SCHOOL BASKETBALL TEAM had the reputation as the best team in the state in 1960. Midland had already easily beaten the BORGER BULLDOGS twice this season. Also known as the Purple Giants, Midland was to play Borger once more to see who advanced to state. Word was out that Midland was so confident that they already made reservations in Austin. A funny thing happened to Midland on the way to state.... BORGER 56 MIDLAND 55

I still think this is one of the biggest upsets in TEXAS HIGH SCHOOL Basketball. BORGER went on to play Austin High in the semi-finals. Borger was ecstatic! Buses were reserved and took a full load of students and others to Austin that year. There were not enough hotel rooms available so the hotel cut a special deal with BHS administrators and put cots out, side by side on the Conference Room floor, top of the hotel, maybe 50 to 60 cots. Students slept there after the game.

What still haunts me to this day...with less than 10 seconds in the game, Borger ahead by 1, Austin took the ball, went the full length of the court, made two passes, and then shot the ball. The ball hit the rim, bounced up on the backboard, then FELL THROUGH THE NET AT THE FINAL BUZZER ... AUSTIN 52 BORGER 51. I still think the Timekeeper was a homer...BUT SO AM I.

Officially BORGER placed third in state that year. Maybe **SAMMY SMITH, DON SEAMSTER, JOHN KENT, FRANK SCHAFFER, TRACY COX OR VERNON WELCH** remembers that heartbreaking game, too. TEX HANNA, our coach, was named BASKETBALL COACH OF THE YEAR IN THE PANHANDLE SPORTS HALL OF FAME FOR 1960. It was overall a very good year.

BASKETBALL AT FRANK PHILLIPS COLLEGE 1958-59

Author anonymous

My freshman year at FPC was all about playing basketball on a full athletic scholarship. We had a bunch of mediocre players from Borger, Pampa and Phillips who, under the coaching of **Bud Simpson**, achieved the impossible. By playing together as a team with no stars, having fun and being unselfish, we won the Regional Tournament and finished as the No. 12 team in the nation at the National Junior College Tournament in Hutchinson, KS. We became the first FPC team to reach that goal.

The next year our team was built around one person, **Warren Tipton**, who graduated from Borger High School in 1958 winning all state honors. I was well aware of what Warren could do on the basketball court, having been on the same team when we were in high school together. With the possible exception of **Gerald Myers**, Warren got more out of his athletic ability than anyone I ever knew. He was less than fleet of foot and at the height of his jump shot you couldn't place a playing card between the bottom of his shoe and the floor, and yet he led his team in scoring and rebounding year after year.

One particular game comes to mind when I think of Warren. We were scheduled to play a new junior college in Lubbock, at the customary starting time of 8 pm. Our usual pre game procedure included showing up in the city where the game was to be played several hours early, check into a hotel and relax for a couple of hours. After a pre game meal we would be at the opponent's gym an hour or so before game time to get suited up and go through our warm-up drills.

We had a brand new athletic bus and were headed to Lubbock when Coach Simpson, who was also the bus driver, decided to take a scenic route through Palo Duro Canyon. All went well until we started the steep climb out of the canyon. We had no transmission. Everyone tried to push the bus and we managed about fifty feet. Coach thumbed a ride to the nearest town, Silverton, after giving us strict instructions to stay in the bus and get some rest.

As soon as he was out of sight we exited the bus and enjoyed Palo Duro Canyon...up close and personal. He returned in about an hour with an oilfield truck, which promptly hooked onto the bus and managed another fifty feet toward Lubbock. Back to Silverton to call for help from Borger. This time his instructions to us were a little sterner... but ignored again.

A couple of hours later here came the cavalry in the form of the Borger High School bus. We climbed aboard, most of us completely exhausted from exploring the terrain. Many of us had bloodied hands, elbows and knees from our afternoon outdoor adventure.

The pre game meal consisted of two oranges and two Hershey bars picked up at a roadside convenience store near Lubbock. We were only thirty minutes late for the game, which was held in a grade school gym (the new college gym was unfinished). Score was kept on a blackboard and we had no visible clock to guide our play.

Although we had no pre game warm up drills we could do no wrong during this game. Almost every shot found the basket, our energy level was unbelievable and our defense had our opponent completely out of sync. Without question it was the most perfectly played game I was ever involved with. **Warren** had more points by himself at halftime than the entire other team. Every game we played on the road after that, we requested that we detour through Palo Duro Canyon.

Later that year we played a game in which we were three points behind with four seconds to go. I had two free throws and somehow managed to "squirrel" in the first one and then called time out. I asked Warren on which side of the basket he wanted me to miss (like that was something I had under my control), and he smiled that little sheepish grin he always had in pressure situations and said "It doesn't matter, I'll handle it!" He did and we won the game in overtime.

Warren and I shared very different "lifestyles" but when it came to playing basketball our goal was always the same...winning. I must admit he was much better than I at getting it done. He will always be a reminder to me of what a person can accomplish with hard work, determination and a ferocious will to win. Warren lost his life at an early age from rheumatoid arthritis.

Ch. 14 Outstanding Borger Graduates

Borger has produced many individuals who have gained success in their adult lives. Some who have achieved national or international honors are included here.

John Bayless, child prodigy, composer, famous pianist

[from John Bayless website] Born and raised in Borger, Texas, John Bayless won a scholarship to the Aspen School of Music at age 15, and two years later moved to New York to study with Adele Marcus at The Juilliard School of Music. He started to play piano by ear at age four. His mother, a singer and musician, was his first teacher and guided him to learn to read music with daily practicing. At BHS students would ask him to play a popular song of the day and he could do it from hearing the song and played it "his way". John's childhood heroes were Leonard Bernstein and Liberace. At age 13 he was the youngest church organist in the State of Texas, playing for his hometown Baptist Church and for services at the Synagogue in Amarillo. When he was 15 he won a scholarship to the Aspen School of Music where he met and first studied with the legendary Adele Marcus. At 17, he was off to New York City to attend the Juilliard School of Music and further his study with Ms. Marcus who shaped his musical gifts and encouraged his extraordinary ability in improvisation.

John was invited to participate as a composer in the inaugural class of New York University's Musical Theater Masters Degree Program where he studied with Leonard Bernstein, Julie Styne, Arthur Laurents, Betty Comden and Adolph Green. Maestro Bernstein was particularly intrigued with John's talent at improvisation and composition and a lifelong friendship ensued. John was artist in residence for the London Symphony Orchestra's Leonard Bernstein Festival, performing at a gala for Queen Elizabeth II. He also served as Associate Conductor for the 1981 production of Leonard Bernstein's Mass at the Kennedy Center.

As a performer, both solo piano and with orchestra, his extensive background includes appearances at Carnegie Hall, Lincoln Center's Avery Fisher Hall, Tanglewood, Wigmore Hall in London, Philadelphia's Academy of Music, Davies Hall in San Francisco The Hollywood Bowl and London's Barbican Center. He has appeared with the Philadelphia Orchestra, Boston Pops, San Francisco Symphony, and New York Pops among others. He created special programs for The New York Philharmonic and the Cleveland Orchestra, performed at New York's Mostly Mozart Festival, The Budapest Spring Festival, made four tours of Japan, toured England and America playing *Rhapsody in Blue* with The Royal Liverpool Philharmonic Orchestra, and has frequently concertized in Italy and Germany. Over the past nineteen years John has performed literally hundreds of concerts across the United

States from Hawaii to Maine. Rosemary Clooney invited him to be her guest artist, performing on her pops concerts and her famed Christmas shows. He has been featured on many television and radio programs including NBC's Today Show and Garrison Keillor's A Prairie Home Companion.

As composer and performer he has received commissions from The Newport Music Festival, The University of Maryland International Piano Competition, The Virginia Waring International Piano Competition, The Metropolitan Museum of Art, and from PBS, where his music can be heard on many series and specials. As a teacher John has conducted Master Classes at Juilliard, Kent State, Dennison University, University of Houston and The Royal Academy of Music in London.

A prolific recording artist, John's numerous CD's have been at the top of the Classical and Classical Crossover Charts since the mid-80's and many are still available today. His best selling collections include, Bach on Abbey Road (one of the top ten best selling albums of the 1980's), Bach Meets The Beatles, Romantica, The Puccini Album (Billboard Magazine's #1 top selling album for 19 weeks), The Movie Album, Circle of Life, Christmas Rhapsody, and West Side Story Variations.

In 2001 the legendary Rosemary Clooney invited John to be her guest artist for several pops concerts at performing arts venues in the United States, including a performance with the San Francisco Symphony. One of the highlights of the year was appearing in Ms. Clooney's famed Christmas Shows at the Orange County Performing Arts Center in Southern California and at Feinstein's Supper Club in New York City. He has conducted Master Classes at the Juilliard School of Music, Kent State University, University of Houston and The Royal Academy of Music in London.

In 2008 John suffered a stroke which put his career on hold for awhile. Through a series of chance encounters that began in the stroke rehabilitation unit at Desert Regional Medical Center, Bayless was invited to serve as composer in residence on the board of the Virginia Waring International Piano Competition. John is composer-in-Residence and serves on the Artistic Committee of the 2011 Virginia Waring International Piano Competition. Currently he is orchestrating an original composition for left hand and he will premiere in Moscow's Tchaikovsky Hall with the Moscow Virtuosi Orchestra.

The biennial competition, which began March 27, 2011, hosts aspiring pianists from around the world for a week of competitions, master classes, and concerts. Bayless is composing two pieces — one for junior and one for intermediate musicians — that he hopes will propel these technically competent youngsters from their comfort zone into a more interpretive frame of performance, stretching the boundaries of the predictable to the improbable. John performs still, most recently at the Newport Music Festival, Newport RI on July 11, 2011. John described to me that he practiced reading music while playing the piano about 3 to 4 hours daily as a child. Playing "by ear" was easy but he had to learn to read music in order to progress in the music industry. His parents knew he had a special talent and did what was necessary for him to get scholarships to prestigious schools.

People in Borger remember John. Here are some memories.

Rita Knowles Kirby Watts '60
My Dad managed Myers Music Mart that was located on the bypass next door to Myers Fried Chicken. Johnny's mother used to take him to the store to play the many pianos on display. He was 4 or 5 at the time and he would always choose a grand piano. I can see him still with a wide grin, sparkling eyes and bright red hair sitting on the bench, feet dangling, playing until his heart was content. He was incredible and we knew he was destined to become a concert pianist. He gave my parents many hours of joy for years to come. He was always welcome to practice there. In the early 60's they closed both Borger operations and my parents moved to Amarillo to manage that piano store.

Odene Floyd Mathis '64
Johnny Bayless began playing the organ in our church (First Baptist) when he was around four years old -- too small to reach the pedals! He actually began playing for the worship services when he was quite young -- 10 or 12, I would guess. The church paid him a salary, which was put into a savings account for him to help with expenses when he attended Julliard. He went to Julliard right out of high school and when he graduated, he was asked to teach a class in improvisation. Johnny was a true prodigy. I once heard him accompany Phil and Andy Dietz who were singing a song he had never heard before. He just asked them what key they wanted it in and was able to follow them because of his innate knowledge of chord progression. This was when he was in high school. He is probably the most talented person to ever come out of Borger, TX.

MARVIN G. CASEY '62 Fire Investigator

I watched a special investigation story on television and saw the story of a rash of fires being set in California. As the story progressed they reported a person who investigated fires came up with a novel theory: the arsonist had experience fighting fires. This led to the identification and capture of the arsonist. When they interviewed the investigator I realized I knew the man. It was Marvin Casey, football star and person who dated my sister, Waynel! I called her immediately and told her to watch the show! Here is his story!!

How did I get from Borger, TX to California, where I am today?

By Marvin Casey

The quick answer is that my Mother bought me a one-way ticket on the train and sent me to California. Was I that bad? No not really. After graduating from Borger High School I went to Arlington State College (now University of Texas in Arlington.) Wow! What a change for a Borger student. I guess I got so involved in the fun, I forgot about studying and that was some pretty expensive playing around. That is how and why in 1964, I got the one-way ticket to Bakersfield, CA.

Bakersfield Junior College had no tuition and I could live with my sister while I worked and went to school. After arriving in California I had several jobs –Working for Newberry's, National Guard in Fort Polk, LA, Back to Newberry's, managing a full buffet restaurant, Manager for 3 variety stores. Then an in-law brought me an application for the fire department that paid good wages and had good benefits, which were very important because, by that time I was married and had two children.

That was the beginning of my career with the Bakersfield Fire Department, August 21, 1967. Like everyone I started at the bottom and worked my way up to Captain in 1979. After 3 years as Suppression Captain of a firehouse, I was interested in more challenging and rewarding work. In 1982 I transferred into the arson investigation department, where I developed and honed the investigative skills necessary to later start my own private investigation business. After retiring in 1995 from the Bakersfield Fire Department, I became my own boss offering investigative services.

With the exception of a couple of cases, listing them would not mean much to anyone who did not live in our geographical area. There are however, two that were well known throughout the United States and those were –

1. The abortion clinic fires in Bakersfield, CA and Houston, TX, and
2. the John Orr case.

In different professions, everyone at one time or another, experiences "significant accomplishments" during the career. Some may have one, others may have many, but we all have one that stands out.

I, as a fire investigator, experienced numerous unique situations. Of those, there are about 8 that fall in the category of "significant" but at the top of the list was what can be referred to as a "career case". I was instrumental in not only finding the evidence, but also identifying and helping to convict one of the most prolific arsonists of all times, John Orr.

Numerous venues have produced TV programs, i.e. Cold Case, Forensic Files, British Broadcasting's Education Channel, Firecracker Productions and two programs yet to be completed. An article was published on the case in the Reader's Digest in June 2002 titled "The Arson Investigator".

In addition, the renowned author, Joseph Wambaugh has written a book titled "Fire Lover", which recounts investigative skills in tracking down and identifying John Orr. This book recounts the events of Marvin's investigation and how he was able to identify from the locations of the fires how this coordinated with a person of interest experienced in firefighting.

NOTE: Thank goodness I wizened up in my later years and got my degree. It was sure a lot harder and certainly took a lot longer than if I had done it when I was younger.

Larry Dyke: Outstanding Borgan and Typical "Bulldog"
by **Frieda Lanham Pickett**

Larry Dyke, master artisan and family man of character, has dedicated his career to capturing the beauty of God's creations. His paintings have been admired by Presidents, the Pope and countless others. Larry graduated from BHS in 1961, finishing his high school years as quarterback of the football team and being elected Mr. Borger High. He went to Baylor University, where he met his wife-to-be, Martha. They were married in 1964 and had two children (Lane, Allison).

Larry was born in Minnesota and moved to Texas with his parents and brother, Jimmy. They lived in Amarillo before moving to Borger when Larry was 3 years old. Larry's father was a prominent optometrist in Borger. His father also had part ownership in Borger's semiprofessional baseball team, the Borger Gassers!

Larry showed his artistic talent in high school where he assisted Mrs. Naomi Smock in designing and making multiple decorations for Jr/Sr proms (and anything else she wanted! Ha!) and hallway designs at BHS. During his high school years Larry worked in the oil fields pulling rods on pump jacks. This must have been strong motivation to get a pathway to success based on higher education after graduating from high school. He applied to medical school, dental school and graduate school following graduation from Baylor University. These doors were not opened. When Larry was accepted into a program for veterinary medicine he realized this was not really what he wanted to do, so he took a job teaching secondary school while he considered his career options. Larry ended up teaching science for nine years in the Clear Creek area of Houston. During this time he began pursuit of a master's degree in education. Larry was dissatisfied with education and tried working as a part-time youth director at his church. He sold insurance, did some coaching, even drove a school bus along with teaching school. During this time Larry had been painting for enjoyment. He and Martha had a son and were expecting a second child. Martha asked Larry to paint some animal pictures for their nursery. Larry got the deed done, but the enjoyment was short lived, as Martha lost the child. The paintings became a painful reminder and when a neighbor offered to buy the paintings, Larry made his first "sale". Larry admits he never took a lesson in painting, but learned by trial and error and his own innate talent. The more he painted, the more he liked his results. Larry views his talent as a God-given gift and has dedicated his work to the glory of Him. His work is always captioned with a scriptural verse that represents the theme of the painting.

Larry's final year of teaching school was 1976. He was 33 years old. It was a leap of faith as Larry felt God's urging to devote his time to art. When he gave his resignation to his principal he was asked what he planned to do. "I don't really know" was his answer and he began painting full time that summer while undertaking an extensive job search. Since he had a small collection of works he was able to place them in the Houston area art galleries on consignment. He struggled with doubts that his work could produce enough income to live on and knew prayer was the answer. When the end of summer came and no firm offers had come forth, doubt and discouragement began to rise in earnest. He applied for another teaching position, this time at Alvin High School. At the height of his despair Larry got a call from a gallery owner in Houston to tell him all his paintings had sold and the owner would like 20 more! It was then that Larry knew God had heard his prayers and answered. While adjusting to the life of an artist Larry found himself asking "Can I really make a living working at something that gives me so much pleasure?" He was fulfilled by his work for the first time in his life and he flourished. For subject matter Larry took photographs of the quiet beauty of the Hill country and began to paint from the photos. He found the vegetation, color and landscape variations as an endless source of inspiration. He disciplined himself to paint for 8 to 10 hours each day of the week, taking breaks only for lunch and necessities. His early years in the classroom and the schedule of making lesson plans had been a good training ground for time management. Larry confesses that he still wonders at the fact that he is able to make a good living "doing what he loves". He realizes that God showed him the way in the story of Abraham who waited 25 years for his promised heir (Isaac). There seemed to be a correlation in that it took Larry about 20 years after high school to decide to use his talent. "Sometimes it takes that long to develop the character necessary for the assignment" Larry explained. "God restored the years the locusts had eaten". Larry is quick to give the credit for encouragement to his wife. She always believed in Larry. Larry is convinced the tragedy of losing a child was the catalyst God used to begin something wonderful. Those first nursery paintings are long gone, but not forgotten. Larry would love to have them back, but he is nonetheless a thankful man and one whose talent has become a blessing to others. His satisfied admirers and possessors of his work are numerous and wider ranged than he could have imagined when he took the leap of faith.

Larry is very proud of his family who grew up while Larry ventured into the world as an entrepreneur. Daughter Allison was born in 1979 and graduated from Baylor University. She is married and has made Larry and Martha grandparents. His son, Lane and his wife had four children before Lane developed a fatal illness.

In 2005 Larry developed a blood cancer due to a malignant tumor in his spleen. His recovery from this medical challenge has been long and hard. Thousands prayed for Larry's recovery and his wife, Martha, was there to encourage and support him in his hour of need. In a sincere and thoughtful letter to his childhood friend, Frieda Lanham Pickett, he writes "I am fortunate to have a low grade lymphoma. The spleen was the source, but of course, I still have the lymphoma cells in the blood system. I may or may not have to take treatment. I hope I can just be monitored, which is a distinct possibility." Larry ended the letter (those of you who knew Larry in school will remember his great sense of humor) with a "cruelty joke". "What did the midget psychic who escaped from jail become?" I had to search for the answer (it was "a small medium at large")! Sadly within a year or so after Larry's bout with cancer his wife died suddenly. He now lives in the Hill Country of Texas and continues painting scenes from that area.

Larry's work can be viewed on the internet (www.larrydyke.com). As one's eyes feast on the beauty of his work, one realizes how fortunate we are to know the master artist and be blessed by his creations. Larry and his work will be a special part of the Class of '61 Fifty Year Reunion as his art will be shown at the Borger museum during the month of the reunion.

G. William Miller, BHS '41,1979-81 U.S. Secretary of Treasury

Submitted by Sandra Zimmerman St. Amand, BHS '62

Many people did not know that the 11th Chairman of the Board of Governors of the Federal Reserve from March 8, 1978 to August 6, 1979 came from Borger TX, graduating in 1941. The Borgan annual shows George Miller (as he was known in high school) as Editor of the Annual and the information by his senior picture says "This clever and quick witted young man aptly adjusts himself to whatever task he undertakes to do—goes in for such varieties as debate, math, chemistry and group singing. George has to his credit such achievements as being Vice-President of the Senior Class, editor of the Borgan, member of the NHS and Who's Who."
Wikipedia has the following information:
11th Chairman of the Board of Governors of the Federal Reserve. In office March 8, 1978 to August 6, 1979, succeeded by Paul Volcker. Born March 9, 1925 in Sapulpa OK and died March 17, 2006 at age 81. He was an attorney. George William Miller served as the 65th United States Secretary of the Treasury under President Carter from August 6, 1979 to January 20, 1981.

Early Life and career

Born in Sapulpa OK, Miller and his three sisters and two brothers grew up in Borger TX. Their father, a businessman, moved the family to the Texas Panhandle town of Borger to start a furniture store during an oil boom. When his business failed during the Depression, his father found work in a local carbon black plant. After George attended Amarillo College for the 1941-42 school year, he received an appointment to the U.S. Coast Guard Academy. He graduated in 1945 from the U.S. Coast Guard Academy with a B.S. in

marine engineering and served until 1949 as a Coast Guard officer in the Far East and on the U.S. West Coast. During his time with the Coast Guard, he married Ariadna Rogojarsky, a Russian émigré whom he met in Shanghai during his Coast Guard service. He received a law degree from the Boalt Hall School of Law at the University of California, Berkeley in 1952, and joined the law firm of Cravath, Swaine & Moore in New York City.
In 1956 Miller joined Textron, Inc. He became a Vice President of the company in 1957 and President in 1960. In 1968 he became Chief Executive Officer of Textron and was elected Chairman and Chief Executive Officer in 1974, a post he held until he came to the Federal Reserve Board. Early in his career, Mr. Miller was credited with turning the small, Rhode Island-based textile-manufacturing company (Textron Inc.) into a global conglomerate. Its goods included Sheaffer pens, Speidel watchbands, Polaris snowmobiles and the Bell UH-1 "Huey" helicopters that were essential military hardware during the Vietnam War.
At the time he joined the Federal Reserve Board, Miller was a director of the Federal Reserve Bank of Boston and of several corporations. He was also a member of the Business Council and the Business Roundtable and Chairman of the Conference Board and of the National Alliance of Businessmen.
From 1963 to 1965 Mr. Miller was Chairman of the Industry Advisory Council of President Kennedy's Committee on Equal Employment Opportunity and in 1966 and 1967 he was a member of the National Council on the Humanities. He was also a member of the Business Council and the Business Roundtable and Chairman of the Conference Board and of the National Alliance of Businessmen. Miller served as a member of the "think tank" Club of Rome. In 1968, he aided Hubert Humphrey's presidential campaign as chairman of a Democratic-leaning business group.

Federal Reserve and Treasury Secretary

Miller was Fed Chairman for just over a year when Carter appointed him Secretary of the Treasury. He was the first Treasury Secretary to come from a corporate background, rather than economics or finance. He inherited a high-inflation economy and his policies did not have an obvious impact. In August 1979, Carter appointed Miller Secretary of the Treasury, replacing Michael Blumenthal as part of a cabinet shuffle. Carter appointed Paul Volcker to replace Miller. Miller thus became the only person so far to serve as both Treasury Secretary and Chairman of the Federal Reserve. As Treasury Secretary, Miller is best known for his role on the Chrysler Loan Guarantee Board, which oversaw management of a $1.5 billion loan to rescue the carmaker from bankruptcy, saving thousands of jobs, keeping people off of welfare and continuing to collect income taxes. Chrysler recovered in the early 1980s, and paid the loan early. Part of his eagerness to help Chrysler was described by himself in an interview where he stated ""If we don't have Chrysler, part of the market for fuel-efficient cars that it could serve will be picked up by foreign suppliers, and we would lose it forever for the United States." Unfortunately Chrysler did not invest in fuel efficient cars and the U.S. has certainly lost much of the automobile market.

Miller had a long-standing commitment to jobs programs and promoted good relations between Carter and the AFL-CIO. Miller is also known for managing the freezing and partial unfreezing of $12 billion in Iranian funds held in the United States during the Iranian hostage crisis. He also pushed through an accord with labor unions on wage-price guidelines that had been "stalemated for months." He was described as "a feisty little guy, with a boyish grin and a broken nose, and that spontaneous, optimistic American attitude that trouble is inevitable but everything is possible."
Miller's plan to improve the economy was to find the fundamental causes of the country's economic problems and attack those. He got Congress to extend unemployment benefits and encourage private investment by cutting taxes for individuals. While Miller was an able administrator, his economic policies failed to contain inflation and had little impact on rising unemployment rates. The poor state of the economy was a major factor in Carter's 1980 defeat by Ronald Reagan.

Later years

After Carter's administration ended, Miller founded G. William Miller & Co., a Washington private investment company and held positions on a number of charitable and nonprofit organizations (American Red Cross, Washington Opera). He served as chairman of the Washington-based H. John Heinz III Center for Science, Economics and the Environment. William Miller died on March 17, 2006 from lung disease.

Bill Dees, Song Writer and Musician

Submitted by Jack Pribek, July 2008

Bill Dees was born in Electra, Texas on January 24, 1939 to Dorine and Beecher Dees. Beecher was a sand and gravel man. He provided for Dorine and the three boys, Val, Bill and Mike, by working a land lease seven days a week. The family moved to the Panhandle area around Borger in 1943. Beecher found a good deposit in Fritch and eventually supplied all of the sand and gravel for the Sanford Dam on the Canadian River that forms Lake Meredith and is the main water supply for North Texas.
Borger was the quintessential boomtown. Bill remembers it as being "hot, and smelling of oil refineries". It was in this "work hard, play hard, when you get the chance" atmosphere that the music bug first bit Bill. Beecher and Dorine would sometimes host house parties attended by the local townspeople and area roughnecks. There was

always a barrelhouse piano player at these affairs and Bill, supposed to be in bed, would hide in the shadows studying the piano man's every move.
Dorine was the one who really got the music rolling though. She started teaching Bill the ukulele and piano at five years old and all three brothers the art of singing harmony. The boys excelled and landed a regular spot on an RC Cola sponsored radio show out of Amarillo. When Bill was in the third grade, he won a gold watch at the county fair for singing his rendition of "I'm A Lonely Little Petunia In An Onion Patch".
At Phillips High School, a music teacher, Mrs. Hubbard, recognized Bill's talent and got him together with four other students, **Bill Baker, Eugene Richmond, Melvin Webb and H.F. Ritchie**. The ultimately formed the **Five Bops**, a singing group. The Five Bops enjoyed local success, playing high school dances and clubs. Word spread and in 1957, renowned producer, Norman Petty, invited them out to Clovis to record. They cut two songs at the session, H.F. Ritchie's "Jitterbuggin'" and Bill's "Unforgotten Love". Dees described Petty, who played organ on the latter as being, "serene and laid back". "Jitterbuggin'" became a regional hit and, on the strength of airplay in Amarillo, the boys were offered the chance to open for Roy Orbison at a couple of shows in Wichita Falls and Amarillo. Orbison, who had yet to reach anything like household name status, was a known entity in that part of Texas and Bill was a fan.
The next year, the two crossed paths again. The Bops were now going by the name **"The Whirlwinds"** and went to an Odessa TX radio station to cut another record. Upon pulling into the parking lot, the boys spied an orchid colored Cadillac. It turned out that the regular recording engineer was sick and Roy Orbison was there to fill in for him. They cut two songs that night, H.F.'s "Angel Love" and Bill's "The Mountain". The bands harmony and songwriting ability impressed Orbison. After the session, he invited the boys to a late night, truck stop breakfast. At one point, both Orbison and Dees were reaching, at the same time, for sugar to put in their coffee. Roy noticed Bill's work hardened hands (from spending many hours swinging a sledgehammer for Beecher at the sand and gravel plant). Roy, always impressed by a strong work ethic said, "Do you really work that hard?" To which Bill replied with innocent honesty, "doesn't everybody?" Looking back at that night Bill said; "I don't really know how to explain it but, in that one moment, that one little thing, I knew we had made an instant connection."

The record from the session was never released and soon, the band fell apart. Bill continued to write and play what gigs he could find.

Harmonica man Dan Woods recalls that he and Bill would set up "most anywhere" for an impromptu performance. Dan also remembers that some of the things that Bill would play were early versions of songs that later resurfaced, completed or re-worked including, "Borne On The Wind", a song inspired by a true story of a man who drowned while trying to save his two children.
In 1962, Roy Orbison played a show in Borger. Bill, who was now married and faced with supporting a family, was in between jobs. He found out that there was a party after the show and, the rumor was that Roy would attend. Bill crashed the party, re-introduced himself to Orbison who, as it turned out remembered Dees, and asked him if he was still writing. Bill sang what he had on "Borne OnThe Wind" and Roy must have liked what he heard because a couple of weeks later, Bill got the call to come to Nashville and write with Orbison. The session was productive, if not immediately lucrative, and yielded, most notably, a finished "Borne On The Wind". At this time, Orbison was still co-writing a string of hits with Joe Melson. The next year, Orbison produced Bill as a singer, with the Bob Moore Orchestra, on three tracks, "Blackie Daulton", "Summer Love" and "This Is Your Song", recorded at the RCA Victor studio in Nashville. The sides were never officially released. Bill went back to Texas and, after working a series of odd jobs, trying to make ends meet, in early 1964 made the decision to move to Nashville.

Now, some people might think that the idea of moving to a strange city, with no solid prospects, in the dead of winter, with a wife and four kids would be a huge risk. However, Bill has always operated on faith and, he was chasing a dream so, he packed up a 1955 Pontiac, given to him by the aforementioned Dan Woods, and headed for Music City with the family in tow. What he didn't know, at the time was, that Orbison had just cut "Borne On The Wind" and, though it wasn't released in the States, it was on its way to #4 in the U.K. Dees knew that he was going to pursue working with Orbison in some fashion but he was bound and determined to find gainful employment, establish a foothold, before he looked Roy up. He got a job running a tow motor in a warehouse and, a second job as piano man in the house band at The Palm's nightclub on Dickerson Road.

Roy was surprised to see him when Bill came knocking on his door but, the two quickly settled in to a productive writing partnership. Over the next few years Orbison/Dees was the credit on 67 songs that Roy cut (he also released a few that Bill wrote on his own; "Sleepy Hollow" is one of the better known). "It's Over" was released in April, 1964 and went top ten in the U.S. and to #1 in Britain. Bill recalls hearing the song on a transistor radio several times a day while driving the tow motor. The song firmly established Orbison and Dees as a songwriting team. The method was similar to what they did on "Borne On The Wind". Bill came in with a song he had been working on, Roy dissected it, and together they re-invented it. "It's Over" continued the use of unusually sophisticated melody and chord structure that the pair had developed. Bill would often play a baritone ukulele and Roy would play guitar in the writing sessions. Bill says that using the uke enabled him to find different chord sequences that he would play on guitar. Fred Foster, the founder of Roy's label, Monument Records, and a brilliant recording engineer, pulled off a monster of a session on "It's Over". Using the full Bob Moore Orchestra (36 musicians), they did over thirty takes of the song. Bill recalls that he went to see Roy the following morning and found him sitting Indian style, in his pajamas, listening to a two-track reel-to-reel mix of the song, and grinning from ear to ear. He had been up all night listening again and again.

1964 was turning out to be a good year for Bill Dees but, he had no idea how good a year it was going to be. He had a solid hit record under his belt, but money was still tight. He was able, however, to get an advance from publisher Acuff-Rose to buy some furniture for the small apartment in which the family was living. Meanwhile, he continued to work and write with Orbison. The writing was evolving. Orbison had a true partner in Dees, for Dees has a remarkable voice of his own. If Bill had a melodic or phrasing idea, he could demonstrate for Roy, in Roy's range. Bill, thanks to those early lessons from Dorine and an uncanny natural ability, could also sing harmony on top of Roy's lead part. Both were big fans of the Everly Brothers and they were experimenting with that style of two-part harmony but taking it to new places, in terms of both chord structure and range. Then, one afternoon that summer, the magic happened. The story has been told many times. This is the way Rolling Stone had it in their "500 Greatest Songs of All Time" issue. Orbison said he told Dees to "get started writing by playing anything that comes to mind... My wife came in and wanted to go to town to get something." Orbison asked if she needed money. Dees cracked, "Pretty woman never needs any money." The rest was easy. They wrote the bulk of the song "Oh, Pretty Woman" before Claudette returned from the store. When Fred Foster heard the song, he told the guys that they needed an ending. Dees says, "We wrote most of the song in a matter of minutes, it took us a day-and-a-half to get the, 'What do I see, she's walking back to me.' part." When, producer Wesley Rose, first heard it, he thought that they should cut the song without drums in order to preserve Orbison's image as a balladeer. Luckily, that logic didn't win out.

The record was the right combination. All of the components, the vocal, the drums, the riff, the bridge, the ending and Foster's mix worked. One key part, that went un-credited, was Bill's harmony singing. The record which by the way, was a recent addition to the Library of Congress National Recording Registry, would not be the same without that part. Things moved fast and furious. Bill says, "We wrote the song on a Friday, the next Friday we recorded it, and the next Friday it was out." Roy, getting ready to hit the road, asked Dees, "Are you still working at that warehouse?" Bill was, and Roy said, "If you can get your hands on an electric piano, over the weekend, you won't have to go back to the warehouse on Monday".

Incredibly, one of the first gigs Bill did with the Candyman was the Ed Sullivan Show. The show, at this time, was a huge deal. Orbison needed a hit record, the British invasion was coming and this one show, was almost a make or break situation. Orbison, Dees and the band delivered a flawless performance and the record blew up. At one point, it was #1 in 22 countries during the same time period. Bill had gone from being unemployed in the hard country of the Texas Panhandle, to co-writing and singing on both sides of the biggest record in the world (On the flip side, "Yo Te Amo Maria" Orbison and Dees actually switch parts and Dees sings lead on the chorus), in a matter of months. In addition, he was a member of the road band of one of the biggest acts in the business. Bill toured with Roy for more than a year, going to Europe twice and appearing on shows with The Beatles and The Rolling Stones.
Some now consider Roy's 1967 feature film, "The Fastest Guitar Alive", universally panned by critics, a camp classic. The soundtrack album was the first record to feature Bill Dees' name on the cover and collectors seek it today as well. After these few prolific years, Orbison and Dees moved on. There was no official break-up. In 1986 Roy and Bill reunited in Malibu and once again got down to the business of writing songs together. "Windsurfer", which appeared on Roy's "Mystery Girl" album, came from those sessions.

In 1971, Dees moved the family to Ozark, Arkansas. Once again, the move defied conventional wisdom. Out of sight, out of mind was how Music City operated and Dees was taking a risk by taking himself out of the loop. In 1990, was the year that saw the release of the huge blockbuster, Richard Gere, Julia Roberts movie, "Pretty Woman", that, of course, featured the song "Oh, Pretty Woman". The movie has become a part of the popular culture and only furthered the status of the song in that regard. In October of 2006, the Rock and Roll Hall of

Fame had a weeklong event celebrating the life and music of Roy Orbison that included "An Evening With Bill Dees". It was a festive atmosphere that brought Bill some long overdue recognition. Dees has continued to write songs, perform and record songs.

Ch. 15 Roy Orbison comes to Borger

Frieda Lanham Pickett ('61)

In 1962 when Roy Orbison performed at the Dome, our local band, **The Arcades (John Henderson, Kent Tooms, Joe Atherton, JP Jones**), opened the show and we had a great time dancing. Sharron Chambliss won the prize of dancing with Roy by selling the most tickets to the event. Sharron was a GREAT dancer, but Roy wasn't! It was Bill Dees (from Phillips) who co-wrote **Pretty Woman** with Roy and Bill sang harmony on the record. Anyway, when Roy Orbison came to Borger the entire community came out to see him, even many parents! I remember jitterbugging with Durwood Williams (great dancer) and Larry Fletcher (another great dancer), and, well, anyone who asked me! Ha! What great days "growing up in Borger".

"Oh, Pretty Woman" is a song which was a worldwide hit for Roy Orbison. Recorded on the Monument Records label in Nashville, Tennessee, it was written by Orbison and Bill Dees. In 1964 the song sold more records in its first ten days in release than any other 45rpm single in history.

Orbison posthumously won the 1991 Grammy Award for Best Male Pop Vocal Performance for his live recording of the song on his HBO television special *Roy Orbison and Friends, A Black and White Night*. In 1999, the song was honored with a Grammy Hall of Fame Award and was named one of the Rock and Roll Hall of Fame's 500 Songs that Shaped Rock and Roll. In 2004, *Rolling Stone* magazine named it as one of the "500 Greatest Songs of All Time.

Larry White '64

One of the ministers of the church I attended at Second and Deahl streets was Jack Orbison, a cousin of Roy Orbison. I remember a sermon or two about song's lyrics of swinging and swaying hips and such. Quite funny at the time because we all knew who Jack was talking about.

Ch. 16 The Big Snows in 1956, 1964 and "Black Dusters"

By Bob Holmes '64

Talking about snow...do y'all remember the huge snow, backed up by wind in about 1956 that had drifts up to the roof line. I was living in Phillips then, and we couldn't get out of one side of our house. The other thing about snow I remember was making "snow ice cream", a favorite at our house, but....you had to get out there and get the snow before it had a fine coating of black on it. Damned carbon black. The last interaction I had with Carbon Black was when I was in college and had a job working at the scrap yard along the railroad tracks. I was cutting torn down steel plating into smaller pieces with a cutting torch....it was 110 in the shade, everything around me was black, absorbing heat and me with a cutting torch. (Now I live in Las Vegas, just about the same, huh?).

Another weather memory: Who remembers the "black dusters" also from the mid-50's? Again, out in Phillips, I remember breathing through handkerchiefs (about as old as the buggy whip) and it was actually dark outside at noon. I remember standing under a streetlight, only once in a while being able to see it, looking straight up, to tell that it was "on" and it was. I think that happened twice. What a strange thing. Haven't seen anything like that since...or even heard of it (except from pics from Iraq).

On **February 2, 1964**, a great blizzard was in progress across the Texas Panhandle. This blizzard ended on the 5th, dumping 26 inches of snow at Borger, 23.8 inches at Miami, and 23.5 inches at Claude.

Eddie Derr -- '65
I vividly remember the Great Blizzard. My Dad and uncle had a garage / wrecker service. They took one of the wreckers, and welded wheels together for a 'home made duelly'. Then my Dad went to Lewis Hardware and bought a 'spool' or large chain. I helped them as we custom fit the chains around the custom duelly tow truck, had to take the fenders off. It was a successful venture (and quite creative I think), as we even pulled other wreckers out of the snow. My sister, Marcia ('59), remembers a big sled on the back of the truck and dad driving around Borger, calling all the kids who ran out to see them to "Get in!" and pulling them all around Borger! FUN! That was all before cell phones, and 2 way radios. Funny thing that some may remember, we had a couple of old car hoods that we turned up side down, and used them as sleds in the streets, pulled by whatever would go. I thought it especially interesting that school was called off, but there we were riding on 'car hood sleds' in BHS parking lot. Those were the days, my friend.

Richard Cornelius '66

'64 snow storm memory-School was let out early on Monday due to the forecast of 6-8 inches of snow (Dan True's TV forecast). After heavy overnight snow and wind, all school activities were cancelled (including our basketball game in Amarillo) for Tuesday. When it kept snowing they closed the school the rest of the week. Funny thing, Tex Hanna expected us to be at basketball practice Tuesday. We had the game in Amarillo on Wednesday even though the roads were bad and the Friday game went on as scheduled. Dan True was on air the next few days in a China man disguise, saying "Honorable Dan go to China where weather more predictable". The snow had drifted roof high in our back yard.

Don Chase '64

Someone mentioned the big snowstorm of 64. I, like most of our 60s timers at BHS, remember this day. I was in Ms. Lane's English class when it really started to come down and at the back of the room a window was cracked and snow was starting to blow in. The kid in the back row by the window had some snow blowing in on him through the big spaced chicken wire window screen and put it down. Ms. Lane (bless her old heart) walked back and put the window back up and said "You people need to know that it is winter and it will be cold and snowy". After a while the kid, freezing, got up and put the window back down. Ms. Lane didn't say anything, possibly because she never noticed he did this. I hope Glen Eldridge is reading this. He knows who the "kid" was.

Edith Guynes (Twyla's sister '61)

I remember a snow storm in 1964. My children were 2 and 1 at the time and they loved all 26 inches. The drift in front of the house was taller than they were. The car was blocked in from behind for at least a couple of days. I still smoked then, and I remember rummaging in the car ashtrays for cigarette butts, since I was out and it took a while for one of the neighbors to walk to the nearest store on the corner of Union and Wilson St. Our house was built in an 'L' shape with the open side on the southwest. The snow banked up clear to the eaves of the house in the corner.

Bobbie Green Barton '64

Re the snow storm of '64. Many people were stranded in their own homes, as well as on the highways. My brother rode horseback during the worst of the snowstorm to deliver medicines, milk, baby formula, & many other essentials. Residents were calling the police department to ask for food or medicines. All the other services in the city were already stretched to the limit. The fire department used their biggest trucks and water trucks for rescue. If anything was mobile and had enough ground clearance, it was put into service.

Reminds us how people stuck together back then. We knew our neighbors well enough to know when they might need help. And those were the "good old days" which we could certainly use again.

Frieda Lanham Pickett, Class of '61

Well, it is interesting reading these accounts of the big snow and wind that caused huge snowdrifts. I don't recall the year, maybe '54, but I was still living in Borger at the corner of Takewell and Country Club Road and there was a drift about 9 or 10 feet tall blocking the road to the golf course. It ran from the Voet's house across the street to our house, blocking CCR. My step-father, Wayne Lanham, worked at the Borger News Herald. He walked to work that day (well, I believe he was walking and some city vehicle picked him up and drove him on to the newspaper on Main street), but when he returned home later he had some food. That had to be the '57 snow!

Judy Hardy

The year of the big snow-our house was covered up to the top of our roof with it and my Dad and other's dug a tunnel out from our door to the walk way so we could get out of our home. They also went and helped others in our neighborhood. We did not have church that day I remember. I was 15 years old I think at that time. We seemed to think it was real neat since we did not have to go to school. I believe, but do not know for how long that was, probably not for long. I also remember making snow ice cream but we had to sometimes take the top part of the snow off and get the snow under it because carbon black would be on top of it! ha I remember having to take clothes off the cloths line one winter because it was so cold and they were so frozen stiff you could stand them up --my brothers had lots of starch in their jeans!
I have told these stories to my family and friends over the years and they just look at me like I'm spinning some kind of Texas yarn.

Susan Parker Miller '64

I remember several huge snow storms but the one that is even more memorable for me was February '64. My Dad and a number of other men with pilot licenses did food drops to people stranded on the highway. There were a number of deaths. The blizzard was one of the worst in the Panhandle according to my Dad. I think it was one of those with little warning, very strong winds and lots of snow.

Ch. 17 The Day it Rained MUDBALLS....

Cleo (McGraw) Morrison Class of 1949
I have been reading your different comments about the famous Dust Storm of the 1950's. So I took a trip to the Borger Public Library according to The BORGER DAILY HERALD it happened on the 19th of February 1954.

Headline reads: **DUST STRANGLES PANHANDLE**
Sub title : WHO'S COMPLAINING ABOUT CARBON TODAY?

Sue Schmitz '55....

In our senior year (1954) the dust storm was so bad they announced over the PA for the boys to wet their hankies and give them to the girls and then for the girls to tie them over their faces and for the boys to wet the fronts of their shirts and pull them up over their noses. Next day they had the fire department come and hose down the high school building.

I was born in Borger in 1936 and my mother said it was so dusty in those old tar paper shacks they had then that she wet a sheet and put it over my crib...when it got muddy she would put a clean one on me and wash that one. It doesn't get much worse than that....and I was an asthmatic baby.

Fred Payne '62

Now this one I remember. It started raining while the dust was in the air, next thing I know we had mud falling from the sky, I remember my Mom came to school to get me yelling and crying that the world was coming to an end. I've never seen her so frightened.

Take a peek below--

Frieda Lanham Pickett '61

Yes, it was very dark when we got out of school that day. I was at Central Elementary. It was the first time in my life that it was dark (like midnight) when I got out of school. I remember it was raining and I got spots of mud on my clothes. I heard kids at school laughing and saying "It's the end of the world!!" And I wondered "Really?" My father picked me up that day at school (usually I walked home), then we picked up Linda, then down to Gateway Elementary to get Waynel. Kim was not in school,

I don't think. Anyway, the next morning it was better. They said it was dust coming down from Kansas where they did not farm properly.

BOBBIE GREEN BARTON '64

YES, IT WAS 1954. I HADN'T LIVED IN BORGER VERY LONG. THE TEXAS PANHANDLE WAS QUITE DIFFERENT, AN ALIEN WORLD TO ME. WE LIVED ON HARVEY STREET. MY BROTHER AND I WALKED HOME FROM SCHOOL THAT DAY. IF MY MEMORY ISN'T PLAYING TRICKS ON ME, BIG FAT RAIN DROPS STARTED TO FALL BEFORE WE COULD GET HOME. OF COURSE, THE RAINDROPS WERE MUD BALLS BY THE TIME THEY HIT THE GROUND. I GUESS I'VE SEEN IT "RAIN" EVERYTHING BUT CATS AND DOGS. I GOT PELTED BY SMALL FROGS AND SMALL FISH ONCE, BUT THAT WAS LIVING NEAR A LOT OF WATER. SEEMS THE CRITTERS WERE SUCKED BY A WATER SPOUT, TRAVELED OVER LAND AND CAME DOWN AS RAIN.

Mary Bess Moore '64

I remember Helen Hunter lived across the street from Central and her dad coming to take her home after it started raining that afternoon. He had mudballs on his slicker. Danny and Carol Ann Cornett's mother had taken my brother and me to school that morning. Mrs. Cornett had to follow the tail lights ahead of her and hope they were going the right direction. My mother hung wet blankets over the doors and windows to keep out the dust. That wasn't the only time she had to do that. My uncle was in the Air Force and was home on leave. He picked us up after school. At 75, he can remember the exact dates he was home on leave during his 20 year career.

Mike Crouch 58

I think it was in the early 50s when we had the huge "black dusters" which were so strong and thick a person couldn't see but a few feet in front of their face.....I think we endured several of them.......I remember my mother stuffing dishcloths and towels in all the cracks of the windows to try to keep the dust out (didn't work because the dust was so fine and the windows of our house in Coronado Addition didn't fit all that well...and she did not have enough towels)......you could see the dust clouds coming in from the north and west (the awesome sight of the approach of those clouds). As I recall, on occasion, they lasted for a couple of days.

We had recently moved to Borger and that was the closest we came to leaving, until my parents finally moved to OK in 63.

Wayne Renfroe, '62

I remember that dust storm. I was in 5th grade at Phillips Elementary. My mother's surgery had to be canceled that day. The school served us oranges for lunch. I also remember another time when we had dust, rain, and hail all in one day. I think that was the same time my sister wrecked her 56 Pontiac on the highway between Amarillo and Dumas. She was 13 years older than I and working for Phillips in Cactus. The Panhandle of the 50's had unpredictable weather, and probably still does.

Mary Lynne Bishop Tiner '64

I remember the dirt blowing so hard I couldn't breathe and then it started raining. Everything in Borger was covered in red mud. It took Daddy over an hour to get from his lab to Huber School to pick us up because he couldn't see the road. They closed he schools in Borger but buses didn't run that day.

Danny Stephens '62

The school buses didn't run after school; some moms/dads picked us up, but others couldn't get there and some kids had to stay at the school overnite.

Our poor old house in the Patburg Camp was so "leaky" that we had to shake our sheets to get the dust off of them before going to bed at night. A couple of rooms in the back of the house had newspapers glued to the wall for wallpaper - no insulation or anything, just some boards and newspapers.

Mike Harrington, Class of '65

Cleo McGraw Morrison's post triggers my memory that I lived through two dust storms during elementary school. She's cited the first: February 19, 1954. I was in Mrs. Parris' First Grade class at Central Elementary. But there was a second such storm the next school year, 1954-5, and I believe it's that *second* storm that also involved the "mudball" rain. Coming back-to-back in consecutive school years, more than 50 years ago, it's little wonder that the two dust storms are easily confused today.

Ernie Lollar '64

Ernie tells the story about the big snow storm that he was quite the entrepreneur. Once he had cleared his folks' yard and the cars, he got a snow shovel and hit the neighborhood clearing drives and sidewalks for $5.00 a yard , worked all that day , broke one shovel , bought another and worked a couple of more days. By the end of the storm he had $5.00 bills coming out all his pockets. He also tells stories about playing baseball in some of those dust storms when the game would be called because you couldn't see from the mound to home plate.
My parents were stationed in Wichita Falls in the early '50's and mom has talked about having to rewash diapers she had hung out to dry because of the dust storms. I do not remember because the diapers were mine (HA!HA!). It has been fun reading the stories. I've learned a lot of Borger history. I can understand why all of you have such a special place in Ernies' life. Life in Borger in so many ways was very different from growing up an "Air Force Brat" who moved around and went so many different places. We never really

had a hometown to associate with until we came to Montgomery. It's great to hear about your small town life.

Alice Rittenhouse Scully '64

From what all has been said we experienced a lot of dust storms-one in my third grade was especially harrowing for my mother when she had taken a trip to Amarillo with a friend who thankfully had electric windshield wipers-not all cars did back then. My sister's wedding shower in 1964 was the weekend of the giant snow. At the time we lived on Monroe and my dad tried to walk to work that next week when the snow was still deep. Not necessarily a wise thing to do.

Ch. 18 People and "things" remembered...who knew?

The Year They Brought Back the Candy Bars

by Gary Jackson '58

The year I was in first grade at West Ward School Hershey Bars came back to Borger. I was six years old and I remembered clearly what a Hershey Bar was—little brown squares of goodness that melted in your mouth. I remembered what those little brown squares were, but not where I had tasted one before. This deficit out of some dim three-year-old's memory I imagine. It probably occurred because one of my uncles brought one home after basic training to share with me and my cousins, before he shipped out for the Pacific. Otherwise chocolate candy was unavailable during the war years. Sugar and meat and gasoline were rationed, but the Hershey Bar was the only sacrifice that stuck in my mind.

The word spread rapidly through the bicycle grapevine: *Big Heart's had a box of Hershey Bars and they wouldn't last long*. I pedaled fast as I could from my home on Meredith Street in Hughes-Pitts to Big Heart's store across Hedgecoke Street from the High School. Kids rode in from all over town. Any time school was in session Big Heart's was usually packed, a big open room with display cases along one wall where all the prescribed school supplies were on sale, everything from Big Chief tablets and those cigar-sized red pencils the first graders used, up to two ring binders and pre-punched paper for high schoolers. In the back was Big Heart's grill where he fried up his not-100%-beef burgers and served french fries in greasy paper sacks. Any time I was in there the kids were elbow to elbow, but that day the big room was empty except for a single line that started at the candy case and ran directly across the room to the opposite wall and then along the wall and out onto the sidewalk. The Hershey Bars were gone before I got in the door.

Something else unexpected and a whole lot less welcome came to Borger that year, a cruel and relentless plague that struck at random, mostly at children, a few of whom it killed and the rest it crippled. It struck next door at the Hailey family. The neighborhood kids clustered together under an elm tree as they loaded Thomas Hailey into one of Blackburn Shaw Brown's hearses. In that day the funeral home hearses doubled as ambulances, and they loaded Thomas in the back and took him away. For weeks afterward Mrs. Simpson, the school nurse, took the kids from our neighborhood to the office each day to take our temperature and look in our throats and listen to our heartbeats. After a time I guess, they decided infantile paralysis was not contagious so the daily checkups became less and less frequent and finally ceased altogether. They did require school kids to go to the high school and take a polio vaccine on sugar cubes.

In the neighborhood our vocabularies soon included words like polio, iron lungs, braces, crutches and wheelchairs. After a year the Blackburn Shaw Brown hearse brought Thomas home from the Scottish Rite Children's

Hospital in Dallas. Thomas had a wheelchair, but his older brother, Oliver, encouraged him to get up and walk with his crutches. It was hard work and Thomas didn't want to do it, but Oliver was relentless, until the day Thomas fell down the steep front porch steps and broke his leg. He never walked on crutches again.

Thomas was three years older than I, but after his year at Scottish Rite he returned to school in the class two years ahead of me. David Hatcher, a neighbor across the street was in that class. Meredith Street was a boy's neighborhood. I had two sisters, Charlene and Bette, and across the street lived the Winters twins, Mavis and Marcia, with their little sister Karen, but every other kid in the neighborhood was male. The Hatchers, Bob and David, the Sults, Johnny and Billy, across the street, the Haileys next door and John Alan and Roger Morris up the hill next door to the Haileys. John Alan and Roger were part timers; their parents were divorced and they periodically came to live with their grandparents. Before they came to Borger none of us had even *heard of* divorced parents.

The boys in the neighborhood altered the baseball diamond we had laid out between our house and the Hailey's so Thomas, who became full time pitcher in his wheelchair, could reach home plate with at least some of the old zing on his fastball. We played with a tennis ball because he was so close, he was in some danger from a line drive. We gave Thomas a few feet off the distance from pitcher's mound to home plate, but that's all we gave him.

The houses in Hughes-Pitts were relatively new in the late 40s and early 50s, shiny white with asbestos siding, young elm trees in the yards. Few had garages and none of those were attached. Driveways were parallel ribbons of concrete wide enough for the tire treads. Solid concrete driveways were several years off in the future. For most of our parents, just after the war and the Great Depression, these were the first homes they ever owned. They didn't stay white long. Borger was surrounded by Carbon Black plants. **"The Carbon Black Center of the World"** proclaimed a sign at the edge of town and was the byline at the top of the local newspaper. You didn't really need the sign. The black fog that settled over the town told the story. A walk across the lawn blackened us to the knee. Mothers got the clothes in off the clotheslines before sundown, because the plants really turned loose the smoke after dark.

Thomas loved sports and would have been a good athlete if polio hadn't sidelined him. His parents tried to compensate by buying him every new sports game that came on the market. I remember he had Photo-Electric Football—the player on offense selected a card about the size of a sheet of notebook paper and slid it face down on the light tray. The defender slid his defensive formation, face up, on top of the offense card. As the guy on offense slowly drew the shield from the light tray the light beneath shined through the card and traced a path between the dots of the defensive formation. If the runner's path hit a black dot, he was tackled. If it hit a red dot, he fumbled. I loved that game and played for hours with Thomas in his room. During baseball season Oliver tacked all the major league team pennants on Thomas's wall, both the National and American Leagues. Thomas never missed the Mutual Game of the Day, and each day Oliver rearranged the pennants so they reflected the current league standings.

By the time Thomas was in 10th grade the new high school was open at its present location at First and Bryan. In those days, before the Americans with Disabilities Act, there were no provisions for a guy in a wheelchair—no ramps, no elevators. When Thomas needed to get up to the second floor he would park at the bottom of the stairs. The first four football players to come by would grab his chair, tilt him back so he wouldn't fly out, and run up the steps with him. I'll never forget the expression on his face—a mixture of abject terror and total bliss.

Sometime after high school Mr. and Mrs. Hailey separated and she moved with the boys to Dallas. Oliver went off to the University of Texas, then he went off to the Air Force and then he went off to Yale to become a playwright. Thomas got a journalism degree from SMU. Oliver worked for a time for the Dallas Morning News, where he met and married another young employee, Elizabeth Forsyth. Oliver and Elizabeth moved to Studio City, California, where Oliver became a successful television writer (most notably *Mary Hartman, Mary Hartman* and *MacMillan and Wife*). Elizabeth wrote a best-selling novel, A *Woman of Independent Means*. Oliver moved Mrs. Hailey and Thomas to Studio City to make their home with him and his family.

In the 1990's I visited Thomas in Studio City. By that time his dad was gone and Oliver too. His mother was nearing 90 and in failing health. He said he never expected to outlive any of them, but now it was clear he would outlive them all.

All the families I knew on Meredith Street moved on in the 50s and 60s. Big Heart's is gone. The old high school became Borger Junior High for awhile and West Ward School disappeared, absorbed into the new Central Elementary. You have to be past fifty to remember polio. And they sell another box of Hershey Bars every day before noon at the Wal-Mart store.

Moving to Borger by Mike Crouch '58

I am going to depart from department store venue.....my family and I (parents and sister Francile '61 and Chris '64) moved to Borger "permanently" in 1948. We had lived there during WW2 when my father was an engineer working on construction of "the Rubber Plant."

We moved into town in early January and there was a light covering of snow all over the ground and it was COLD. My dad had a job with Manhattan Construction Co. then, building the Rice and Alamo plants at Phillips. We stayed for a few days in the Hotel Black before our house was ready. We moved into 1315 Haggard Street in Coronado Addn....all our "stuff" was in a trailer which we pulled behind our car from Iowa where we had lived the previous year.

Coronado was still under construction as we moved in. Next door lived Marshall and Nettie Dyke, sons Larry and older bro Jimmy ('56). Marshall was an optometrist and owned the Borger Gassers, which was great for my dad (who played semipro baseball for a few years while doing his real job....I have lots of memories of the Gassers and games at Huber Park). The Dykes moved and the Smith's moved in. Don't remember names of parents but Kenny (60?) was son and Betty Sue the younger daughter.

On the other side lived Elmer Williams and his wife - "Blackie" was from PA and worked at Phillips; his wife had TB I think and never came out.

Next to them lived the Bogans - Linda, Sandra and David. Behind them across the alley lived Richard Green and his family.

Across the street from my house lived the Walstead's with son Billy Ray Cannon and daughter Diane (who would have been in class of '58 had they not moved). Next to them lived the Stafford's - I can remember only Carlene's name - she was a year ahead of Francile.

Behind the Dyke-Smith house lived the Voet's - parents were both PhD. chemists (I think) at Phillips. These folks had fled Holland from the Nazis. There was an older daughter and older son Donald, Marion ('58) and Martin. They later moved to Takewell Street, across from the Lanhams.

On the NE corner of Haggard lived the Matthews.....Lee was the only son. He and I played a zillion games of Monopoly (I always won). He had a black Cocker Spaniel who ate raw carrots. I remember playing in Lee's yard the day the Korean War started.

Next door to the Matthews lived the Bond's....I took (and hated) piano lessons from Mildred for a few years.

Other kids living in Coronado whom I met at play or at school included Jon Kyle and Carmen Evans who lived next door to each other (both '58). Glenda Adams ('57?) lived on the same block as did Scooter Darden (at the other end) and the Beamguards, Gordon and Larry.

The Bonifields (Ann was '58) lived in that direction as well.

Randy Hudson and Rodney Escoe, (both '58) who were cousins lived in Coronado as did, for a while, Bob Fleishner whose dad was manager of the Chamber of Commerce.

There was a small park with playground equipment located at the intersection of Haggard and (can't remember the next cross street) only a block away from our house. On that park Ronnie, Jeff, Julee Levine and his parents lived.....and up that cross street (which name I cannot remember) lived the Strovas family (Jerry '56? and Frances '58) and the Pelleys (Richard 61)....Mrs. Pelley was a teacher and we played football in her side yard. I have a scar on my arm from running into an exposed nail in her window and Richard Green has a scar on the back of his head from getting tackled into the fire plug on the corner. He bled like a stuck pig and I thought I had killed him. Jeff Levine was watching, almost fainted himself, so much blood.

All those kids went to East Ward....our favorite pastime in walking to school (which we almost all did) was kicking cans from the edge of the addition across a vacant area (probably about 300 yards or so) then covered in tall weeds, to 10th St. where the school ground was.....my Mom would fuss at me all the time for wearing out the toes of my shoes kicking cans.

I can remember a zillion other things......like the day Rodney Escoe and I saw a flying saucer move straight up from (what appeared to be) the hill behind the radio station KHUZ and go straight up and disappear....this while we were walking home from school and kicking cans.

We moved from Coronado St. at Christmas 1954 to 1710 Boyd St...where our house backed up onto the highway, right next to "the Circle." At that house brother Chris had several terrapins that would come out from the sides of the yards when he called them!

Pot Parties and other bad behavior among BHS students

By Mike Crouch

Well, given it's been 50 years, I suppose any statute of limitations has long since expired, so I can now go public.....and confess.....while I was in high school we had **Pot Parties!** ....Yep, that's right boys and girls, **P O T** PARTIES....among BHS students!!

About twice a month (more often in the Fall and Winter) and most often on a Saturday afternoon or evening, several of us would gather in Terry Patchin's basement or Frank Castleberry's living room for **pot** parties which could last for several hours. The usual lineup of miscreants at these sessions, besides Terry, Frank and me, included Jimmy Hines, Troy Tooms, Dumpy Green, Larry Black, Mike Connelley and often John Wilkinson and Henry Turner. I'm sure others who I have now forgotten would also join in the debauchery.

What kind of **pot** you ask?......well, the **pot** in this case, was not the hallucinogenic kind, though occasionally "long green" was involved, the **pot** we indulged in was **the "poker" kind**.

We always played dealer's choice, and Terry was by far the most creative in naming the hand to be played....when it came his turn to name the game, everyone would moan and roll their eyes in anticipation of some off-the-wall variation, and Terry did his best to insure that expectation was not met with disappointment. He especially liked Mexican Sweat (we were naively politically incorrect in those days) with odd combinations of wild cards. So in addition to the joker, he would call (for example) 3s and/or one-eyed Jacks and/or 8s and all would be scratching their heads trying to figure out what they had.....and various ones would have to ask, "now tell me again what is wild?"

The **pots** were usually only a couple of dollars, as the betting was nickel, dime quarter .....so big winners for the day walked away with maybe $10 or $12 and few losers would acknowledge their losses at more than $2 or $3, though most often the arithmetic sum of the final reported results did not equal zero.

People would bring soft drinks and chips or other stuff to munch on, and in the fall we usually listened to the play-by-play of some college football game on the radio (remember that device, now seen only in your car, people used to have these in their homes) because there was poor TV reception in

Borger. The signal came from Amarillo and it was 45 miles away! But what I remember *most* is that **we had a blast!**

Stella's Grave **By Gail Warren**

On a full moon night a car tops the hill and slowly pulls to the side of the dirt road to stop. Below is a valley, dark in shadows, the mesquite trees casting images that deceive the eyes of a human. The car lights blink three times as a beacon to the unseen, and the occupants get out of the vehicle. Down in the valley, at first what seems to be a swirling fog, forms into a white ghostly apparition. With white hair cascading freely around her head and the white dress rustling in the Panhandle wind, Stella roams the valley protecting her land from those who want to take it away from her. The frightened spectators, not sure of what they are seeing, lose no time in getting back into the car and leaving. They will have their story to tell about the night they saw Stella.

A road that is now closed to the public wound its way from the back of Phillips, Texas down to the Spring Creek area. As you topped the hill, you could see down into the valley. After crossing the creek bed, there is a grove of trees on the right which at one time had a grave covered with rocks and a small headstone. More than one citizen of Hutchinson County – adults, teenagers, and children - have claimed for years to have seen Stella near her grave or in her valley. Is she there, was she real, what is the story of Stella?

According to one of my sources, Roy Haley, "There is a creek and a pretty good size grove of trees. I don't know if the rope that they hung her with is still there, but it was for many, many years. The grave is back behind the grove of trees. There is a cement deal. It could have been for something else, but that's what we always called it, cause it was real heavy. I think it was a grave at one time. I think someone went out to do a monument or something."

Roy continued his story by telling me, "She (Stella) owned all of the land in the valley. Her husband had passed away. They lived in a canyon in kinda of a cave house which they had dug out. The oil field people knew where she lived and they had tried to get her to let them drill on that land and she wouldn't do it. Bunch of wildcatters got drunk one night in Borger, and went down there, and pulled her out of the dug out with her screaming and scratching and going on. She was a pretty rough lady herself to have survived boomtown Borger. So they took her and hung her. There are oil wells down there and I don't know who got the mineral rights, but she had no family or children." Roy told me that he has taken "lots and lots of tours down there and some nights they haven't seen her. They want to see her so bad that anything white that moves is her. Mostly when you see her, it is on a full moon night." He assured me that "she will come looking for you." Roy concluded by saying "with an old white dress and old white hair, she just looks terrible. If it's real or not, it sure looked it to me."

Some sources I interviewed agreed with Roy Haley's story of Stella with only minor changes -you need to call out "Stella, Stella" or you need to blink your car lights three times. Other sources disagreed with the story. One source, who didn't want their name revealed, said that Stella was buried at the Plemons Bridge. Another person I interviewed told the story this way. "Stella and her boyfriend were parked out there and were murdered so Stella haunts the hills." Whatever the story, Stella seems to have touched the lives of many county residents and their guests, especially teenagers, and almost everyone has a personal story to tell of Stella.

I asked Roy Haley in what time period he thought this was supposed to have happened and he said that he guessed the latter part of the 1920's probably around 26 or 28 or maybe even a little later, 1930, as that was the beginning of the oil boom in the county.

Now, could this story be true?

As a genealogist, I know that sometimes there is a smidgen of truth to even the wildest stories that are told. So I began my research of Stella by trying to find a person by that name in that time period. My first research was checking the census records of Hutchinson County. According to the 1900 and 1910 censuses of Hutchinson County, there is no one with the first name of Stella, or Estella listed. The same is true of the 1920 census. However, in 1930 there are sixteen (16) listings for Stella. Upon eliminating those too young to have been a wife, that leaves ten (10) possible. After eliminating those with children, there are three (3) remaining - one was single living with her mother and sister, one married and living in that household were four step children and the husband worked at a filling station. The remaining Stella was a landlady who had a rooming house on Harvey Street. My first effort in finding Stella was fruitless.

My next step in the research was to check for a newspaper article substantiating the hanging of a woman by a group of men. Research showed no early newspaper articles on the hanging of a woman or murder of a couple. Also, there are no court records proving the fate of Stella. Land records were researched and there is no evidence that Stella owned that parcel of land. In fact, the land in question was owned by the same person for many years.

Therefore, it is conceivable that the story of Stella is a myth. Could the ghost story be true? Is there a ghost in the valley? Do you believe in ghost? One never knows for sure. It may not be the ghost story that we have all been told. Perhaps there is a ghost haunting that valley - maybe she traveled through this area years before it was settled, died, her family buried her, and now she walks the valley in hopes they will come back. Or perhaps she was a captive of the Indians, or a long-dead race of hunters who encamped in the valley. She could have traveled in the party with the 16th century Spanish conquistadors in their silver chest armor and bladed helmets as they journeyed through that valley in search of gold. Now that would be another story.

No matter the negative conclusion of my research, it would be very difficult to convince those who have seen Stella in the past that she is not a real ghost that roams that valley.

Oh, by the way, as to there being a grain of truth to even the wildest of stories, remember the grave that some believes is Stella's resting place. I have information from a very reliable source that there was a family in Phillips who had a beloved collie dog. When that dog died, they took their pet to the grove of trees down behind Phillips and there they dug a grave. After burying their pet, they carried stones to cover the grave. As a final tribute, they placed a marker on the grave. It was quite a big to do at the time. You might ask Constable Ron Cromer to confirm this story!

Wrestling in Borger

Chris Crouch '64

Wrestling was big in the Texas Panhandle and one of the famous wrestlers, Dory Funk, hailed from Amarillo. Others of notoriety were Fritz Von Erich, and Lou Thesz. These guys were some the best of all times. Imagine what these guys could make today in their prime. Dory made appearances all over the Panhandle and came to Borger several times, often invited by the influential management of Phillips 66. Here are some of the recollections.

Has anyone mentioned the wrestling arena near the traffic circle? It seemed like those weekend matches always attracted a pretty big crowd. Perhaps the last one we saw was when a spectator was bashed over the head with a folding chair. I think after that incident my parents thought it best that we stay away from the arena.

Linda (and Harold) Alexander--class of '63 and '60 respectively

Speaking of the wrestling arena on the north end of Borger: I remember several of our parents' friends telling us the story of how my dad, "Alex" Alexander provoked Dory Funk at the arena and Dory came out of the ring and completely pummeled him. Yes, I guess ole Harold (now called "Alex", too) got his rowdiness legitimately! Ah-hah! Yes, I think that was our dad, Wilbur (Alex) Alexander, who was bashed over the head by Dory Funk! Thanks for reminding me it was more than fisticuffs!

Joyce Griffing Trigg '64

The ProWrestling Place was down on the east side of Main St. close to the circle--very large building (Leslie Derr had that building for awhile in later years for welding shop?). My Aunt Margie Kerwin & son would go to all the events. On special occasions, they would give away free "oil changes" etc, really a "big deal" to my Aunt Margie. Her son, Gene, and I would get the wrestlers' autographs. There was this one older wrestler --"Dizzy Dean" I think anyway, he was the one that I was trying to reach for an autograph for my Aunt Margie. He said--sure I'll give you an autograph, if you'll give me a "yankee dime"? I did not know what that was and I said--but I spent all my money and I don't have a Y-dime! Ok, I'll give you the autograph anyway. I was about 7 or 8yrs old. So, I ran to tell my Mom & Aunt M. She was so excited!!! She said you go tell him--that I'll give him 2-Y-dimes!!. They all laughed at me--so did my cousin G. What a story! I think the other wrestler was Dory Funk. My AM---just loved them . It was really fun & very exciting to go to those matches.

Drag Racing in Borger by **Fred Payne - Class of 62**

I do remember the Drag Racing well, I think Elton Brown and myself had the fastest cars, I had the 57 Pontiac 2 door hardtop with a 421 engine, 2 four's converted Hydramatic, the whole ten yards. Elton had the beautiful 56 black Chevy Bel Air with a 350 engine and just about every goody you could put on one at the time.
Saddest thing that happened was when Doug Cole was killed drag racing. He was a great guy and a good friend. My sister was going steady with Doug when he was killed and my Dad unfortunately had to take care of the funeral back when he was a Funeral Director and Mortician. To this day, I don't think Borger had a bigger turnout for a funeral than Doug's. Any one going to admit to drag racing and playing "chicken" going all out towards the one lane "Plemons" bridge? I seem to recall seeing more than just a couple of those, especially Ed Vidaurri's '55 Ford 4 door sedan, but I never did participate. Ya think?

KBBB Radio Station - David Hogg '59

KBBB - 1600 Khz - Top 40 - Now that brings some memories back to me... It now has new call letters - but back then it was only a little 500 watt station - but I had just passed my FCC 1st class license and I was the "chief" engineer - that should also read "only" engineer. I worked there from '59 until '62 while attending Frank Phillips before going on to Texas Tech - grad '64 BSEE. The DJ's were Dean Robertson - Dale Keith ('59) & Dick Guthrie ('59) - they played the really true "golden oldies" music of the 50's & 60's.
Why can't we have more music like the '50's music?? [I've wondered the same thing. When one listens to the music of the 50s and 60s it is melodious, with meaningful words, beautiful music one never tires of listening to. My daughter even likes to listen to the "golden oldies". Recently I tuned into a "golden oldies" station and they were playing music from as far back as...1972! Another era has passed...)
While working at KBBB - I did a stupid stunt by holding a 4 foot fluorescent bulb out the window trying to "light" it up by holding it "near" the transmitting antenna - - YES it did light for an instant - BUT I got too close

and I got a jolt of RF from the antenna and it burned a small hole in my palm as I fell backward and dropped the bulb - - - I was lucky...

Horse Races on Canadian River By Gary Huffman '65

There used to be a horse race track along the river past Electric City about a mile West of the highway, South of the river bridge. Sheriff Hugh Anderson was usually always in attendance for the weekend races. (You can get more information from **Zoe McGough**, as her dad used to own and or run the place.) There was a lot of money that changed hands as rich ranchers from Oklahoma would bring their prize quarter horses over for match races. Some of the races weren't always on the up & up. There was always a lot of beer drinking and gambling down there. Phillips owned the land but leased it out until the 70's when they closed the area due to the liability of the salt caverns below ground where many barrels of hydrocarbon are stored. Punkin' Edwards was the last to lease it. He also owned the Fish Trap (eating place) next to Bunavista Drive-In.
Don't know who built the track but since betting was not legal at the time you bought the horse you thought would win. There was also a track in Bunavista just west of the ball park and across the HWY of what we called the **"Spanish camp".** I believed Donny McKinney or Bill McKinney dad's had something to do with it. There was a man that worked at the Phillips 66 station that used to fix our flats for free. His name was BJ who got most of his money back from us when we visited his establishment in HS. Most boys know what I mean.

Lake Meredith and Alibates Flint Quarries
By Frieda Lanham Pickett '61

When I was in junior high school I heard my stepfather talk about the city manager, A.A. Meredith and his vision for damming up the Canadian River to make a lake. The water would be ideal for providing water to communities in the Panhandle, many who were using the aquifer under the Panhandle area for water, and there was concern the aquifer was diminishing. He felt it was a lost cause, as the amount of money needed was enormous. This shows that a man with commitment to a vision and ability to have an eye for the future was in Borger. The beautiful deep blue water of Lake Meredith offers the answer to every fisherman's dreams and this is a dream come true whether from the shore line or private boat ramp. I recall while at Frank Phillips College going out to the newly formed Lake with a group, hoping to do some "night fishing" and putting up our light to attract the fish, only to see the head of a water moccasin swimming toward us out of the water. That did it for me, up the ridge and into the car...wasn't going for it.
Sometimes you would see someone skiing down the long stretch in the middle of the lake, navigating to miss the graceful sailboats utilizing the frequent winds in the Panhandle.

The hustle and bustle of city life seems miles away as the family picnic includes sending the children to search for "arrowheads", most constructed from the famous alibates flint that comes from the Panhandle area. For thousands of years, people came to the red bluffs above the Canadian River for flint, a unique type of stone, vital to their existence. Demand for the high quality, rainbow-hued flint is reflected in the distribution of Alibates Flint throughout the high plains area and beyond. Today this area is protected by the U.S. National Park Service and can only be viewed by ranger-led guided tours, which must be made in advance.

Alibates Flint Quarries

Of major interest are the flint quarries located on the south side of Lake Meredith used by Indians since the 13th century. The Alibates Flint Quarries is the only National Monument in the state of Texas, and is an integral part of the Lake Meredith Reservoir. Although termed "flint," the stone is technically a silicified or agatized dolomite quartz occurring in Permian-age outcroppings. These deposits, exposed as slightly undulating layers, are unique to the Panhandle area. But regardless of what the stone is called, none of the terms captures its startling beauty. In hues and tones of the evening sky, colors range from pale gray and white, to pink, maroon, and vivid red, to orange-gold and an intense purplish blue. Patterns in the stone are varied, with many containing bands of alternating color create stripes and a marbled effect. Researchers have speculated about the statistically significant occurrence of red Alibates in sites, and whether the color might have invoked magical connections to the blood of animals. It may have been the exotic appearance of Alibates flint rather than its workability that attracted prehistoric toolmakers. Modern-day knappers report that the material has a resistant quality and hardness which makes it more difficult to flake and shape into tools than other stone, such as the Edwards cherts found abundantly in the Edwards Plateau to the south. Finely flaked and fluted Alibates flint projectile points were found at the Blackwater Draw site in eastern New Mexico. There are still dug out areas suggesting quarry sites among the hills.

References

Borger history:

Newspaper supplement, Borger News-Herald, March 7, 2007

Book: *Borger, Texas* by John H. White, Library Binding Co.:Waco TX, 1973.

Ace Borger:

http://www.rootsweb.ancestry.com/~txhansfo/bios.html

Boomtown painting and artist:

Book: *Seeing America: Painting and Sculpture from the Collection of the Memorial Art Gallery*, Chapter 52 Thomas Hart Benton *Boomtown (1928)*, pages 211-214.

Thesis: History of Hutchinson County for Master of Arts, by L.J. Garner, August 1930; submitted to faculty of SMU, Dallas Texas. (copy in Hutchinson County Library)

Adobe Walls

Book: St. Clair, Lucia."Ride the Wind: The story of Cynthia Ann Parker and the Last Days of the Comanche". Ballantine Books:New York, 1982, pp. 580-85.

Derrick, R. Adobe Walls: Trading Post and Historic Battleground. (http://www.panhandlenation.com/adobe_walls.htm).

Neely, Bill. The Last Comanche Chief, 1995, Wiley & Sons, pp. 83-101)

Olive K. Dixon. Life of Billy Dixon. 1914; revised edition 1927 (Dallas Turner). Also http://www.tshaonline.org/handbook/online/articles/DD/fdi22.html.

G. Derek West. The Battle of Adobe Walls. Panhandle Plains Historical review 1963;36.

The Handbook of Texas Online (http://www.tshaonline.org/handbook/online/articles/AA/qea1.html).

Fort Adobe in Hutchinson County, by Wes Phillips:
http://www.panhandlenation.com/history/hutchinson_county_history/17.html

Civic Leaders

A.A. Meredith: Amarillo *Sunday News-Globe*, April 14, 1963. Hutchinson County Historical Commission, *History of Hutchinson County, Texas* (Dallas: Taylor, 1980). *Handbook of Texas Online*, s.v. ","
http://www.tshaonline.org/handbook/online/articles/MM/fme45.html (accessed March 11, 2010).

Lake Meredith Project: http://www.crmwa.com/History.htm

BHS Football and Gene Mayfield

Borger News Herald, sports pages

Obituary of Gene Mayfield"". *Lubbock Avalanche-Journal*, October 3, 2009.

Coach E.B. "Tex" Hanna

Amarillo Globe-News, Sept. 19, 2004

Biography written by Hanna family.

Made in the USA
Charleston, SC
13 September 2011